LOST LINKS

Forgotten Treasures of Golf's Golden Age

LOST LINKS

Forgotten Treasures of Golf's Golden Age

DANIEL WEXLER

CLOCK
TOWER
PRESS

Clock Tower Press, LLC
320 North Main Street
P.O. Box 310
Chelsea, MI 48118
www.clocktowerpress.com

Printed and bound in Canada.

10 9 8 7 6 5 4 3 2 1

Library of Congress Cataloging-in-Publication Data

Wexler, Daniel.
Lost links : forgotten treasures of golf's golden age / by Daniel Wexler.
p. cm.
ISBN 1-932202-03-X
1. Golf courses—United States—Design and construction—History. 2.
Golf course architects—United States—History. I. Title.
GV981 .W475 2003
796.352'06'0973—dc21
2002155220

For all who continue to play by the rules despite being told that it's okay to cheat.

And to the memory of Harry Vardon, a truly great champion.

TABLE OF CONTENTS

INTRODUCTION

❧

*W*hy another book on golf courses that no longer exist?

In publishing, as in any other commercial endeavor, the obvious answer is "because the first one sold well." However—and I offer my word on this right up front —such was not my primary motivation here. Indeed, with several other interesting projects in the offing, the prospect of a sequel to *The Missing Links*, my first book on lost courses, initially held little attraction.

What changed my thinking was the knowledge, slowly gained, that this book would not be a sequel at all but rather a companion volume; an entirely separate collection of material which, together with its sister, might provide a complete picture of an American golfing landscape long ago demolished in the name of population growth and economic progress.

This change in thinking came about primarily as a by-product of my research into the original designs of hundreds of still-existing courses from golf architecture's pre-World War II Golden Age. For in the process of acquiring old aerial photographs of these many gems, I frequently noted additional courses nearby, defunct layouts whose names and specifics seemed to

have slipped away through the cracks of time. In many cases they were rudimentary facilities, holdovers from the "Eighteen-Stakes-on-a-Sunday-Afternoon" days of prehistoric golf design. But others, such as the Palm Beach Winter Club (a Seth Raynor layout which I stumbled onto quite by accident) were splendid courses of a genuinely classic nature.

Naturally, such blue-chip discoveries were somewhat more the exception than the rule. Yet if one appreciates the style, strategy and originality that permeated most Golden Age design, they will surely look with interest upon the 15 additional Donald Ross courses included here, the eight by Devereux Emmet, six by William Langford, three by A. W. Tillinghast, and so on. Sadly, several dozen more "big name" layouts will forever remain a mystery, having expired, with little ground-level documentation, before the widespread use of aerial photography in the late 1920s. But a veritable beating of the bushes has produced the 74 courses included herein which, combined with those featured previously in *The Missing Links*, surely comprise a most thorough and satisfying study.

Where *The Missing Links* dwelled heavily upon the

very finest lost layouts, *Lost Links* is intended to be a broader, more comprehensive volume. Thus it includes former courses and holes from more than 20 states, as well as maps detailing the locations of deceased facilities in 8 additional metropolitan areas. Also, more than a dozen Golden-Age architects not mentioned in *The Missing Links* have at least one of their works presented here.

In keeping with this more comprehensive approach then, I have chosen to divide this volume into five sections, arranged as follows:

I. The Golden Dozen - Twelve first-class layouts on par with most of *The Missing Links'* featured 27, omitted (or, more frequently, sidebarred) previously due to lack of verifiable information. They are presented here, in full, for the first time.

II. Lost Links - Fifty more lost layouts of genuine distinction, built by the master designers of the Golden Age.

III. Lost Nines - Twelve of the best, several from very famous clubs.

IV. Missing Holes - From San Francisco Golf Club in the west to Quaker Ridge in the east, many of today's most hallowed layouts are not 100% intact. This section highlights the holes missing from the architect's original, unaltered designs.

V. Metropolitan Area Maps - Illustrating the locations of lost courses in 8 more major cities from coast to coast.

Finally, several relevant points.

First, the astute reader will note that the majority of these prewar designs played quite a bit shorter than today's 7,300-yard Goliaths. What this says regarding the unchecked advancement of the game's equipment is frightening, yet it is also interesting to see the more intricate design strategies frequently employed on the shorter holes of the past, as well as the remarkable proximity in which many tees, greens and fairways were built. Practical in today's litigation-happy world? Perhaps not—but can the expanded acreage required for twenty-first-century golf be anything but a detriment to what is already an expensive, land-hungry game?

Second, to quote from *The Missing Links*: "While the maps appearing in this volume have been prepared as accurately as possible, the vagaries of dated material and the tendency of early architects to vary their plans significantly in the field have occasionally made an exact presentation difficult." Specifically, as these layouts have been drawn from even further out of the 75-year-old limelight, some information (often in the form of precise hole yardages) is virtually impossible to find. Thus more frequently will the reader find the scorecard distances estimated; scaled, in fact, from the best available aerial photos and total yardages listed in period publications. Though such scaled numbers will seldom be exact, they have generally proven themselves quite close—which, when the alternative is leaving the course out altogether, seems entirely good enough.

Similarly, as courses inevitably evolve, the versions presented here may not represent a particular layout's original (or final) configuration, but rather its arrangement at the time of the best (or only) available photographs.

Finally, in the interest of limiting redundancies, I have minimized the presentation of certain historical facts (e.g., architect biographies) where they have previously been provided in *The Missing Links*. Likewise no course is mapped in both volumes, allowing as much space for new material as possible.

I offer then another set of ghosts from golf's great and glorious Golden Age, this colorful collection of *Lost Links*.

Daniel Wexler
Los Angeles, CA

THE GOLDEN DOZEN

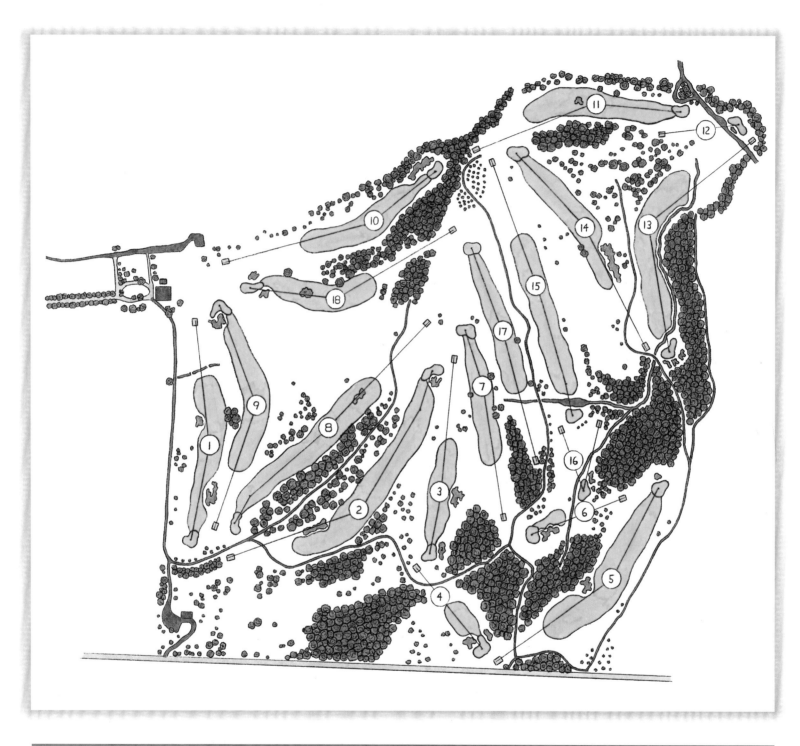

AUGUSTA NATIONAL (1934)																			
400	525	350	190	440	185	340	500	420	3350	430	415	150	480	425	485	145	400	420	3350	6700
4	5	4	3	4	3	4	5	4	36	4	4	3	5	4	5	3	4	4	36	72

AUGUSTA NATIONAL GOLF CLUB
AUGUSTA, GA

꙼

DR. ALISTER MACKENZIE AND BOBBY JONES (1933)

We are quite willing to have low scores made during the tournament. It is not our intention to rig the golf course so as to make it tricky. It is our feeling that there is something wrong with a golf course that will not yield a score in the sixties to a player who has played well enough to deserve it.

— Bobby Jones, 1960

Some may consider it dubious to kick off a volume on lost golf courses with a facility which not only still exists but is, at least for one week each spring, the very center of the golfing universe. Indeed by the author's own rather subjective standard, the fact that Augusta National's original hole-routing remains approximately 90% intact might itself remove the club from any such consideration.

Yet Augusta, by its very nature, is different.

For the home of The Masters stands essentially alone among golf courses in its pedigree, its intended uniqueness, and the degree to which this uniqueness was deliberately and explicitly documented.

The pedigree, of course, is well worth noting, for Augusta's creators were no less than the most famous golfer and preeminent architect of the game's Golden Age, Bobby Jones and Dr. Alister MacKenzie. Talk of this collaboration has become so commonplace as to lose a good deal of its impact, its mention blending with the weather report and obligatory foliage shots that annually precede the televised golfing action. Yet such a partnership is in fact genuinely unrivaled, with only Harbor Town's pairing of Jack Nicklaus and a fledgling Pete Dye even meriting comparison.

More important, however, was Augusta's intended uniqueness, for therein lay the crux of its greatness. Both Jones and MacKenzie were emphatic in their belief in strategic, variety-laden holes, wide fairways, heavily contoured greens, and a judicious use of the ground game as played, for time immemorial, in Scotland. They were equally united in their dislike of rough, a nonhazard which MacKenzie believed caused "a stilted and cramped style, destroying all freedom of play." Finally, both men revered the classic old holes of the British Isles, a truly relevant point given that not less than half of Augusta's original design was in fact replica-inspired. In short, Jones and MacKenzie set out to create something unprecedented in American golf—a roughless, thinking man's layout which on its opening day featured only 22 bunkers, yet offered multiple options on each and every shot.

To be fair, many of the changes that have so affected Augusta took place while Bobby Jones was still a fixture at the club; in fact if one is to believe longtime majordomo Clifford Roberts, Jones may even have been at the root of several. Also the fact that Augusta is the lone permanent site of a Major championship suggests more frequent applications of the once-a-decade sort of tune-ups associated with many familiar U.S. Open or PGA championship venues. And finally, as it is surely not Augusta's fault that golf's governing bodies have abrogated their responsibilities with regard to regulating equipment, the lengthening of many holes will not be considered as relevant here.

However...

The simple fact is that while the routing remains largely the same, Augusta's present course bears little resemblance to its unique and wonderful original, having been methodically transformed into a less strategic, less exciting, distinctly modern affair.

Its minor alterations are far too numerous to mention but the major changes—more of which are likely taking place even as this book makes its initial rounds – run as follows.

The 575-yard downhill second initially played to an L-shaped green guarded front-right by a single bunker. It required a powerfully drawn tee ball to negotiate a vast left-side carry bunker, then a low, running fade if the green were to be reached in two. This wonderful balance was altered in 1953 when the extension of the green behind a new left-side bunker created its modern T shape. Thirteen years later, the carry bunker was replaced by a right-side hazard posi-

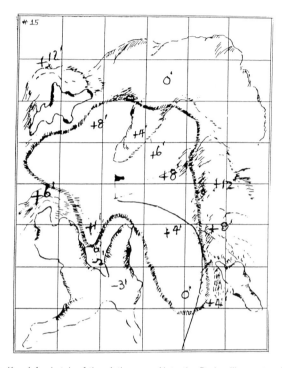

Dr. MacKenzie's sketch of the sixth green. Note the Redan-like contouring as illustrated by the line indicating the ideal method of approach.

tioned in what had previously been the "safe" portion of the fairway, effectively making the preferred left side the easier target and removing much strategic consideration from play.

The 205-yard fourth was the first of four consecutive holes built to loosely replicate the great holes of Scotland, in this case #11 (colloquially known as the Eden) at St. Andrews. A key to the Eden's difficulty is the severe back-to-front slope of the putting surface, a point which led MacKenzie to write that "Most copies are failures because of the absence of the subtle and severe slopes which create the excitement of the original hole." The doctor was char-

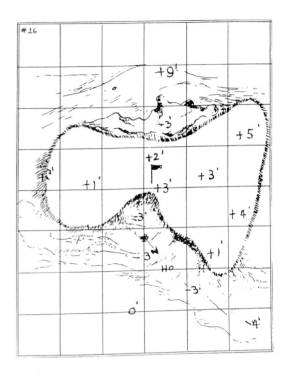

Dr. MacKenzie's sketch of the seventh green. The imitation Valley of Sin was graded below the fairway, leading to a moderately elevated green.

The par-4 seventh is more thoroughly changed, having once been a 340-yard approximation of the home hole at St. Andrews, complete with imitation Valley of Sin. Apparently at the suggestion of Horton Smith, its green complex was completely rebuilt in 1938, resulting in a steeply pitched, sand-ringed putting surface distinctly inhospitable to the originally intended run-up shot. Recently extended to 410 yards, with its driving area nearly strangled by trees, the seventh is now a thoroughly penal hole holding nothing in common with its MacKenzie/Jones original.

Having completed the preliminaries, we soon reach Augusta's most seriously altered stretch, beginning with the 420-yard ninth. What's missing here is MacKenzie's original green, a large boomerang-shaped creation offering distinct pin placements on either side of a single deep bunker. This spectacular design was a favorite of the doctor's and one which surely provided as much of his favored "pleasurable excitement" as any feature at Augusta. Though today's newly extended 460-yard version is certainly difficult, it offers little in the way of strategy or inspiration by comparison.

The 10th began life as a wonderfully strategic 430-yard par 4 whose green was perched on the hillside some 35 yards short and right of the present putting surface. For the player capable of placing his drive on the elevated right side of the fairway, an open, downhill pitch was the result. Those who found the lower section of fairway generally utilized by modern professionals, on the other hand, were, in MacKenzie's words, "called upon to play a difficult second shot over a large spectacular bunker, with small chance of getting near the pin." Sadly, Perry Maxwell's 1937 construction of the new green quickly rendered this grand hazard little more than a hood ornament—though with continued unchecked equipment advances, it may soon be in play off the tee!

The 490-yard par-4 11th also began more manageably,

acteristically confident that his own Augusta version would "compare favorably with the original"—but once the club had former MacKenzie partner Perry Maxwell flatten the putting surface in 1938, any further comparisons were rendered moot.

A similar fate has befallen the 180-yard sixth, which was initially modeled after North Berwick's most-pilfered Redan (see page 34). MacKenzie called this replica "a much more attractive hole than the original," yet one wonders how he would feel about Maxwell's relative leveling of this putting surface as well, minimizing the front-right-to-back-left fallaway that is the strategic essence of the Redan.

at 415 mostly downhill yards. In addition to a green perched famously above a bending corner of Rae's Creek, the hole originally featured a deep, invisible bunker near the center of the fairway, a Jones-inspired tribute to so many similar hazards at St. Andrews. Though clearly one of the layout's most fascinating holes (MacKenzie himself claimed not to "know another quite like it"), it was modified—with a longer, realigned tee, a rebuilt green complex and the removal of the fairway bunker—in 1950.

Among the most interesting alterations are those at the famous 12th and 13th holes, which MacKenzie initially planned to be bunker-free. At #12, evidence suggests that the single front bunker was constructed prior to opening, while the back pair were added sometime later. It is also worth noting that the hourglass-shaped green was less symmetrical and more contoured than at present, with a much shallower right half elevated noticeably above the deeper, more forgiving left.

At #13, photographic evidence suggests that despite being left out of MacKenzie's plans, three rear bunkers did exist from the beginning. The fourth was added more than 20 years later, essentially replacing a front-left section of putting surface which had featured a very neat pin position just above the tributary of Rae's Creek.

At the 440-yard 14th, a 75-yard-long MacKenzie fairway bunker was inexplicably removed in 1952, making the favored right side as easy to find as the more difficult left.

At the 500-yard 15th– in addition to adding, then removing fairway mounds, planting trees, and introducing the pinballish gimmick of scalping the greenfront above the pond—a small bunker replaced a mound adjacent to the right edge of the putting surface in 1957. A change of minor importance? Compare Dr. MacKenzie's stated reason for utilizing the mound (that the "courageous player will, aided by a large hillock to the right, be able to pull his second shot around onto the green") with the clearly penal nature

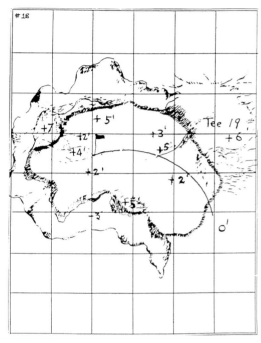

Dr. MacKenzie's sketch of the ninth green. The boomerang turned out even more pronounced than the drawing suggests but the adjacent 19th hole (planned as a bet-settling par 3) was apparently never built.

of the bunker and one garners an illuminating sense of how greatly both Augusta and the game itself have changed.

And on the subject of change, none of Augusta's holes have undergone more of it than the 16th, originally a 145-yard par 3 modeled after the seventh at the Stoke Poges Golf Club in Buckinghamshire, England. This early version played from alternate tees on either side of the 15th green and continued on in the same westward direction, culminating in a wide, shallow target backed by sand and fronted by a narrow creek. Because the hole was clearly on the short side (Clifford Roberts maintained its actual length to be only slightly more than 110 yards), it was replaced by

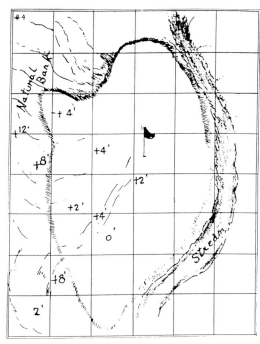

Dr. MacKenzie's sketch of the 13th green. Clearly his original intention was for it to be built bunker-free.

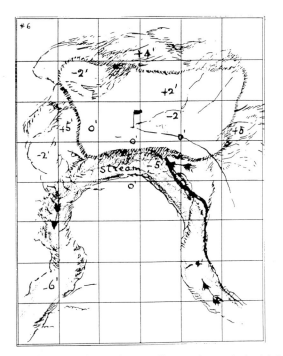

Dr. MacKenzie's sketch of the 15th green. Noteworthy are the back-left fall-away, the shape of what initially was only a fronting stream and the right-side mound—since leveled and replaced with a bunker.

Robert Trent Jones's present-day 16th, a pretty, often dramatic affair with little more than one-and-a-half useable pin placements.

Following the vastly altered 17th (where added bunkers and recent tree plantings have removed all of the original strategy) comes the finisher which, following its 2001 renovation, seems far more suited to closing a U.S. Open than a Masters. MacKenzie's 18th challenged the player to fade his drive around the dogleg corner, opening the ideal angle of attack for an aggressive approach. Subsequent renovations to the green complex have minimized the advantage of so dangerous a play, however, and the newest changes

have succeeded in turning the hole from a potentially dramatic finisher to a drudging march of survival.

So, as probably the most regularly altered facility in the history of the game, Augusta National begs an answer to the obvious question: is it a better golf course today than at its inception? Sure—if one supports the USGA "Protection of Par" doctrine that gave us knee-deep rough, Oakland Hills, and the "modernization" of literally dozens of other classic Golden Age designs. But Augusta was explicitly intended to be different, to yield the dramatic final-round birdies and eagles (mixed with the occasional eight) that annually made the Masters so excitingly unique.

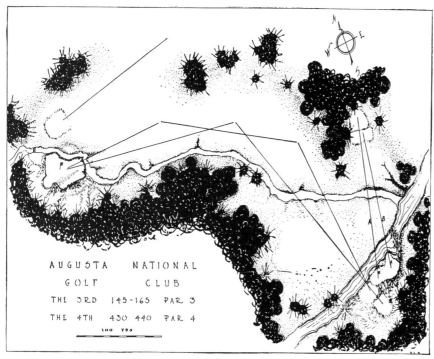

Dr. MacKenzie's sketch of today's 12th and 13th (originally the third and fourth). The 13th is clearly bunkerless and planned as a par 4—but neither idea actually came to fruition.

What it has become is a poor-man's U.S. Open track, its accent on drama and thrills deliberately traded for a plodding sort of difficulty entirely antithetical to the stated goals of Bobby Jones.

And that was before they grew rough.

How Augusta Would Measure Up Today

From whose perspective?

As a fun, engaging golf course in an era of reasonable equipment, there can be little doubt that MacKenzie and Jones's quirky, strategic original was infinitely better. But whatever its initial intent, today's Augusta is, first, last, and always, about the Masters. So is the present version better for Major championship play? Perhaps—if golf's once-greatest event has taken simply to aping the U.S. Open and PGA championships. But as we continue to watch Augusta's calculated emasculation of all that made it unique, one can't help but notice that yielding low scores in recent Open championships has not ruined St. Andrews, and that a great deal of the old excitement has been missing from most recent Masters Sundays.

What would Bobby Jones be saying now?

Craig Wood watches as Gene Sarazen prepares to close out their play-off for the 1935 Masters. Note the encroaching tree on the golfer's right side of the fairway. (*Golf Illustrated*)

This very early shot of the 13th tee gives some sense of the initial contour and bunkering of the 12th green. (*Golf Illustrated*)

BOCA RATON (NORTH) (Approximate)																				
345	325	380	440	525	210	410	150	575	3360	360	405	345	415	145	455	415	160	440	3140	6500
4	4	4	4	5	3	4	3	5	36	4	4	4	4	3	5	4	3	4	35	71

BOCA RATON RESORT & CLUB (NORTH)

BOCA RATON, FL

WILLIAM FLYNN (1926)

When discussing a list of the world's finest 36-hole facilities, names like Winged Foot, Royal Melbourne, and Sunningdale come quickly to mind. As the conversation expands, Baltusrol, Ballybunion, and, depending upon El Niño's state of mind, the Olympic Club may gain a mention, joined, among the newer vintages, by Oregon's Bandon Dunes Resort.

What separates these facilities from a host of other contenders? Primarily the usual ingredients: strong architectural pedigrees, storied tournament histories, and, for the less-initiated, the ever-present magazine ratings. But in the end the truly elite offer something else that other multicourse clubs don't: balance. The sense that while one layout may surely stand among the world's very best, the second is indisputably deserving of similar acclaim in its own right. And while many are the clubs that offer one great and one very good, few genuinely offer two 18s of authentic top-shelf quality.

Lacking detailed information regarding the con-touring of green complexes, it is difficult to judge how well William Flynn's lost 36 holes at Boca Raton would have measured up with the above-listed giants. But considering their length, hazard placement, sandy terrain, and proximity to Atlantic Ocean breezes, the smart money says they would have made a strong case.

As chronicled in *The Missing Links*, the Boca Raton Resort & Club was the brainchild of the Mizner Development Company, an organization run chiefly by Palm Beach architect and eccentric savant Addison Mizner. Though the scion of a distinguished California family, Mizner was ill and nearly destitute upon reaching south Florida in 1918. Yet within seven years he was the toast of Palm Beach society, designing all manner of buildings for the rich and famous in a style frequently termed "Bastard-Spanish-Moorish-Romanesque-Gothic-Renaissance-Bull-Market-Damn-the-Expense." Eventually, bitten by the easy-money bug of pre-Depression America, Mizner elected to expand his operation by moving 20 miles

The Cloister Inn, circa 1930: any golfer's vision of midwinter paradise. (*The American Golfer*)

General view of the Boca Raton facility. The small bunkers and grassed-over terrain suggest this may be part of the short practice course that originally existed immediately behind the hotel. (*The American Golfer*)

down the Gold Coast to develop his own rich man's town, Boca Raton.

During the mid-1920s boom years, Addison had help from his brother Wilson, a well-known wit, con man, and convicted gambler. It is Wilson Mizner who is generally credited with coining the phrases "Never give a sucker an even break" and "Be nice to people on your way up because you'll meet the same people on your way down." Armed with aphorisms for any occasion, Wilson actually headed the "Social Committee" which determined who might be allowed to purchase property in Boca Raton, though he is surely better remembered for his "wisdom" – such as advising chronic pugilists: "Always hit a man with a bottle—a ketchup bottle preferably, for when that breaks, he thinks he's bleeding to death."

With Addison designing the buildings and Wilson helping to attract/fleece the customers, it isn't surprising that Boca Raton was an instant hit. Real estate sales in 1925 – the height of the Florida boom – were tremendous and the opening of the $1.25 million Cloister Inn (the initial version of today's Boca Raton Hotel) a year later drew a veritable Who's Who of seasonal customers.

Yet if an aura of malfeasance may have lingered a bit around the Mizners, there was no skimping of quality with regard to the resort's recreational amenities. Toward that end Donald Ross was briefly engaged to design 18 holes (a real estate map details his proposed routing on the site), then was replaced by William Flynn, for reasons unrecorded, when the Mizners instead elected to construct 36.

Though remarkably little documentation exists regarding the specifics of Flynn's North and South courses, certain facts have been pretty well verified. To begin with, the North was the earlier layout by two years, opening in 1926. As such, it occupied the land immediately adjacent to the Cloister Inn, a large, sandy expanse bordered to the west by North Federal Highway and the south by the resort's grand entrance road, El Camino Real. Several period publications were agreed in listing the North's length at 6,500 yards but accounts varied as to its earliest par (either 71 or 72). It was firmly established at 71, however, by the 1950s.

Genuinely an excellent layout, the North might well have garnered a good deal of national attention had it not been usurped by the long-lost South course in 1928. Indeed the South was so frequently singled out for player and media acclaim that the North was relegated to secondary status almost immediately, particularly after four of the South's holes were cited in a 1934 *The American Golfer* series featuring America's finest tests. Yet in hindsight, a careful examination suggests that aside from being more tightly routed, the North was, in most respects, very much the equal of its famous sister.

The North began rather modestly with a pair of medium-length par 4s, but from there forward, the front nine represented as strong a stretch of golf as one might hope to encounter.

The third, a 380-yard par 4, doglegged nearly 90° to the right, daring the aggressive player to ride the prevailing breeze across the vast beach which guarded the corner. The 440-yard fourth and 525-yard fifth were similarly challenging, with great expanses of native sand flanking both sides of each. The fourth in particular was likely one of Flynn's toughest creations, allowing a chosen angle of attack in the finest tradition of C.B. Macdonald's Cape holes, yet mandating that a substantial stretch of the hazard be crossed for the green to be reachable with one's second. The fifth, in turn, may well have been reachable in two by longer hitters, though the various nooks and crannies of the adjacent sand created fascinating angles of play throughout.

Though the 210-yard sixth and 410-yard seventh were

Early view of the 150-yard eighth shows the initial shaping of Flynn's greenside bunkers. (*The American Golfer*)

of obvious stature, the North's most memorable challenge surely came at the ninth. For here, at roughly 575 yards, stood a massive three-shot par 5 built on a scale similar to the South course's celebrated ninth and 17th holes. Though the tee shot was relatively simple, danger loomed on one's second, where the fairway's leftward sweep around a huge waste area required a most accurate cost-versus-benefits analysis. Laying back safely was always an option, of course—but with the tiny green situated tight to the sand, the prospect of a mid-iron third would hardly have been inviting.

The North's inward half was slightly shorter and took on a bit of the back-and-forth routing seldom seen on the South, yet it too offered several excellent holes. The stretch from 11 through 13 was particularly absorbing as it included three wholly different par 4s in rapid succession. The 405-yard 11th required a mid- to long-iron approach to a deep, narrow green while the 345-yard 12th was more on the order of a drive-and-pitch. But the 415-yard 13th was the real star of the group, requiring another Cape-like drive across sand in order to leave a reasonable approach to a narrow, angled green. Those bailing out to the right might still get home in two (providing they missed a prominent fairway bunker) but would have to flirt with a huge hazard encroaching short and right of the putting surface to do so.

The North's finishing holes were equally memorable, beginning with the narrow 415-yard 16th, a long, sandy two-shotter. The 160-yard 17th, played to an exceedingly narrow green pinched between massive bunkers, certainly bore the general configuration of a Redan. Though hardly a regular ploy of Flynn's, he had built a rather straightforward replica at the Homestead Resort's Cascades course prior to designing Boca Raton, so he was clearly not averse to the concept.

Finally, the 440-yard into-the-wind 18th was an obvious bruiser but may have been more forgiving than an initial glance might indicate. For once a tee shot had successfully avoided three fairway bunkers, a long-iron or wooden approach could generally be run onto the relatively open putting surface.

Given the North course's immediate proximity to the hotel, its post-World War II survival was preferred to that of the more distant South, though the integrity of Flynn's design was scarcely maintained. By the 1950s, nearly all of the character-giving native sand had been grassed over, leaving a layout that differed little in appearance from countless other Florida courses. In addition, Red Lawrence (1947), Robert Trent Jones Sr. (1963), and Joe Lee (1988) all performed substantial renovations, before a complete 1997 overhaul by Gene Bates buried whatever traces of William Flynn might somehow have been left.

How Boca Raton Would Measure Up Today

One suspects that the North course might mirror the relationship of Winged Foot's East course with its bigger, more famous sister: somewhat shorter and thus frequently overlooked, but at the same time more varied and, in spots, more challenging.

Yet even more compelling is the image of the entire 36-hole Boca Raton facility and how, in anything resembling its maiden form, it would tantalize the golfing world today. For without an artificial lake, waterfall, railroad tie, or double green in sight, this was natural design at its finest. Thirty-six unique and challenging holes roaming adventurously across the native Florida landscape, offering as attractive a test as anything in William Flynn's portfolio this side of Shinnecock Hills.

Winged Foot, Royal Melbourne, and Sunningdale?
Perhaps.

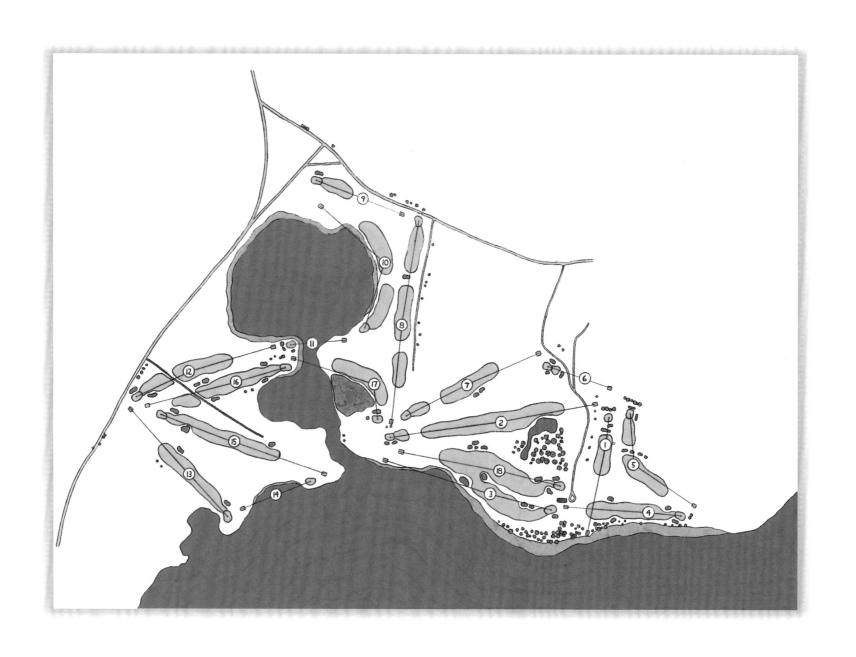

CEDAR BANK LINKS

EASTHAM, MA

✤

QUINCY SHAW (1928)

Throughout golf architecture's long and fascinating history there have been many reasons for men of means to build private courses, personal bastions strictly reserved for the use of themselves and their friends. In some cases it was the elemental desire to create something lasting and great. In others it was simply about following the trend, building a golf course because – as we have seen again during the 1990s – the game's popularity made it the fashionable thing to do. In still other cases it was about convenience—for many are those who've simply grown tired of crowded conditions at the local club. But in the long annals of private golf course construction, the Cedar Bank Links enjoyed a *raison d'être* that likely stands unique: mental illness.

Indeed Cedar Bank was the creation of one Quincy Adams Shaw, a certified Boston Brahman who also happened, for the rather impressive span of 10 years, to be certifiable. Scion of a family fortune made in the copper mines of upper Michigan, Shaw suffered a nervous breakdown in his middle 40s, the result being long-term confinement to the McLean mental hospital just outside of Boston. Upon his release in

1925, Shaw's doctors advised him of the need to absorb his mind completely in a new project or vocation, something all-consuming and, essentially, unfinishable. What pointed Shaw toward golf is not a matter of record. Nevertheless upon making his decision, the Harvard graduate found himself well prepared to build his own private course, as his family owned ample acreage in Eastham, a small coastal town on the Atlantic side of the Cape Cod peninsula.

And what land it was, perched on bluffs high above Nauset Bay and favored with the sort of rolling, links-like terrain that had spawned the Royal and Ancient game once upon a time in Scotland. The Shaw homestead was not pure linksland, however, permeated as it was by several sizable salt- and freshwater ponds and dotted with scatterings of scrub pine, bayberries, beach plum, and other indigenous growth. But by any measure it was land well-suited to golf and in 1925 the bearded, ex-mental patient set about building his ideal course.

Curiously, despite his great affluence, Shaw spent very little money on design and construction, planning the holes himself and utilizing only a handful of local

The only known aerial photograph of Cedar Bank. A close look reveals the presence of several bunkers and holes not a part of Quincy Shaw's original design. (National Archives)

laborers, a single horse and an earth scoop to bring them into being. Not surprisingly, this imposing crew took nearly three years to fully execute their employer's plans. Equally predictable was the fact that so primitive a construction process could only result in an extremely natural golf course. Cedar Bank, it seems, was the poster child for minimalism 75 years before the phrase took hold as a modern architect's buzzword.

Playing out of the Shaw family cottage (which doubled conveniently as a clubhouse of sorts), the links began benignly enough with a simple drive-and-pitch par 4. The 535-yard second likely served as a bit of a wake-up call but it wasn't until the dangerous third that things really picked up. Stretching 450 yards directly into the prevailing wind,

this monster required a truly heroic tee shot played across the rocky bluffs and a small pond, all to set up a long-iron or wooden approach to a modest green laid nearly in the shadows of the clubhouse. As volume of play was seldom an issue on Shaw's personal layout, one can well imagine smarter players bailing out deliberately into the adjacent 18th fairway, turning the third into a distinct three-shotter. Curiously, as Cedar Bank was alternately listed with a par of 72 or 70, it can be surmised that both the third and 15th may, in their earliest years, have played as par 5s. This appears to have been changed, however, by the early 1930s.

The 340-yard fourth was also dangerous, primarily because of the stark seaward slope of its fairway. Described in a manner similar to the famously slanting ninth at Pebble Beach, this shorter version obviously favored a right-to-left tee shot working against the incline, keeping one's ball from tumbling downward onto the beach.

The remainder of the front nine appears to have been relatively long but somewhat nondescript, a condition which changed abruptly at the 410-yard 10th. Here was a long par 4 turning left-to-right around the large salt pond, requiring as courageous a tee shot as one dared to set up a manageable approach. Laid-up drives were probably common, especially given the decidedly unfriendly break in the fairway near the 250-yard mark. But their result was an into-the-wind second aimed at a small, water-guarded green.

The 140-yard 11th, easily Cedar Bank's shortest hole, was made memorable by its forced carry over the pond, with both tee and green perched atop modest bluffs. Aside from its obvious all-or-nothing nature, the 11th also required players to cross the hazard on a small barge, powered by rope and pulley. In his quest for naturalness, apparently, Quincy Shaw was loath even to construct a bridge.

Water next came into play at the 13th, a straightforward 385-yarder whose green was paralleled by the rocky shoreline of the bay. But this paled in comparison to the forced carry required at the 190-yard 14th, a dangerous par 3 played to a green perched right at water's edge. Though otherwise hazardless, this putting surface surely proved itself an elusive target, especially on windier days when the prevailing gusts required one's long iron to be aimed well out over the surf to avoid being swept far left of target.

Following the 445-yard 15th (something of a brute after its apparent reclassification as a par 4), the 410-yard 16th required another dangerous approach to yet another bluff-guarded green.

Then came what was perhaps Cedar Bank's most fascinating hole, the 310-yard 17th. Here, as at #10, the primary challenge was determining just how much of the salt marsh might be carried with a driver. On this occasion an all-out blast for the green was a real possibility, though the carry was fully 250 yards, quartering against the prevailing wind.

Though not quite as difficult as the adjacent third, the 425-yard 18th was still a suitable finisher—yet one wonders if Shaw was ever tempted to reverse the two holes in order to provide a truly epic close.

Like most "estate" courses, Cedar Bank received comparatively little play, though several important golfers including Bobby Jones and Massachusetts favorite son Francis Ouimet did visit. More frequently, however, it was just a few of Quincy Shaw's closest friends, spending summertime weekends away from the big-city heat of Boston or New York. Shaw himself seldom visited after Labor Day, instead passing his time at a Boston town house on Exeter Street, a North Shore family estate or a winter beach house in Nassau, Bahamas.

Architecturally, it is curious to note that by the late 1930s, significant bunkering and perhaps even a new hole or two appear to have been added to Cedar Bank, though no record exists as to who precisely did the work, or when. What is known is that by the late 1940s, an aging Quincy Shaw was visiting hardly at all, and the facility was ultimately allowed to grow over in 1948. Though maintaining the clubhouse (which had never even been equipped with a telephone) for many years, Shaw's heirs sold much of the property to the federal government in 1959, upon the establishment of the Cape Cod National Seashore. Few if any golfing features remain visible upon the site today.

How Cedar Bank Would Measure Up Today

The primary question would be the course's ownership. For with a fair number of less-than-inspiring holes, only a wealthy individual unconcerned with turning a profit likely could have resisted the urge to "strengthen" things in several places. But left in its original form, Cedar Bank would surely be among the most talked about courses in New England, not so much for its overall challenge but rather for its marvelous setting, unique history, and conspicuous cache of All-World holes.

30

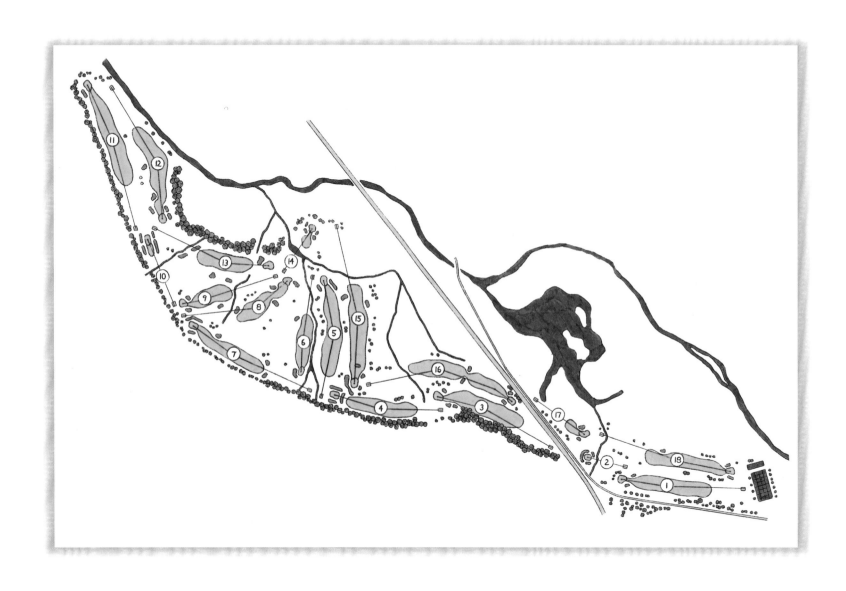

GREENBRIER (NO.3)																				
420	130	430	353	370	300	415	360	300	3078	220	440	455	400	160	480	500	190	420	3265	6343
4	3	4	4	4	4	4	4	4	35	3	4	4	4	3	5	5	3	4	35	70

THE GREENBRIER (NO. 3)
WHITE SULPHUR SPRINGS, WV

SETH RAYNOR (1924)

The game of golf, at least so far as it has prospered in America, has long been a private club affair. One need only compare the design, conditioning and general player etiquette on display at most public facilities with those seen at private clubs to quickly reinforce this conclusion. But if further evidence is needed, a quick glance at the major golf magazine rankings tells us that roughly 80% of our consensus Top 100 courses are distinctly private in nature. Similarly, the U.S. Open has visited only three nonprivate sites (Pebble Beach, Pinehurst, and, most recently, Bethpage) in its 100+ year existence. Thus it is not unreasonable to conclude that in the twenty-first century, it is behind guarded gates that the heart of the American game will continue to lay.

But such was not always the case. In fact, some may be surprised to learn that during the final decade of the 1800s, well before the founding of so many of our most distinguished private clubs, golf was widely played in all manner of resorts throughout the country. From the mountains of New England to Florida's Gold Coast to the Monterey Peninsula, relatively primitive courses, generally hewn from marginal terrain by whichever

Scottish émigré proved handiest, served as staples of the seasonal vacationer's recreational experience.

Though the Greenbrier came into the golfing derby relatively late (its first course opening in 1910), the game itself reached White Sulphur Springs considerably earlier. For a preponderance of evidence suggests that the very first standardized course in America, the six-hole Oakhurst Links, opened in the tiny mountain town way back in 1884—fully four years prior to John Reid and his Apple Tree Gang's more chronicled operation in Yonkers, New York. But the Oakhurst layout would close within a few short years and soon be forgotten—that is, until a modernized nine-hole version returned in 1994 to capitalize on ancient history.

At the Greenbrier proper, serious golf began with the arrival of the resort's Number One course (known today as the Old White) in 1913. Situated primarily across Howards Creek to the northwest of the famous Georgian-style hotel, this 6,250-yard, par-70 layout was designed by the legendary Charles Blair Macdonald with help – likely in large proportion – from his protégé Seth Raynor. As always, the ratio of

Overview of the 'Casino' and sections of all three prewar courses. The first and 18th of No.3 are visible at left. (*Golf Illustrated*)

work between these two architectural giants remains uncertain, though it can be said that as a rule (and especially on projects far from New York City) Raynor likely did the vast majority of on-site design and construction. Whatever the case, their combined effort at the Greenbrier certainly yielded fine results, with *Town and Country* magazine calling the Number One course "beyond

a doubt one of the finest courses in the country, and probably the very best south of Philadelphia."

Though a nine-hole short course was subsequently erected to handle less accomplished players, golf's enormous burst of popularity would necessitate the construction of a second full-sized layout by the early 1920s. Once again Macdonald and Raynor were called upon, only this time history is clearer as to the division of labor; though C.B.'s name would long be associated with the Greenbrier's Number Three course, he himself wrote that after 1917 only six facilities received any of his personal attention. The Number Three wasn't one of them.

Yet we can hardly pity the grand old resort for by this time Raynor had come into his own, having already completed his enduring classics Shoreacres and Camargo, among many others. His work at White Sulphur Springs was similarly well-received despite being performed on a challenging piece of property. Writing in Golf Illustrated magazine in 1924, one J. Lewis Brown reported that "No. 3 course has not a weak hole in its whole makeup, and when one realizes the obstacles that confronted the builders, due to rough and timbered ground in its virgin state, the finished product appears incredible."

And, at 6,343 yards, par 70, quite difficult as well.

The usual assortment of Macdonald/Raynor replica holes dotted Number Three, the models for which are outlined in detail in *The Missing Links*. High on that list was the Short hole, technically a Macdonald original which had debuted as the fifth hole at the National Golf Links of America nearly 15 years earlier. Featuring a green nearly surrounded by sand and permeated by a prominent horseshoe-shaped ridge, it appeared on the Number Three as the 130-yard second hole.

Though distinctly different from its namesake at the National, the 353-yard Sahara fourth was another outstanding test, requiring an approach of only modest length but great accuracy, its green slightly elevated and ringed with bunkers, and grass hollows.

The 370-yard fifth featured a similarly dangerous green – flanked by bunkers, backed by a steep fallaway – but the short par-4 sixth was perhaps of greater interest. Named Cape on the scorecard, this 300-yarder did not conspicuously exhibit either of the traits associated with

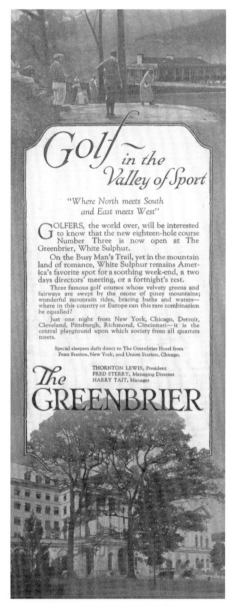

This 1925 advertisement highlighted the opening of course No.3.
(*The American Golfer*)

A fine example of Raynor-style bunkering at the Greenbrier. This unidentified image shows golfers putting on what appears to be the second green. (*Golf Illustrated*)

and-pitch made interesting by the left-side creek.

Number Three's longer back nine began with a favorite Raynor replica, the ever-challenging Biarritz. Modeled after an ancient clifftop hole in Biarritz, France, this 220-yarder featured a large, squarish putting surface fronted by a four-to-six-foot deep swale, and lined on either side by large, geometrically precise bunkers. Surely a wooden club for most during the Golden Age, the Biarritz could always be counted among the very toughest holes on which to achieve par figures.

The back-and-forth 11th and 12th offered little respite at 440+ yards, particularly as the former ran predominantly uphill. Yet for fans of classic design the 400-yard Punchbowl 13th likely held more interest with its green sunk below the surrounding terrain, allowing for elements of both leniency and luck on one's approach. This Greenbrier version was also noteworthy for its tee shot, which required a generous carry of both water and sand to reach its plateau fairway.

The 160-yard 14th, like the original third at Augusta National, was a replica of the Eden at St. Andrews. Like MacKenzie's Augusta version, the Greenbrier's lacked any rear bunkering (generally used to approximate the waters of the Eden Estuary) but featured the usual steeply sloping green and deep frontal bunkers. In reality, both holes were more adaptations than true replicas, but for anyone whose tee shot finished above the hole or in either bunker, par was an excellent score regardless.

Back-to-back par 5s marked one's trip home but the most memorable of the finishers was likely the 190-yard 17th, another Raynor version of the world's most copied hole, the Redan 15th at North Berwick. As with any standard Redan, the smart shot here was toward the right-front of the green, allowing its substantial contour to release the ball naturally toward any center or left pin position. As first-timers frequently learned the hard way, a ball flown

this favored C.B. Macdonald original, namely a bold-as-you-dare dogleg and a green extending outward into a large, often liquid hazard. Despite being famously epitomized by such spectacular renditions as the 14th at the National and the fifth at Bermuda's Mid Ocean, however, the Cape frequently appeared in straighter, shorter versions where the hazarded side of the fairway simply offered the preferable angle for one's second shot. The fifth at the Lido and the 15th at Macdonald's lost Shinnecock Hills layout carried this flag as did the Greenbrier's sixth, a drive-

directly at such a flag, unless perfectly struck, would generally skip long or, even worse, find the deep front-left "Redan" bunker.

Finally the 18th, though not of any great strategic interest, was surely solid, playing gently uphill to a putting surface that had previously served as the last green of the nine-hole short course.

That the Number Three course does not exist today can probably best be attributed to the Greenbrier's continued success and growth. For with its various expansions and reconfigurations, most of Raynor's original holes had already disappeared prior to Jack Nicklaus's complete rebuilding of the facility for the 1979 Ryder Cup matches. Today the land houses holes from both Nicklaus's design and Robert Cupp's more recent remake of the old Lakeside

Number 10, the Biarritz. The bunkering in this photo is far less symmetrical than the Raynor norm—but this shot was taken 12 years after opening. (*Golf Illustrated*)

course, rechristened the Meadows. Though neither provides the classic Golden Age feel of Raynor's defunct Number Three, both are well in tune with today's modern, technologically altered game.

How The Greenbrier Would Measure Up Today

As a blue-chip resort course.

With a bit of standard lengthening, Number Three would rank among the South's more character-filled vacation layouts, though one suspects that given the relative blandness of several replica holes, it would not stand among Seth Raynor's absolute elite. Still, both the back nine and an overall par of 70 would guarantee enough challenge to make us wonder: if able to view 75+ years of step-by-step development with the flawless vision that is hindsight, would the resort wish that it might somehow have rebuilt the older Number One course and kept Raynor's Number Three intact?

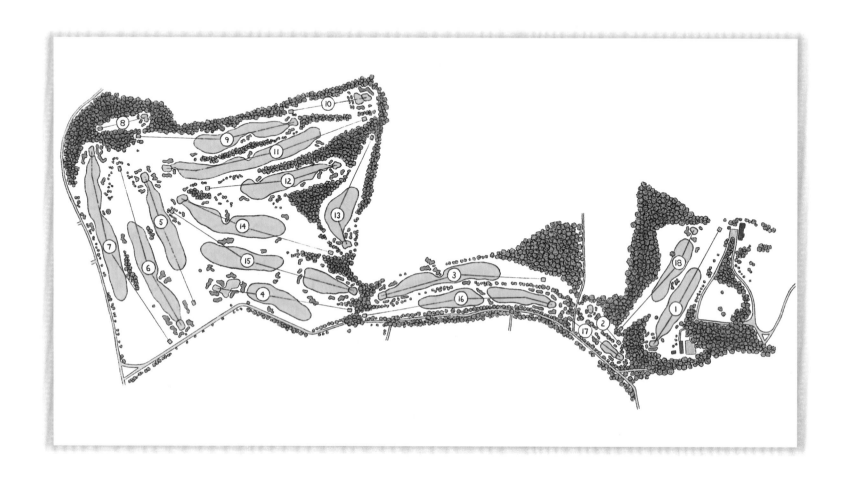

HUNTINGTON CRESCENT (WEST)																			
350	140	445	370	360	448	590	135	445	3283	210	570	340	315	445	540	520	190	330	3460	6743
4	3	4	4	4	4	5	3	4	35	3	5	4	4	4	5	5	3	4	37	72

HUNTINGTON CRESCENT CLUB (WEST)

HUNTINGTON, NY

✧

DEVEREUX EMMET & A. H. TULL (1932)

Few indeed are the American country clubs whose active operations date back further than the Huntington Crescent Club, which began life as the Crescent Athletic Club of Brooklyn in 1888. Located in Bay Ridge, where they enjoyed a commanding view of the Narrows and Upper New York Bay, the Crescents adopted golf as early as 1896 when a rudimentary nine-hole facility was built. Three years later another nine was added and though bisected by roads and hemmed in by all manner of urban development, this basic layout was something of a metropolitan area star based solely upon its incomparable vistas.

But with the growth of golf's popularity and the invention of the rubber or "Haskell" ball came an evolved sense of what constituted suitable playing conditions. Many early club courses were rapidly deemed obsolete and replaced, quite literally, by greener pastures further out in the country. In such a context, it seems somewhat surprising that the Crescents remained in Bay Ridge right up until the latter years of the Roaring Twenties—but only then, with the city ready to swallow them up, did they finally elect to move.

A relatively remote Long Island site was selected, for the town of Huntington lies a full 35 miles east of Bay Ridge. But here, on the old Roy Rainey estate, the Crescents found their ideal property: 300 acres of rolling woodlands and meadow, complete with the beautifully landscaped Rainey mansion to serve as a clubhouse. Intended was a gamut of recreational activities to rival the grandest of clubs, including golf, tennis, all manner of field games, a winter toboggan slide and nearby beach and yachting facilities on Huntington Bay.

As excellent as their planning was, however, the Crescents' timing was comparably awful. For the great Depression was just setting in as the new club came to life, ultimately crippling most every aspect of its development. Thankfully there was time at least to complete construction of the golf facility, a highly ambitious project of 36 holes.

Chosen as architect was then-69-year-old Devereux Emmet, veteran designer of over 85 courses and possessor of connections within New York's high society that even his good friend Charles Blair

The expansive bunkering of the par-4 fourth illustrates both A.H. Tull's shaping style and the sandy nature of the terrain. (*Golf Illustrated*)

Macdonald might envy. One assumes it was such entrée that landed him the plum Crescent Club assignment, but the club's choice could hardly be questioned. For by 1930, Emmet had built or rebuilt at least 50 layouts in the New York area—a number unequaled by even his more famous rival, A.W. Tillinghast.

It must be mentioned that by this relatively late stage of his career, Emmet had taken on a design partner, Alfred H. Tull, a British émigré whose more free-flowing bunker style began to creep into the partnership's work just prior to 1930. Such bunkering would prove a hallmark of both courses at the Crescent Club and though not altogether true to Emmet's solo style, it certainly worked out well enough in Huntington.

Constructed literally in double time, the shorter East course opened first, on July 4, 1931. The 6,743-yard West course would come on-line the following summer and was, in its day, among the longest and toughest layouts in the golf-rich Metropolitan section.

Following short-but-precise openers at the first and second, the West's long par-4 third gave ample hint of what lay ahead. Stretching 445 yards, it was one of four two-shotters measuring at least this length, no small thing even with the expanding popularity of steel shafts. Like most of Emmet's longer par 4s, this one allowed the player a bit of leeway on his approach, with seven bunkers forming an alleyway into the green, but the front of the putting surface left unguarded.

Though less publicized than the brawny 10th, the 135-yard eighth was an all-or-nothing Emmet classic. (*Golf Illustrated*)

The 370-yard fourth set out across more open terrain whose sandier nature was exploited in the form of seven decidedly large bunkers threatening the approach. The uphill fifth and long, downhill sixth proceeded back and forth, leading to another staple of an Emmet design, the immensely long par 5. In this case the seventh ran 590 yards, much of it proceeding up a long, gentle grade. Though obviously not reachable in two, it nonetheless required a relatively aggressive drive played close to a cluster of right-side trees, for a leftward bailout added enough yardage to make getting home in three not altogether certain. Ultimately one's third (or fourth) was played to a small putting surface set back against the trees and framed by large, distinctly Tull-like bunkers.

Indicative of Emmet's proclivity for greatly varying his hole lengths, the eighth then measured all of 135 yards from the very tips. Yet a more appealingly dangerous hole one could little imagine, for a line of three very deep bunkers fronted the shallow green, making for an inspiring all-or-nothing sort of shot.

It goes without saying that the 445-yard, tree-lined ninth was an impressive test but it's entirely possible that many players looked right past it, to the 210-yard 10th. For here was a showpiece, a long par 3 requiring a 185-yard carry over a very deep ravine whose precipice was dotted with small, rough-edged bunkers. Clearly a hole of real distinction, it was singled out in a 1934 *The American Golfer* article by four-time Major champion Jim Barnes as one of the finest in America. Barnes happened to be the Crescent Club's professional at the time so some element of bias can be assumed. Yet in this same piece, Barnes eloquently spelled out the perceived weaknesses of wind-free inland golf when he wrote of the 10th: "It's showy, and shooting to carry that ravine is a thrill. But it is always a cut-and-dried 185-yard carry. If that hole were sitting out on a windy headland, sometimes that carry would be an easy iron and sometimes, in the face of the wind, it might be impossible for any drive. Then this hole would be something to write about; but they don't rise to supreme distinction without the spice of the salt sea breeze."

Well said.

The 570-yard 11th was another behemoth, requiring a tee shot played back across the ravine, but little beyond brute strength thereafter. A brief respite was offered at the 12th and 13th before the 445-yard 14th required a very long and accurate approach to a somewhat elevated green.

Now standing far, far from the clubhouse with holes running out, Emmet ate up a good deal of interceding real estate with back-to-back par 5s. At the 540-yard 15th, a large left-side bunker required negotiation off the tee if a

Golfer tees off on the difficult 445-yard 14th, played to the elevated green visible in the distance. (*Golf Illustrated*)

and woods left little margin for error. The 330-yard 18th, on the other hand, offered a wide fairway and the opportunity to be aggressive. Such a short par-4 finisher was yet another of Emmet's favored schemes, though in this case a particularly delicate approach shot made birdies a well-earned commodity.

Hard-pressed for cash during the Depression and war years, the Crescent Athletic Club sold off most of the land which encompassed the championship West course, retaining the shorter but more centrally located East. Much of its Emmet & Tull routing remains in play as today's Huntington Crescent Club layout, though at least four holes have vanished altogether (see page 208) and substantial alterations have been made on many of those that remain. The sole enduring traces of the West course are holes one and 18, retained as the 15th and 16th in the current configuration.

How Huntington Crescent Would Measure Up Today

As one Devereux Emmet layout still capable of challenging in the modern age.

Generally built on smaller tracts of land, many of Emmet's remaining New York-area designs suffer from a marked lack of length—an affliction from which Huntington Crescent's West course would largely have been immune. With its massive par 4s and 5s, and its two splendid par 3s, the West would surely measure up well among so many fine Long Island neighbors. Additionally, if the East course joined it in remaining consistent with Emmet's original design, today's Huntington Crescent Club would stand behind only Winged Foot and Baltusrol as the Metropolitan Section's best 36-hole facility.

line of cross-bunkers were to be comfortably carried on one's second. At the narrower 520-yard 16th, the second offered three distinct options. The most aggressive player could attempt to cut their approach along the property line in hopes of getting home in two. The more conservative might try to place his ball between the various flanking bunkers, leaving himself a wide-open pitch. The most careful, however, could always lay back short of the sand, a relatively risk-free play but one leaving a much longer approach.

Running flush against Flower Hill Road, the 190-yard 17th followed Emmet's model of allowing long-iron approaches room to run up, though the adjacent bunkers

The 18th green of Huntington Crescent's East course (see page 208) sits before the Men's Locker House, a free-standing facility located a short distance from the main clubhouse. (*Golf Illustrated*)

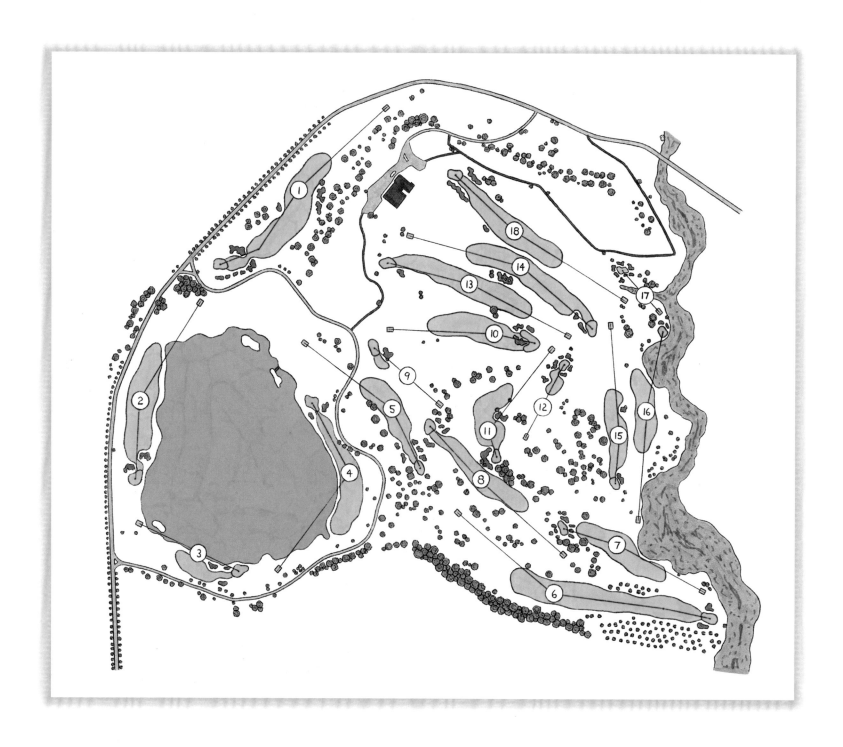

LA CUMBRE																				
500	420	240	425	365	620	320	400	190	3480	330	300	180	425	450	340	405	110	465	3005	6485
5	4	3	4	4	5	4	4	3	36	4	4	3	4	4	4	4	3	5	35	71

LA CUMBRE COUNTRY CLUB
SANTA BARBARA, CA

⚬

GEORGE THOMAS & BILLY BELL (1925)

For all the purported good it does for ailing economies, wartime has seldom, if ever, benefited the game of golf. On a small scale, the everyday economic challenges experienced by nations embroiled in conflict have threatened the well-being of countless courses, often in the form of reduced maintenance practices, sometimes in the permanent loss of certain hazards or holes. In more extreme cases, the large, open stretches of well-located land proved ideal for training grounds or air bases, leading to the takeovers of such courses as the Lido or Scotland's Turnberry by Allied forces during World War II. At Turnberry, one Mackenzie Ross (a more perfect name cannot be imagined) renovated the Ailsa course to an entirely new standard, turning it into a world-ranked classic and regular host of the Open Championship. At the Lido, American naval construction consigned the once-elite C.B. Macdonald/Seth Raynor layout to oblivion. At most other facilities, the end results of wartime austerity lay somewhere in between.

The difference between the La Cumbre Country Club, a Santa Barbara mainstay since 1918, and so many other war-affected clubs was that La Cumbre survived the actual years of conflict relatively unscathed. Certainly some bunkers became overgrown and things were in a relative state of disrepair, but the fundamental changes that ultimately ruined the golf course actually took place after the war was over.

But we get ahead of ourselves, for the La Cumbre story does indeed date back to Tom Bendelow's building of an 18-hole course on the site in 1918. Like many Bendelow-designed facilities, however, this 6,089-yard, par-70 layout lacked a bit of inspiration and was renovated at least once, by persons unknown, in the years soon to follow. But it wasn't until 1925 that La Cumbre would take its place among the Golden Age greats, a quantum leap facilitated by the hiring of Captain George C. Thomas Jr. to supervise a substantial renovation.

Thomas, renowned designer of such enduring Southern California standards as Riviera, Bel-Air, and the Los Angeles Country Club, was aided in his labor by his regular sidekick, Billy Bell. He was also helped by the acquisition of real estate not available to the club at the time of Bendelow's work, specifically a large piece of acreage to the course's southwest. This land

Aerial photo diagrams the newly available land utilized during the Thomas and Bell renovation. Some original Bendelow holes are visible at left. (*Golf Architecture in America*)

was largely occupied by Potter Lake (alternately referred to as Laguna Blanca) and would become home to the layout's opening five holes, the first of which followed Thomas's frequent prescription of a downhill, potentially reachable par 5.

But it was at the 420-yard second that the fun really started. One of several La Cumbre holes diagrammed in the Captain's landmark 1927 book *Golf Architecture in America*, it was a dogleg-left played across a corner of the lake and into the prevailing wind. Though similar in concept to C.B. Macdonald's Cape hole, Thomas added his own ripple by sprinkling a series of small mounds up the center of the fairway, effectively dividing the preferred left side from the more conservative right.

Perhaps even more celebrated was the 240-yard third,

simultaneously one of the toughest and most strategic par 3s in the history of American golf. Angled across the corner of the lake and requiring a massive carry to reach its left-side pin positions, it was in fact a modified version of the ubiquitous Redan, with green sloping properly from right to left. Embodying similar principles to Thomas's fourth at Riviera and 13th at Bel-Air, the third was made somewhat more manageable by the subtle slope of its fairway, allowing one to aim safely away from the lake yet still maneuver a well-played stroke onto the putting surface.

As difficult as the third might have played, the fourth may well have been tougher, its 425 yards doglegging nearly 90° around the lake. Given the progressive narrowing of the fairway as it rounded the hazard, the safe play appears to have been the expedient one—but what a long and intimidating second shot it must have left.

Following a mid-length par 4 came one of the longest holes of its era, the 620-yard sixth. Yet this was in many ways one of La Cumbre's less imposing tests, owing to its downhill terrain, relative lack of hazards, and generally favorable wind. The seventh, by comparison, was far more interesting, requiring the skirting of a large barranca off the tee to open the best line of approach to a heavily bunkered green.

The eighth and ninth were both steady enough but it was at holes 10 and 11 that Thomas's flair for the innovative again galloped into play. At the 10th, a 330-yarder with an extremely wide fairway, the captain utilized one of America's earliest boomerang greens to inject a massive dose of strategy: place your drive on the correct side of the fairway relative to the day's pin placement and face an essentially simple pitch. Find the wrong side and four became a good score. At the 300-yard 11th, the decision was even more plainly defined: clear a bunker guarding the dogleg – a nearly 200-yard carry – and the simplest of wide-open approaches remained. Lay up safely to the right, on

Fine image of the seventh green, detailing Thomas and Bell's intricate bunker work. (*The Links*)

The amazing 10th green, its boomerang shape creating strategic questions all the way back to the tee. (*Golf Architecture in America*)

the other hand, and a much-longer second had to cross the course's largest bunker to find the small putting surface.

Following the reverse-Redan par-3 12th, the 13th and 14th added some brawn to an otherwise-short back nine, with each providing a ground route for one's long-iron or wooden second. The drive-and-pitch motif returned briefly at the 15th before the player turned for home with one of the most spectacular golf holes ever built.

La Cumbre's 16th has been listed at anywhere from 365 to 416 yards, though the 405 referred to by Thomas seems to match up best with early aerial surveys. The key to the hole was the positioning of its green well out upon a ledge on the far side of the barranca. A large hillside tumbled down from its left, perhaps helping a pulled approach but also obscuring one's view of the putting surface from the left side of the fairway. Consequently it was important to

place one's drive as close to the barranca, trees, and rough as possible. Yet even from position A, the mid- to long-iron second must surely have been among the most daunting of all time.

As a fascinating sidelight, Captain Thomas disclaimed any credit for the design of this legendary hole, writing, "No. 16 hole was laid out and built by the chairman of the Green Committee, Mr. Peter Bryce," and that, "the credit for this beautiful hole belongs to him." A brief fit of modesty? Astute readers of *Golf Architecture in America* will notice that beneath its photo of the 16th green, in the lower right-hand corner reserved for architectural credits, there appears only one name: Bryce.

The barranca crept around, in somewhat less menacing form, to the tiny 17th, a beautiful hole requiring a deft touch to avoid six bunkers and hold the shallow green. The

The green of the 405-yard 16th—offering as dangerous and exciting an approach as any hole in golf. (*Golf Architecture In America*)

The tiny 17th green, surrounded by trademark Thomas and Bell bunkering. (*Golf Architecture In America*)

uphill 18th, though on the surface a bit anticlimactic, likely made for fascinating finishes as its relative shortness and open-fronted green surely tempted most capable ball-strikers to have a go at it in two.

So where is La Cumbre today?

Still very much in business on the same site. However attempting to trace its slide from epic George Thomas design to today's rather pedestrian track is no simple task. Clearly the decay began during an extended World War II closing, a fact confirmed by midconflict aerials which show many bunkers already overgrown and disappearing from the scene. At least three separate postwar remodelings have since resulted in an essentially new golf course, with housing filling most of the land previously occupied by holes 8, 11, 12 and 15 and only a handful of current holes utilizing the same corridors as the originals. Among this latter group, the par-3 third still exists (as the 215-yard 13th), though its green complex has been modified and an alternate island green added! Similarly, today's 402-yard eighth occupies essentially the same land as the exceptional

16th—but with the barranca filled in and large-scale tree growth blocking much of the right side. How much has the once-legendary hole changed? On his first visit, noted architect and historical expert Tom Doak gave up his search, concluding that the 16th, like so many of La Cumbre's best holes, simply no longer existed.

How La Cumbre Would Measure Up Today

A scary thought is that holes number two, three, and four all offered considerable room for lengthening and thus would measure something like 470, 255, and 485 yards today—apparently desirable distances to our modern, discombobulated USGA. But on the whole, La Cumbre would look less like Riviera and Los Angeles Country Club and more like Bel-Air or the lost Bell and Thomas collaboration at El Caballero: eccentric, fascinating, highly strategic tests with enough all-American holes to make them entirely worthwhile in any era.

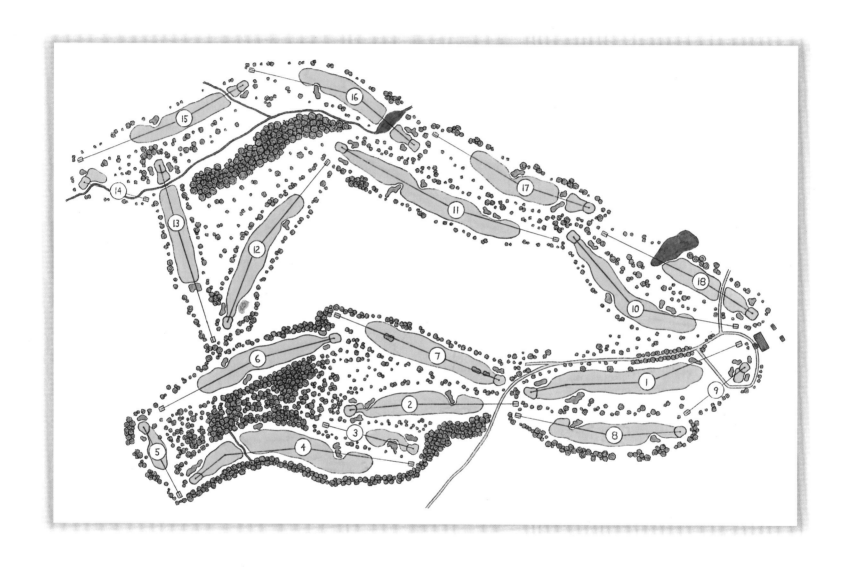

OVERHILLS																			
450	375	205	509	172	417	384	360	150	3022	422	510	411	387	146	385	395	371	380	3407	6429
5	4	3	5	3	4	4	4	3	35	4	5	4	4	3	4	4	4	4	36	71

OVERHILLS GOLF CLUB
OVERHILLS, NC

❦

DONALD ROSS (1911)

*C*harting the history and evolution of a golf course initially constructed more than 80 years ago can frequently be a difficult task. Such early layouts came into being, for example, prior to the onset of aerial survey photography—or, for that matter, most other manner of substantial documentation. Complicating matters further are the occasions where the property's purpose was altered, economic turbulence descended, or wartime dictated its standard vagaries of alteration and neglect. But even more challenging, the researcher quickly discovers, are those circumstances where the story line lacks consistency, where varied accounts provide discordant information and thus demand some highly educated guessing nearly a full century after the fact.

Donald Ross's Overhills Golf Club, located on land now owned by the United States Army in Manchester, North Carolina, very definitely falls among the latter.

The Overhills story – at least those parts of which we can be certain – is a fascinating one, dating back to the early years of the last century when Mr. J.F. Jordan of Greensboro acquired 40,000 acres of undeveloped sandhills real estate for use as a hunting and equestrian paradise. Golf, too, made an early appearance, with Donald Ross being brought aboard, perhaps as early as 1910, to provide a state-of-the-art layout. It has been reported that Ross built nine holes initially, then added nine more in 1918, yet considerable evidence exists to suggest that the entire 18 was actually completed in 1911. A property survey map dated 1913, for example, illustrates 18 holes and a *Golf Illustrated* article from February 1917 makes clear reference to a fully completed facility. Furthermore, an undated set of Ross drawings illustrates changes planned for 16 out of 18 holes, suggesting that perhaps there was a 1918 visit, but that it was strictly to renovate an already-established layout.

Whatever the precise dates of Ross's involvement, a new twist was encountered in 1915 when a syndicate headed by Mr. Percy Rockefeller purchased half of Jordan's land. It has generally been accepted that Rockefeller's intention was to turn the golf course into a private estate facility and over time its usage was in fact enjoyed exclusively by his family and friends. However, the 1917 *Golf Illustrated* piece is most

The slightly downhill approach to the 411-yard 12th, one of Overhills' tougher par 4s. (*Golf Illustrated*)

emphatic in discussing Overhills' development as a commercial resort, highlighting both its private railway stop and the impending construction of a hotel to be called the Vanderbilt Inn. What sidetracked these plans is not altogether clear, though the federal government's condemnation of 18,000 acres for an expansion of Fort Bragg must surely have played an important role. Regardless, Rockefeller bought out Jordan's remaining interest upon the latter's passing in 1920 and with that, it appears, any notion of a public-oriented facility expired.

Equally intriguing is the evolution of the course itself, a layout which, even into the early 1990s, was being billed as "virtually unchanged" from Ross's original design. Unfortunately, such claims seem erroneous on several counts. First, like all Southern courses of the period,

Overhills began life with sand greens. Therefore, lacking any evidence of additional World War II-era involvement by Ross, we can safely conclude that whatever contouring the green complexes enjoyed following the war represented a tangible change.

Beyond this inevitability, there is ample evidence to suggest that following the course's reduction to nine holes prior to the Depression, the "restored" back nine of the modern era was substantially altered from Ross's version. To wit: its routing differed noticeably from the property's 1913 survey map, in direct contrast to the front nine which matched perfectly. More conclusively, postwar accounts placed Overhills in the 6,000 to 6,100 yard range, whereas both the 1913 survey and the 1917 article had it extending beyond 6,400. Indeed, as late as 1989, front-nine yardages

The over-the-pond approach to the elevated 16th green, a genuine Donald Ross classic. (*Golf Illustrated*)

were a precise match to a nine-hole scorecard dated 1940, which in turn was nearly identical to both the 1913 survey and Ross's undated renovation plans. Back nine lengths and pars, however, matched none of the above.

Regardless, what does seem clear is that following Ross's early renovation work, Overhills was among the very finest layouts in the South. Of course, this is hardly surprising given both the well-chronicled advantages of the sandhill country for golf (see Pinehurst) and the fact that, according to *Golf Illustrated*, Ross was provided with his choice of 3,500 acres and an unlimited budget. J.F. Jordan instructed Ross – as it seems every developer in history has

told his architect – to create "a course that will have no superior." Whether Percy Rockefeller, who likely was on the scene by the time of Ross's renovation, cared either way is not a matter of record.

Overhills began innocently enough, first with a typically short Ross par 5, then a manageable par 4. The 205-yard third stepped up the challenge a bit but still served largely as a warm-up before the course's first really fine hole, the 509-yard fourth. Here the combination of the fairway's right-to-left sweep and a small creek crossing near the 400-yard mark required a tee shot played boldly over the single right-side fairway bunker, for anything placed left would leave little option but to lay up one's second. A perfectly positioned drive was only half the battle, though, as the continued turning of the fairway mandated a long, hard draw if a huge right-side bunker was to be avoided on one's second.

The 417-yard sixth was another hole that received its share of notoriety, with its tee shot requiring threading between two awkwardly angled bunkers. The 384-yard seventh, on the other hand, demanded one's full attention on the approach as two bunkers placed short and dead-center mandated either a purely struck aerial shot or a skilled run-up brought in from right to left.

The 150-yard ninth, played to a tiny, heavily bunkered green, closed the outward half in birdie-or-bogey style.

The tougher back nine commenced with one of Overhills' longest stretches, beginning with the 422-yard 10th. Here, like at number four, the angle of the dogleg was a key component, for an aggressive drive over the right-side bunkers left a manageable approach while a leftward bailout mandated an extremely long second.

Following the club's longest hole, the slightly uphill 11th, came another noted par 4, the 411-yard 12th. Bending gently from right to left, this hole offered plenty of fairway for an aggressive drive but narrowed considerably on the approach, a mid- to long-iron threaded between a large right-side bunker and sandy waste area left. Curiously, this waste area began life as a swampy depression but was filled in – complete with transplanted wire grass – during the Ross renovation.

The 387-yard 13th was an oddity in the Ross catalog, offering forced carries on both shots, though the waters of Muddy Creek were situated fairly well shy of the putting surface. This hole appears to have survived relatively intact into the modern era, though the creek was at some point widened into an attractive and dangerous pond.

The 1917 *Golf Illustrated* article singled out the 16th, 17th and 18th as all being among Overhills' five best holes, suggesting that if nothing else, the layout certainly closed in style. The 16th in particular was a beauty, gently doglegging nearly 400 yards across a small pond to an elevated, well-bunkered green. The 371-yard 17th was more strategic, its key being a large, wire-grassed mound situated just right of the putting surface. Because of this man-made obstacle, a left-side tee shot was vastly preferable—no simple affair as it required a 200-yard carry over a large, deep bunker cut into the face of a natural rise.

The drive at the last presented more of a psychological challenge, requiring a carry of roughly 150 yards to negotiate a modest lake. This left a mid-iron approach to another elevated green, the face of its left-side bunker planted with wire grass.

As mentioned previously, Overhills remained in play (with at least nine original holes) until the late 1990s when the Army purchased the land to incorporate into its 160,000-acre Fort Bragg complex. Reports at that time wrote the course off as doomed and it was quickly allowed to become overgrown. Of late, however, based upon economic and environmental concerns, there has been talk of restoring the facility to its previous specs, a move which, if successfully accomplished, would place Overhills among the very best of the country's military golf facilities.

How Overhills Would Measure Up Today

Better than most Donald Ross courses of the period.

Because of the general spaciousness of the property, Overhills would be relatively easy to extend, with most holes offering plenty of room for lengthening. Measuring, say, 6,800 yards, it would remain a wonderfully classic test, one capable of standing up to all but Pinehurst #2 among Ross's sandhills creations. In short, it would genuinely fit one of golf design's most overused marketing phrases:

"A true Donald Ross gem."

PALM BEACH WINTER (Approximate)																				
555	380	325	130	365	480	160	335	370	3100	530	350	215	340	450	370	335	180	465	3235	6335
5	4	4	3	4	5	3	4	4	36	5	4	3	4	4	4	4	3	5	36	72

PALM BEACH WINTER CLUB
NORTH PALM BEACH, FL

C.B. MACDONALD & SETH RAYNOR (1925)

Particularly today, in what we universally refer to as the "Information Age," it is difficult to imagine any social, business or sporting event of substance not being chronicled with abundant accuracy, the specifics of its existence a matter of record for all to behold. This would especially be true for any recreational entity well-heeled enough to occupy 100+ acres of valuable real estate, be constructed by the highest-profile builders of its day, and include numerous people of affluence among its clientele. A Donald Trump building ignored? A Steve Wynn casino resort overlooked?

Inconceivable.

Imagine then for a moment a golf club established during the heart of the game's Golden Age, located on Florida's affluent Gold Coast and built by the famed Palm Beach developer Paris Singer. Imagine its course being planned by the very father of American golf, Charles Blair Macdonald, and his renowned architectural protégé Seth Raynor. Imagine a clubhouse built by legendary architect-to-the-wealthy Addison Mizner. And finally imagine that such a facility could come into being and then, despite so glorious a pedigree, lapse into extinction almost completely beneath the radar screen of history. Impossible, you say?

Welcome, then, to the Palm Beach Winter Club.

Located between the Intracoastal Waterway and what one period publication described as "the tropical loveliness of Della Creek," the Winter Club was in fact the brainchild of Paris Singer, heir to the sewing machine fortune and general partner-in-crime of legendary architect Addison Mizner. Singer became involved in Palm Beach real estate development accidentally, initially commissioning Mizner to build a World War I soldiers hospital, then converting the structure into the sumptuous Everglades Club when the war ended before the hospital could open. From his position as Everglades Club czar, Singer reigned supreme, not only by running the elite club but by actually deciding, at his own pleasure, who would be granted membership privileges at the outset of each new winter season.

Ultimately wishing, like Mizner, to develop his own version of paradise, Singer eventually purchased a small spit of land immediately north of Palm Beach and christened it Singer Island. That this planned development lay very close to the site of the Winter

This image, from 1953, is likely the earliest remaining survey shot of the Winter Club. It is interesting to note
the many subtle changes that have taken place since the time of the earlier aerial. (National Archives)

Club is immediately obvious. Thus, while records of the club's origins are rather sketchy, it is not unreasonable to assume that its creation was intended as a blue-chip amenity to the luxurious subdivision.

Though not a golfer by reputation, Paris Singer clearly grasped the game's importance in attracting his desired level of clientele. As early as 1919, he had commissioned Seth Raynor to build nine rather sporty holes for the Everglades Club, a layout which Raynor would expand to 18 some six years later. It was almost surely during this expansion job that Raynor undertook the design of the

Winter Club, though the new layout would bear several notable differences from its Everglades predecessor.

To begin with, it was substantially longer and tougher, a track built to test players of quality rather than simply entertain less skilled snowbirds. Perhaps more importantly, it was billed as that most scarce of architectural creatures, a Charles Blair Macdonald design constructed by Seth Raynor. Though local press clippings did occasionally mention Macdonald, his well-documented abstention from post-1917 projects makes this claim dubious, suggesting instead that C.B. simply lent his ever-valuable name while entrusting Raynor with the actual work. That Charles Banks, Raynor's protégé, likely handled much of the construction following his mentor's 1926 death adds yet another historical flourish.

In any case, the fruits of the team's labor was impressive. For the Winter Club turned out a full-sized test, complete with ocean breezes, more water than was customary for a Macdonald/Raynor design, and very much the full dose of classic replica holes. It was also terribly undocumented, with the complete lack of recorded yardages necessitating a careful scaling of the published 6,335-yard total to a post-World War II aerial photo.

The Winter Club began abruptly enough with a man-sized par 5, a 555-yard dogleg-right whose staggered bunkering bore great resemblance to some of Charles Banks's solo work. Turning westward, the 385-yard second was equally testing, its relative lack of length (playing with the prevailing breeze) mitigated by several prominent bunkers and the waters of today's Intracoastal Waterway to the right.

After a narrow drive-and-pitch came the fourth, by all indication an adaptation of Macdonald's favored Short hole. Though not as geometrically measured as most Raynor versions, it did offer enough sand to virtually surround the putting surface and, one assumes, the requisite horseshoe-shaped ridge within the putting surface.

Another apparent replica was the 160-yard seventh, a one-shotter likely patterned after St. Andrews' famous Eden. To the trained eye there will immediately be some question here, for while the long rear bunker simulates the dangers of the original's Eden Estuary quite nicely, the standard front hazards appear to have been lacking. Oblique aerial photos suggest that the green was somewhat elevated, however, raising the possibility that some form of grass bunkering existed in their place.

The 530-yard 10th was the Winter Club's longest hole and paved the way for several outstanding challenges to follow. The 11th, a 350-yarder, was the obligatory adaptation of Macdonald's classic Cape hole. Swung along the quiet waters of Della Creek, this version was especially demanding as its fairway proceeded to narrow, pinching tightly between water and sandy waste, the further one drove.

The 12th was the Biarritz, built to full scale at roughly 215 yards but perhaps slightly less ominous over the flat Florida terrain. Like most Macdonald/Raynor versions of this perennial favorite, all evidence indicates that the area before the swale was always maintained as fairway, thus negating the ultimate Biarritz prospect of having to putt through the five-foot-deep hollow.

At only 340 yards the 13th might have appeared a respite, but the angling of the green favored an approach played from the left side of the fairway, the very spot guarded by one large carry bunker off the tee. The carry itself was hardly backbreaking (perhaps 175 yards) but was generally played dead into the Atlantic breeze.

The 450-yard 14th was much longer and, despite the helping wind, an obviously tough two-shotter. The out-and-back 15th and 16th were the only sections of the course to actually cross Della Creek, setting up that most popular of replicas, the Redan 17th. Once again we have a hole of the prescribed 180-yard length, with putting surface angling front-right to back-left and falling away distinctly at the rear. What stands different about this rendition, however, is the extreme narrowness of the green and the greater length of the bunkers, perhaps indicative of Charles Banks's expanded construction role following Raynor's untimely death.

The 465-yard finisher was, by all appearances, a relatively manageable par 5. Yet it must be noted that due to its similarity in length with the downwind 14th, some uncertainty remains as to which was the three-shotter. The combination of wind direction, a very imposing left-side fairway bunker and the green's tight location between sand and

Circa 1930 aerial photo, with the Intracoastal Waterway and the Atlantic Ocean beyond. There's a bit less undeveloped land left in this area today.

maintenance road (far more conducive to a pitched third than a wooden second) strongly suggest that it was the 18th. It is really only the smallness of the 14th green that muddies the matter.

Despite being built by the rich for the rich, the Winter Club seems initially to have been rather a low-key facility, its amenities essentially being limited to a golf course and Mizner's small, stately clubhouse. Unfortunately, like a great number of south Florida facilities, the land bust of the mid-1920s followed by the onset of the Depression put the hammer to Paris Singer's operation rather quickly. By 1940 it was doing business as a unique sort of "open" facility, available for play to anyone already affiliated with one of the surrounding area's social, beach, tennis, or golf clubs. Eventually the property would be taken over by the city of North Palm Beach and a post-World War II renovation, likely by Trent Jones Sr., resulted in an entirely new back nine and material changes to most every Raynor/Banks characteristic on the front. Subsequent work by Mark McCumber in 1990 further genericized the layout.

For fans of the Macdonald/Raynor style of design, the Winter Club's descent into blandness represents an obvi-ous loss. But for the golfers of south Florida that loss is even greater. For while hardly a Hall-of-Fame layout, the Winter Club joins an impressive list of regional facilities which, if still in their original form, would do a great deal to alter the state's reputation as a golf architecture wasteland.

How The Winter Club Would Measure Up Today

As a much-needed Golden Age classic in an area largely devoid of them.

But more to the point, the argument can be made that given their obvious idiosyncrasies, Macdonald/Raynor courses are most accurately judged when compared to others of their own kind. In this context, the Winter Club would hardly have measured up to C.B's National, Lido, or Mid Ocean layouts, nor, for that matter, with Raynor's works at Camargo, Fishers Island, Shoreacres, or Yale. Yet it was undeniably a fascinating creation, especially in its ability to superimpose the various replica holes upon the relatively flat Florida soil.

A jewel in its neighborhood.

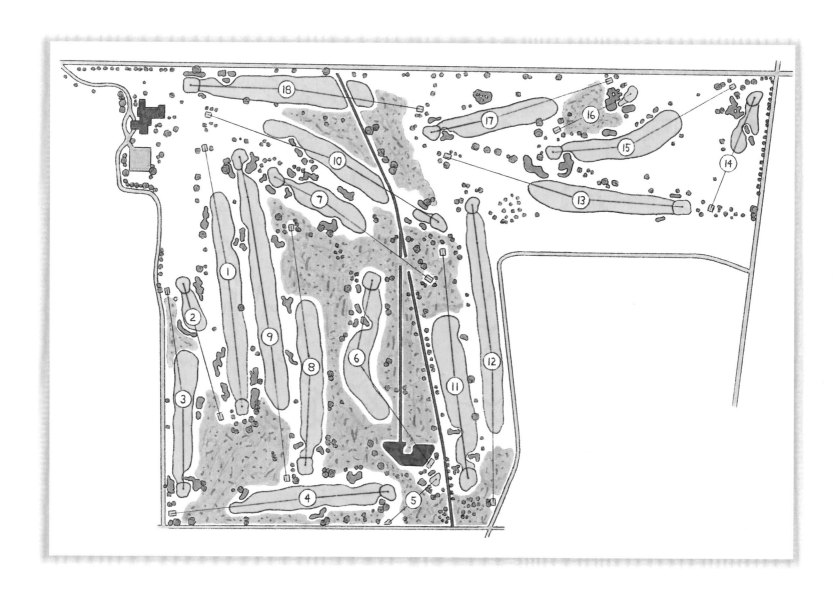

PASADENA																			
450	225	350	385	110	375	305	410	530	3140	425	395	480	430	190	365	140	340	386	3151	6291
4	3	4	4	3	4	4	4	5	35	4	4	5	4	3	4	3	4	4	35	70

PASADENA GOLF CLUB
ALTADENA, CA

GEORGE O'NEIL & JACK CROKE (1920)

*A*t no time in its history has the game of golf enjoyed a greater rush of course construction than in pre-Depression America, a roughly 10-year period in which literally thousands of courses sprang up from coast to coast, many in major metropolitan areas. In line with this national trend, Los Angeles County experienced a boom which was equally remarkable. For according to the highly reliable *American Annual Golf Guide*, 10 courses – six 18-holers and four nines – existed in the county as of 1919. By 1931, only 12 years later, that number had nearly quintupled to 46, with 40 18-holers and six nines.

Such widespread growth obviously touched most inhabited areas of the county including one of its earliest hotbeds of wealth and seasonal visitors, Pasadena. Indeed, with the late nineteenth-century extension of the Los Angeles and San Gabriel Valley Railroad to Colorado Street, tourists from the East and Midwest flocked into the area each winter, many staying at grand hotels such as the Green, the Raymond, and the Huntington. As in most early resort areas, golf became a primary attraction by the early 1900s and it is worth noting that several of these hostelries maintained their own courses. Most were nine-holers and relatively rudimentary, though the Raymond's was generally considered among the better hotel courses in the country and the Green's (located on today's California Institute of Technology campus) was built by that accomplished Golden Age architect Willie Watson.

In any event, such golf-minded resort operators must surely have been happy when, in 1920, a most ambitious golf and real estate venture first opened its doors as the Pasadena Golf Club. Located on the site of today's Altadena Town Golf Course, in the very shadows of the beautiful San Gabriel mountains, the Pasadena Golf Club was intended as Southern California's grandest club, with initial plans calling for three 18-hole golf courses, full tennis facilities, a private airfield, and real estate subdivision. With men like two-time PGA champion Leo Diegel and well-known tour player Eddie Loos on its staff, it was clearly a well-financed operation and the attention paid to it in period hotel ads demonstrates plainly its importance to the resort community.

Ultimately only 18 of the planned 54 holes would ever be built, but such is merely a footnote in examining what was, in many ways, one of the West's most prominent and underrated prewar courses.

The Golf Club was laid out by a pair of Chicago-area professionals who dabbled in architecture on the side, George O'Neil and Jack Croke. Something of a journeyman in the design game, Croke's work was limited to collaborations with other Chicago pros including Jack Daray, Harry Collis, and Joseph Roseman. Pasadena would serve as his only recorded design credit outside of Illinois. O'Neil, on the other hand, was a bit more prolific, launching a solo practice in the late 1920s which included, in rather a neat coup, the Greenbrier Resort's third 18-hole course. O'Neil also maintained social ties to some of Chicago's wealthiest citizens including advertising magnate Albert Lasker, owner of the game's finest-ever private estate course (see Mill Road Farm in *The Missing Links*) and O'Neil's financial benefactor during the architect's later years.

In any event, the Pasadena course was laid out over rolling, sandy terrain that might, to the imaginative, call up romanticized memories of Pine Valley. Beyond some extensive desert-like waste areas, its predominant features were a narrow ridge bisecting the property from north-to-south and its parallel-running canal and reservoir, an unnatural but largely unobtrusive hazard. Interestingly, promotional sketches of the period suggested this reservoir might be a rather large hazard but early aerial photos prove that a less-expensive construction route was obviously chosen. Also worth mentioning is the fact that the course's nines were periodically reversed, with the configuration presented here appearing to be the most frequent.

Pasadena began with a bang at the 450-yard first, a slightly downhill par 4 which may well have originally been intended as a three-shotter. Lest one consider this driver-fairway wood opener a fluke, the 225-yard second quickly followed. Here another long approach was required, first

A general view of the Pasadena layout, illustrating the proximity of the scenic San Gabriel Mountains. (*Golf Illustrated*)

to carry a wide cross-bunker, then to slip between a large right-hand bunker and a seven-foot mound that blended into the green's left edge.

Following a pair of mid-length par 4s came one of Southern California's famous challenges, the 110-yard fifth. Described by Croke himself as "one of those easy three or hard five holes," it played over a sand-filled ravine to a small, slightly elevated putting surface guarded by several deep bunkers. Not surprisingly, this green was the smallest on the golf course and was backed by a number of large mounds as well.

The 375-yard sixth was a sharp dogleg-right around a large waste area divided by the canal. Here the artist's rendering of an expanded reservoir would have made for an impressive Cape sort of hole, though on the ancient theory that a player must continue playing his ball from a sand hazard (whereas he lifts clear of water), the as-built version may in fact have proved tougher.

After the drive-and-pitch seventh – no walk in the park with its huge stretch of sandy waste and seven maintained bunkers – came the beautiful 410-yard eighth. Here the ideal angle of approach lay on the left side of the fairway, but to find it required more flirtation with the open desert. From the optimum spot, one's second was slightly downhill to a large plateau green which fell steeply away on three sides.

The back nine began with what was likely the toughest hole on the entire course, the 425-yard 10th. This dangerous par 4 left little choice but to rip one's best drive directly over a line of five angling bunkers, for a ball pulled left faced more waste and a semiblind second over a large mound. The approach crossed the canal, then climbed to the top of the central ridge, requiring a lengthy carry to get safely home in two.

The ridge next appeared at the 480-yard 12th, an extraordinarily natural hole. Playing steadily uphill, its narrow fairway skirted the ridge top, requiring two or three very accurate shots to reach a bunkerless green situated in a narrow depression.

The 430-yard 13th looks equally deceiving on a map, its primary challenge coming from a deep concavity which crossed the last 80 yards of fairway, very nearly reaching the putting surface. Similarly rugged terrain also flanked

The concrete walls of the canal where it fronted the seventh tee. Admittedly something of an eyesore. (*Golf Illustrated*)

the 190-yard 14th, a longish par 3 played to a green pinched between a left-side gully and right-side out-of-bounds. Aimed directly toward 5,710-foot Mt. Wilson (home of the famous observatory), this was certainly one of Southern California's most scenic holes.

The same concavity which crossed number 13 influenced play at the 15th, 16th, and 17th as well. At the 365-yard 15th, one's approach played directly across it to an elevated green also fronted by a huge bunker. At the 16th, a 140-yard beauty, the ravine fronted the tee and required carrying prior to reaching a small green protected by large expanses of sand. The 340-yard 17th played over the chasm's deepest stretch but only for its first 100 yards, the remainder

The building of a green on Pasadena's desert-like terrain—no small agronomical feat in 1920. (*Golf Illustrated*)

running gently uphill to another ridge-top green.

Though measuring only 386 yards, the 18th was no pushover, primarily due to the dangers in play on one's drive. From a tee perched atop the course's highest point, a long, straight ball was required first to carry the canal, then to avoid a waste area left and out-of-bounds (in the form of today's Mendocino Street) on the right.

The Pasadena course underwent some degree of renovation at the hands of George Thomas's California partner Billy Bell in 1926. Though little is recorded regarding the specifics of this work, comparisons of Jack Croke's detailed written descriptions with the post-Bell layout suggest that the alterations were minor. Major change would come some 12 years later, however, when torrential rains inundated Southern California, doing significant damage to a large number of courses. Situated in a natural drainage area

beneath the San Gabriels, the Pasadena layout was virtually obliterated. As a result, Billy Bell would again be called in, this time to build an entirely new layout on the western half of the original property. That facility – the nine-hole Altadena Town Golf Course – remains in play as of this writing.

How Pasadena Would Measure Up Today

The big question here would be one of maintenance. If O'Neil and Croke's original layout retained its open, sand-strewn look, Pasadena Golf Club would be one of the most talked about courses on the West Coast. If, alternatively, it was grassed-over and heavily treed (like so many of its early California brethren), it almost certainly would languish in complete anonymity. Just another medium-length, moderately hilly Golden State layout that once was something special.

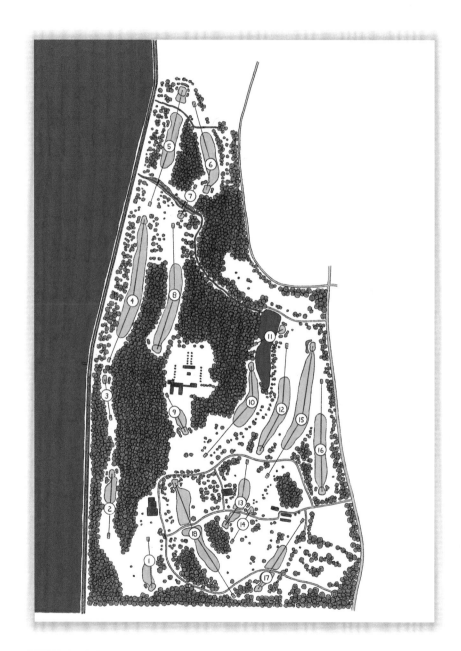

ROCKWOOD HALL																				
220	237	160	585	450	360	122	465	180	2779	397	140	430	275	136	527	407	284	463	3059	5838
3	3	3	5	5	4	3	5	3	34	4	3	4	4	3	5	4	4	5	36	70

ROCKWOOD HALL COUNTRY CLUB
TARRYTOWN, NY

✗

DEVEREUX EMMET (1926)

During golf design's Golden Age, when America's population was smaller and its wealth vastly more concentrated, step one in developing a first-rate country club was often the acquisition of a grand country estate. Such homesteads, many of which extended into the hundreds of acres, dotted the suburbs of most major cities, generally built by famous financiers or captains of industry in the late 1800s and early 1900s. The benefits of such properties to a fledgling club organization were several. For aside from providing well-located, undeveloped land whose terrain was nicely suited to golf, they generally offered a stately old mansion whose size, layout, and choice location were ideal for conversion into a clubhouse. Combine these attributes with numerous ancillary practicalities (well-established access roads, power sources, secondary structures, etc.) and it is easy to see why so many of America's finest clubs were born through such estate acquisitions.

When one examines the various criteria mentioned above then, it quickly becomes clear why so much excitement surrounded the establishment, in 1924, of Rockwood Hall. For Rockwood Hall was not to be built on just any rich man's retreat. It would occupy the former residence of Mr. William Rockefeller, brother and frequent business partner of the legendary John D. As such, Rockwood Hall was not simply a great Hudson River estate, it was *the* Hudson River estate, encompassing 400 acres of prime real estate with panoramic views up- and downriver.

The club was to be centered around the eponymous mansion, a turreted gray stone affair that bore more than a passing resemblance to a medieval castle and included, among other amenities, a glass-enclosed dining room. Several additional structures lay within easy walking distance including stables and a building designated for conversion to a gymnasium. A boathouse and pier were already in place on the Hudson and a modest lake (which would affect play on two golf holes) was well situated for summer canoeing and winter ice skating. Additionally, Mr. Rockefeller had installed miles of bridle and walking paths over the years, providing access to the estate's most prominent feature, its flora.

For William Rockefeller was a monumental lover of gardens and trees. So much so, in fact, that his great

The former Rockefeller mansion, surely one of the stateliest golf clubhouses of all time.
(*Golf Illustrated*)

hobby over the 40 years that he owned the estate was the constant improvement of its landscaping. Trees and shrubbery from all over the world were imported and formal gardens erected. English parks were studied and special equipment devised to relocate trees from place to more-idyllic place. The end product, undeniably, was an acreage of almost unparalleled botanical beauty, where one might truly savor the simpler pleasures of nature. But was such a carefully vegetated tract particularly well-suited to golf? Articles of the period screamed yes—but then what golf course architect of any era hasn't trumpeted the great possibilities incumbent to a prospective site?

Given that the club's founders were a group of New York City social and business leaders, it seems natural that the man chosen to integrate a golf course into so pastoral a setting was that mainstay of Metropolitan golfing society, Devereux Emmet. Actually, Emmet's initial mandate was to create two courses, and it is here where a bit of mystery begins to loom. For it is apparent from period aerial photos that despite reports to the contrary, no construction was ever undertaken on a second 18. Further muddying the early organizational picture is the apparent alteration of eight holes extremely late in the design process—so late, in fact, that a 1927 scorecard shows incorrect yardages for all eight, with each entry corrected by hand. Were these changes economically motivated? Were they the result of some reassessment of the available terrain? Whatever the case, they clearly represented something of a "Plan B" as the resultant layout began, rather uniquely, with three consecutive par 3s!

A smaller mystery also lingers regarding the involvement of Emmet's eventual partner A.H. Tull in the Rockwood Hall project. Specifically, published information has, in the past, listed Tull as codesigner, yet this seems highly unlikely. For while Tull did join Emmet's firm as a junior associate in 1924, he did not achieve full partnership (and begin receiving design credits) until 1929. No other pre-Depression Emmet design lists Tull as a partner, and given that Rockwood Hall demonstrated no sign whatsoever of Tull's uncommon bunker style, it seems a good bet that the credit is simply erroneous.

Emmet's design commenced with a hole which was utterly spectacular in its location, if not its play. Angled down a gentle grade, the 220-yard first began close to the elevated mansion and ran directly south, thus enjoying the dazzling view downriver which extended all the way to the Manhattan skyline some 20 miles distant.

The second hole turned back north and was the first of the altered bunch. A difficult 237-yarder carved through a heavily wooded patch, it had initially been planned as a 375-yard par 4, and early aerials confirm that a much larger swath (doglegging slightly right) had been cut through the trees. As with all of the alterations, we will likely never know the reason for the change.

Following the tightly forested third (built 40 yards shorter than initially planned) came two of Rockwood Hall's more memorable holes, the par-5 fourth and fifth. As one might expect from the variety-loving Emmet, the pair differed dramatically, with the former stretching a back-breaking 585 yards but offering little in the way of obstacle or strategic interest. The latter, on the other hand, measured only 450 yards but challenged the player with two narrow ravines and an elevated, well-bunkered green.

The first of these chasms was also integral to the 122-yard seventh, Rockwood Hall's shortest hole. Typical of a tiny Emmet one-shotter, it required a pinpoint pitch, down a hill and across the hazard, to a small green fronted by four bunkers.

The inward half was considerably more orthodox, playing to a standard par of 36. It began with the 397-yard 10th, running downhill off the tee, then around a leftward bend to a green bordered right by the lake. The beautiful 11th followed, only 140 yards but requiring a forced carry over

Aerial view of the estate prior to the club's establishment. The 18th hole, routed neatly between existing trees, would finish immediately in front of the mansion. (*Golf Illustrated*)

the water. Widely photographed during its brief heyday, it was surely the very private club's most recognizable hole.

Next came the long, uphill 12th, then a quick downshift to the diminutive 13th and 14th. On each of these shorter holes, one of the estate's paved access roads came prominently into play, especially at number 14 where it fronted the putting surface. Thus despite measuring only 136 yards, this final par 3 could be quite dangerous as a ball flown just slightly short might bound far, far over.

The 527-yard 15th was cited in period articles for the splendid prospect of its downhill tee shot, though on the whole it was the first of two long but rather mundane holes.

The 122-yard seventh, downhill and across the ravine. A typically demanding short Emmet par 3. (*The American Golfer*)

The 284-yard 17th was shorter and, so far as aerial photographs reveal, only somewhat more intriguing. The 463-yard 18th, however, definitely required some thought, snaking its way through the woods before emerging, past one prominent tree, for a gently uphill approach. Surely representing a good opportunity for one final birdie, the 18th was also well situated for club spectators with its putting surface positioned squarely upon the mansion's former front lawn.

It is perhaps worth noting that in response to the altered course's limited length, a prominent *American Golfer* article of 1927 mentioned the extension of several tees "back into the forest, bringing the length of the course to well over six-thousand yards." Beyond this easily foreseeable change, it has been frequently reported that A.W. Tillinghast was retained by the club in 1929 to perform a renovation, supposedly including the construction of five new holes. That Tillie did in fact work on the course has never been disputed. Yet a 1938 aerial photo clearly indicates no appreciable change to the original corridors of play, strongly suggesting that no new holes were ever constructed.

More clearly on the record is the fact that by 1929 the club was in real financial difficulty, its plans for a second 18 long since scrapped, its head remaining only just above water. Further hammered by the onset of the Depression, Rockwood Hall managed to stagger along until 1939 when, after operating briefly as the Washington Irving Golf Club, it shut its doors for good.

How Rockwood Hall Would Measure Up Today

It is difficult to envision so offbeat and unbalanced a layout surviving intact into the modern era, and even with its reported extension to over 6,000 yards (or even a bit more), Rockwood Hall would still be terribly short by today's standards. Given the difficulty that such a facility

The semiblind tee shot on the dogleg-left 10th provides a sense of the estate's wooded splendor. (*Golf Illustrated*)

The all-carry 140-yard seventh, played across a lake used for skating during the off-season. (*The American Golfer*)

might have in attracting affluent members in golf-rich Westchester, Rockwood Hall thus would seem an ideal candidate (like nearby Briar Hall) to have been purchased by a big-name developer for conversion into a real estate-oriented, overcooked modern facility.

This approach to an unidentified green (likely the 18th) required a deft touch to negotiate four bunkers and a three-level putting surface. (*The American Golfer*)

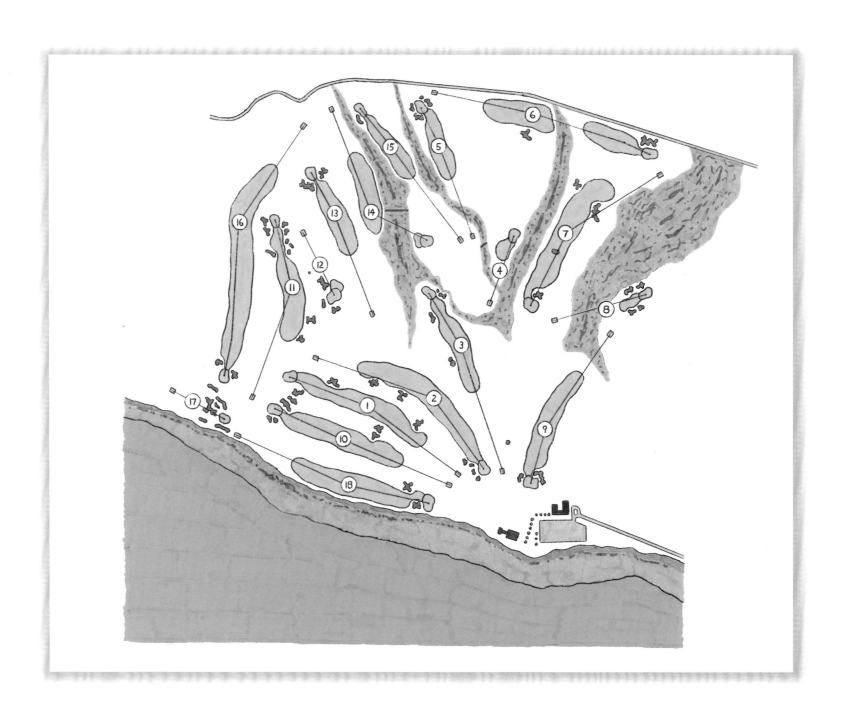

432	467	416	152	300	494	415	206	360	3242	411	380	150	308	365	343	565	128	442	3092	6334
4	4	4	3	4	5	4	3	4	35	4	4	3	4	4	4	5	3	4	35	70

THE ROYAL PALMS COUNTRY CLUB
SAN PEDRO, CA

⌘

BILLY BELL (1927)

With over 400 miles of Pacific Ocean coastline, the state of California would seem among the most likely of places for excellent seaside golf. The catch, of course, is that unlike Florida and much of the Atlantic seaboard, the California coast is mostly rocky and cliff-laden, providing countless inspiring views and secluded beaches but little in the way of British-style linksland. Thus with only a handful of exceptions, the Golden State's most famous seaside layouts are of the distinctly clifftop variety—though few are likely to suggest that Cypress Point, Pebble Beach, or Olympic's original Ocean Links were much the weaker for it. Indeed most knowledgeable observers would agree that these three were the finest coastal layouts built in California during the last century. But not far behind – particularly if one places a heavy emphasis upon the spectacular – was Billy Bell's finest solo creation, the Royal Palms.

Located at White's Point, on the southwest corner of Los Angeles County's dramatic Palos Verdes Peninsula, the Royal Palms was the brainchild of Mr. Aloi J. Amar, a successful area businessman and native of nearby San Pedro. A member of the Los Angeles Athletic Club, California Yacht Club, and the Jonathan Club, Amar wished to develop a facility of similar caliber closer to his peninsula home. Thus in the mid 1920s he put together an all-star cast of local financial types and set about acquiring the rights to the White's Point property.

And what a parcel it was, 350 clifftop acres situated above a secluded section of Pacific Ocean beach, its entire spread offering unparalleled views across the San Pedro Channel to Santa Catalina Island. On this exhilarating tract Amar planned the ideal private community, a seaside village which would include a full spectrum of recreational facilities, private dwellings, and a resort hotel, all situated around what was initially called the San Pedro Golf Club. The projected capital outlay for the development was a staggering $2.5 million which, if nothing else, confirms the intention to do everything on a truly first-class level.

Situated initially upon a flat, clifftop plain, then the rather severe foothills behind it, Billy Bell's golf course featured a degree of topographical change not frequently encountered among Golden Age layouts. In fact, simply finding a playable routing on such a site – a routing which incorporated four separate mesas and three canyons – was something of an accomplishment. Not surprisingly, Bell reserved his clifftop frontage for his finishing holes, but otherwise allowed each nine to take equal advantage (or disadvantage) of the often-rough terrain.

The course began in very difficult style with three long par 4s, only the last of which benefited from the incoming sea breeze. A bit of wildness was tolerated at the 432-yard first but not so at the 467-yard second, a brutal dogleg-right whose heavy bunkering surely raises the frequent Golden Age question of whether the hole might originally have been conceived as a par 5.

At 416 yards, the third has held a position of cultish fame over the years, for this was the hole primarily fea-

tured in a grainy old photograph in Captain Thomas's book *Golf Architecture in America*. Rather generically captioned "General View, San Pedro Course, California," this photo is perhaps the only shot in existence which adequately illustrates both the magnitude of the Royal Palms' terrain and the attractive way that Bell wove his golf holes through it. A gentle dogleg-left running into the base of a canyon, the third was also the only hole on the entire course where a tree came into play.

Climbing atop the property's central mesa, holes four and five marched steadily uphill, paving the way for an exciting set of front-nine finishers. The 494-yard sixth was a canyon-crossing par 5 angled close to out-of-bounds in the form of today's West 25th Street. The downhill 415-yard seventh required a careful drive to avoid both canyons and fairway bunkers, but surely took a backseat, at least in terms of difficulty, to the par-3 eighth. For at 206 yards, this ruffian required a long-iron or wood to be played across a canyon and between pairs of flanking bunkers to find a relatively small putting surface.

Following the downhill ninth, the 411-yard 10th returned to flat land and was another stiff test, requiring a well-struck approach in the prevailing left-to-right cross-wind.

The next six holes took on some rather tumultuous terrain, beginning with the uphill, 380-yard 11th. Here one's second was played up a narrow alley between seven bunkers to a hilltop putting surface. The downhill 150-yard 12th was largely a judgment proposition, something of a drop shot requiring the advantage gained by the plunge to be measured against the incoming breeze. The 308-yard 13th, though less spectacular, was a solid drive-and-pitch running up the hillside, bringing the player very near the course's highest point...and the onset of its very big finish.

There can be little exaggeration in stating that the 14th, at 365 yards, must surely have been among the most

General view of the Royal Palms. The third hole is located dead-center, running past the trees, into the lower reaches of the canyon. The bridge connecting the 14th fairway and green is visible at upper-left. (*Golf Architecture in America*)

breathtaking holes in the history of American golf. Little more than a drive-and-pitch due to its downhill tee shot, this sharp dogleg-left was menaced throughout by an enormous chasm, the depth of which can be seen in the background of the photograph of hole number three. As an additional distraction, the view from this tee – down several hundred feet to the shimmering Pacific, then on to the distant camel's humps of Catalina Island – was unsurpassed.

The 343-yard 15th, though distinctly less thrilling due to its uphill nature, was similarly dramatic, its tee shot also skirting the edge of the chasm. Curiously, the single greenside bunker flouted conventional strategic thought by being positioned on the left side (thus encouraging a drive away from the canyon) and we can only assume that it was so placed as a measure of mercy — to prevent slightly mishit approaches from pitching into disaster.

Following the long, downhill 16th, the 128-yard 17th might at first seem a puzzler, because of both its diminutive length and the decision not to perch its green directly at cliff's edge. As for the former, it seems more than coincidental that at nearly the same time he was building the Royal Palms, Billy Bell was also laying out his other lost masterpiece, El Caballero (see *The Missing Links*) some 30 miles north in Tarzana. There too the 17th was tiny (115 yards) but exceptional, with period writers frequently singling out its severely contoured green and all-or-nothing nature. We can reasonably surmise, then, that the green complex of the Royal Palms' 17th was similarly taxing. Why Bell elected to keep it several yards inland, however, we can only guess.

All of which leads us to the 442-yard 18th, a hole which, upon first glance, immediately challenges one to name a tougher or more memorable finisher of the prewar era. Off the tee, a steady crosswind forced a drive aimed very nearly over the cliff to find the heart of the fairway. A similar strategy was also necessary on one's approach and

The Royal Palms clubhouse, circa 1930. This building would survive nearly 30 years past the course's closing. (San Pedro Bay Historical Society)

must have been especially scary when the pin was tucked close to the precipice, behind one of two fronting bunkers.

Given the transportation limitations of its day, the Royal Palms' location – at the far end of the peninsula, in proximity to little more than the San Pedro shipyards – was a problem virtually from the beginning. The economic hardships of the Depression only magnified these difficulties, ultimately forcing the closure of the golf course in 1933.

As an interesting footnote, it appears that had the club managed to survive the Depression, it might well have expired during the 1940s anyway. For during World War II,

This picture, taken years after the course's closing, gives a fine sense of the property's spectacular clifftop location. The golf course was located on the developed parcel at left. (San Pedro Bay Historical Society)

the entire White's Point area was taken over by the military and fitted with training facilities, gun placements, and other defensive positions. Remnants of this wartime presence dot the area landscape to this day, suggesting that much like New York's legendary Lido, the Royal Palms likely would not have seen the modern era regardless of economic circumstance.

How The Royal Palms Would Measure Up Today

Wow.

Though a certain lack of strategy would likely rate the Royal Palms beneath the elite level, its remarkable terrain and world-class views would surely make it a major hit among today's omnipresent magazine rankings. With the requisite lengthening bestowed upon so many classics over the years, it would likely fall behind only Riviera and Los Angeles Country Club's North course among contemporary Southern California's finest—unless such vital criteria as "Conditioning," "Walkability" and "Tradition" were to somehow conspire against it.

And the 18th hole might well be as famous as Pebble Beach.

80

SHAWNEE INN																			
367	500	425	359	108	448	559	400	321	3487	472	344	164	353	449	360	135	486	221	2984	6471
4	5	4	4	3	4	5	4	4	37	5	4	3	4	4	4	3	5	3	35	72

SHAWNEE INN & GOLF RESORT
SHAWNEE-ON-DELAWARE, PA

A. W. TILLINGHAST (1911)

*I*t certainly seems reasonable that when discussing milestones in American golf course design, Charles Blair Macdonald's National Golf Links jumps quickly to the head of the line. Its 1911 opening, after all, broke ground in so many aspects of architecture, ushering in an era that would feature unsurpassed levels of design strategy, variety, and artistic beauty. Macdonald had set out to build the "ideal" golf course, blending superb original concepts with several replicas of great holes he had seen in the British Isles. That he succeeded grandly was universally agreed upon and in many ways, his son-in-law (and two-time U.S. Amateur champion) H.J. Whigham summed it up best when he wrote: "A course has been produced where every hole is a good one and presents a new problem. This is something which has never yet been accomplished, even in Scotland, and in accomplishing it here, Mr. Macdonald has inaugurated a new era in golf."

Indeed.

Yet generally overlooked in such architectural polemic is a course opened during the very same year at Charles Worthington's new Pennsylvania resort, the Shawnee Inn. As keenly aware as most period hotel men of golf's role in attracting clientele, Worthington hired the son of a friend, one Albert Warren Tillinghast, to create his new 18. Though an accomplished player, Tillinghast had little architectural experience prior to taking the Shawnee job, yet he clearly shared a good deal of C.B. Macdonald's conviction that golf courses needed to be diverse, interesting, and above all, strategically challenging. In fact, in 1914 Tillinghast definitively argued for the need to upgrade traditional concepts of design when he wrote that, "The development of Shawnee was of vital importance, for it demonstrated the theory that those who golf really want to play over a course which provides an exacting test."

In assessing Shawnee's significance, then, it is important to recall that Tillinghast was building it simultaneous to Macdonald's creation of the National and not, like so many others, as a reaction to it. Though perhaps aware of C.B.'s ongoing Southampton project, Tillie created at Shawnee a test which arguably was more strategic and sophisticated than any American layout which preceded it. It was, for a 34-year-old neophyte, a truly remarkable accomplishment.

This early aerial clearly shows holes two through 15—not one of which remains in play today.

That nearly none of Tillie's original layout remains today is surely the reason for Shawnee's overlooked place in architectural history, and to the purist this relative lack of attention may in fact be justified. Yet for what it's worth, we must also acknowledge that Tillie himself began the evolutionary process, tinkering considerably with his design during its early years. Such continuous flux makes tracking many of the specific changes difficult, and the course illustrated here is absolutely not the original. It is, however, a faithful representation of the version upon which Paul Runyan won the 1938 PGA Championship, save for one piece of poetic license: by 1938, the second hole played as a mid-length par 4, altered – for reasons we shall likely never know – from its spectacular over-the-water par-5 origins. The earlier version is presented here as much for enlightenment as sentiment.

Things began with the hole that Tillie himself considered the toughest, the 367-yard, creek-threatened first. In a 1913 open event, in the midst of his second American tour, the great Harry Vardon managed an expensive eight here, an occurrence which might well have caused him to emulate the immortal Lord Castlerosse who instructed his caddie to "pick that up, have the clubs destroyed, and leave the course."

But history suggests that Vardon played on, and well he might, for the original 500-yard second was a genuine classic. Built along the lines of C.B. Macdonald's Cape hole (which, we must note again, did not yet exist to be copied), it challenged the player to bite off as much of the river as he dared on his drive, for the left side of the fairway surely provided the optimum angle of approach.

In later years Tillie would become legendary for the dangerous bunkering of his green complexes and while his hazards at Shawnee were not as deep as many later to come, they certainly seemed as strategically prominent. The third was a fine example of this with its tiny green pinched between sand and treeline, while the bunker placement at the fourth dictated a right-side tee ball if a decent approach angle was to be secured. For variety, there was the minuscule 108-yard fifth followed promptly by the difficult 448-yard sixth and the 559-yard seventh, easily the course's longest hole.

At 400 yards, the eighth appeared fairly stout but in reality provided a great opportunity to carve off some yardage by aggressively cutting the corner of the dogleg. The ninth, in turn, was nearly driveable, but its tiny green required obvious precision given its virtual imprisonment by sand.

Perhaps the next hole of real note was the 164-yard 12th, a mid-length par 3 played to a small, punchbowl-like putting surface. The 360-yard 13th was of similar interest

THE SHAWNEE COUNTRY CLUB
SHAWNEE-ON-DELAWARE
PENNSYLVANIA

ANNOUNCES THE OPENING OF THE

NEW GOLF COURSE

ON

SATURDAY, MAY 27, 1911

RAILROAD STATION, WATER GAP, PA.
AUTOMOBILES MEET ALL TRAINS

This simple advertisement announced the opening of an American golf architectural landmark. (*The American Golfer*)

because Tillie himself used its strategy as an instructive example in the years to follow. Here a large area of man-made mounding ("Alps") barged into the fairway's left half, requiring an aggressive, well-struck drive to be carried. The less assertive enjoyed the option of bailing out right, but from there faced a tougher angle of approach due to green-side bunkers and the difficult slope of the putting surface.

Next up was the 449-yard par-4 14th, another strategically engaging affair. On the tee shot, a single carry bunker affected only the weaker player, while the more incursive hazards down the right side only bothered the highly skilled man. The dub then decided whether to attempt to carry the mounded area that divided the fairway near the 375-yard mark, while the scratch attempted to reach the small but relatively accessible green with either a long-iron or wood.

By far the most famous hole at Shawnee – and, thankfully, one of the few that still exists – was the 16th or

Binniekill, named for the branch of the Delaware River over which it was played. Though only 135 yards, this was truly the epitome of the forced carry, for anything short of the plateau green would surely finish with a splash. Aside from being so exciting a challenge, this hole was noteworthy for several other reasons, not the least of which was the early use of a small boat to carry players from one side to the other. Stories of astronomical scores taken here are legendary but one of the best involved the playing of a so-called Tombstone tournament, an event in which each player was allotted the par of 72, plus his handicap. He would play until he used up this total number of strokes,

then deposit his mock monogrammed tombstone at the spot of his last. Tillie himself reported that, "On this day the Binniekill teeing ground resembled a cemetery, although one of the players had remaining 19 strokes when he came to the place where he was going to die."

Though bland by comparison, the 17th and 18th were effective finishers, the former a distinctly reachable 486-yard par 5, the latter a long but relatively open par 3. The 18th currently joins the 16th and the first as the only remaining holes bearing any resemblance to Tillinghast's 1911 originals. The primary reason for this was a 1963 expansion to 27 holes performed by Indiana-based archi-

The frightening tee shot facing the golfer at the famous Binniekill—all carry to a green surrounded by trouble. (*The American Golfer*)

The tee shot at the 486-yard 17th, played directly over the back portion of the 16th green. (*Golf Illustrated*)

tect William Diddel, a move which made great economic sense relative to the available land but little with regard to the potential marketing of a genuine American classic.

How Shawnee Would Measure Up Today

Though hardly as unique, grand, or inspiring as the National Golf Links of America, Shawnee was a golf course whose strategic intricacies likely would not have translated badly to modern golf. Even with some logistically simple lengthening, it wouldn't have been a particularly brawny track but its old-fashioned styling and first-rate history would surely have held it in good stead. As a monument to early golf design in general and the formative years of A.W. Tillinghast in particular, it would be a living shrine.

Or, if you like, a poor-man's National.

LOST LINKS

88

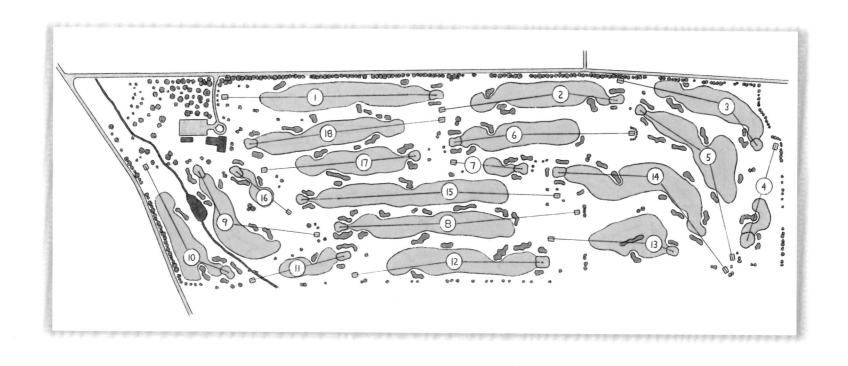

ACACIA (Approximate)																				
490	395	350	220	415	395	155	535	330	3285	320	220	425	280	480	570	150	340	430	3215	6500
5	4	4	3	4	4	3	5	4	36	4	3	4	4	5	5	3	4	4	36	72

ACACIA COUNTRY CLUB
HARLEM, IL

WILLIAM LANGFORD (1924)

Located approximately 15 miles southwest of downtown Chicago's landmark Loop, Acacia Country Club was only the fourth recorded Illinois layout of native son William Langford. A 1908 graduate of Yale, Langford teamed with construction engineer Theodore Moreau to ultimately create more than 20 courses in the Prairie State, and it can be reasonably argued that Acacia was among the four or five best. Oddly, despite being open to the public for several decades, the specifics of Acacia's layout were rather poorly documented. As a result, it is only through careful scaling from a prewar aerial photo (and a bit of deductive reasoning) that the following hole yardages and sequence of play can be presented.

Acacia was in many ways a typical Langford design, featuring his trademark elevated green complexes, profuse bunkering and an ever-present element of strategy, particularly off the tee. One need look no further than the 415-yard fifth for an example, where a large bunker cut into the outside corner of the dogleg, necessitating a tough decision: drive aggressively toward the narrow fairway left of the hazard, leaving a fairly simple short-iron second, or lay back safely to its right, mandating a more difficult approach of nearly 200 yards.

Three similarly attractive holes, the 330-yard ninth, 320-yard 10th and 280-yard 13th, were not only thought-provoking but also served to illustrate the marvelous strategic possibilities inherent in short par 4s. In each case, at least three distinct options faced the player on the tee, ranging from safe lay-ups with irons to all-out drives aimed for the green. Naturally, the dangers increased in proportion to the player's boldness, though with regard to the 13th we can only assume the severity of what was likely a steeply elevated green.

Acacia's narrow, north-south property, located east of Flag Creek adjacent to Wolf Road, was eventually sold off to real estate developers in the 1960s. It is now occupied by the Indian Head Park residential neighborhood and, at its northern reaches, the modern Par Three Golf Club. For the public-course golfers of a major city (for whom tee-time access is always an issue), it is an obvious loss. But for fans of William Langford, few of whose original designs remain anywhere near intact, it is a very disappointing absence indeed.

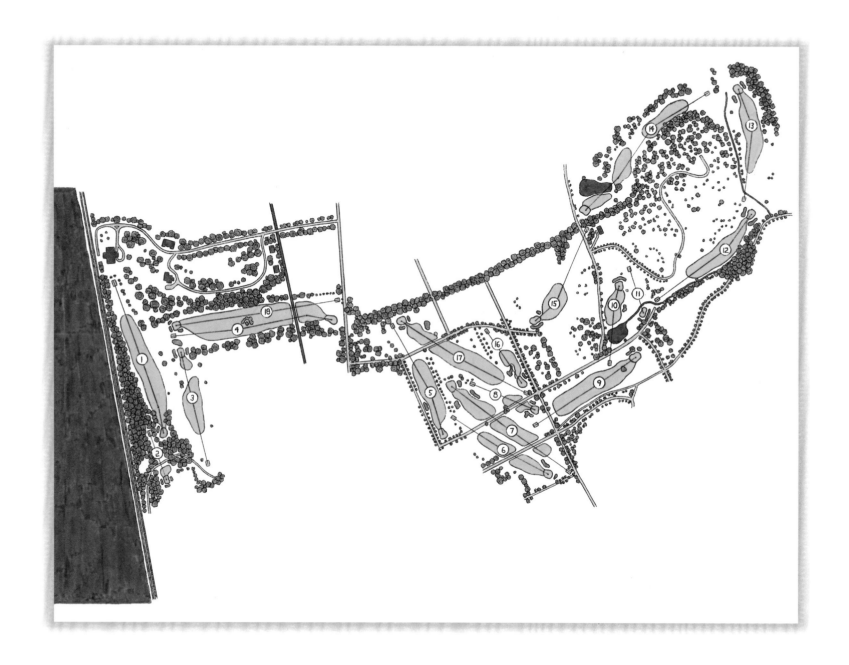

ARDSLEY																			
430	140	350	500	336	370	431	200	360	3117	233	160	366	372	475	300	180	444	483	3013	6130
4	3	4	5	4	4	4	3	4	35	4	3	4	4	5	4	3	4	5	36	71

ARDSLEY COUNTRY CLUB
ARDSLEY, NY

꘎

DONALD ROSS (1917)

With an 1895 opening-day roster that included the likes of John D. and William Rockefeller, J.P. Morgan and Cornelius Vanderbilt II, the Ardsley Country Club may legitimately have claimed the title of America's ultimate rich-man's club. In fact, being ideally located for a crop of millionaires whose palatial estates filled the nearby banks of the Hudson River, Ardsley's membership was estimated to have a combined 19th-century net worth of a staggering $2 billion!

As one might expect, so affluent an operation featured only the very finest of facilities including a grand riverside clubhouse, yacht basin, lawn tennis courts and a private station on the New York Central and Hudson River railroad—a splendid amenity made possible by Vanderbilt's ownership of the line.

For their golf course, the founders turned to the original British golf émigré, Willie Dunn Jr. of Musselburgh, Scotland. Dunn, who by this time had shaped Shinnecock Hills' first 18-hole layout while serving as the Southampton club's professional, created what he would later call his American masterpiece. Though short and somewhat rudimentary by today's standards, this track was certainly exciting, featuring an opening sequence of holes hop-scotching across ravine tops high above the Hudson.

Issues of leased land and surrounding development were soon to pop up, however, and in 1919 Donald Ross was retained to substantially reconfigure the already-altered Dunn layout. Given an odd mix of land parcels and unavoidable road crossings, Ross produced a course which might best be described as uneven, in places being shoehorned into whatever acreage was available, yet elsewhere boasting fine golf holes.

Ardsley's best stretch likely ran from the 11th through the 14th, where the terrain steepened and the holes wound scenically around North Mountain. It also finished in style as the 18th played first across the old Croton Aqueduct, then utilized a St. Andrews-like double fairway for the duration of its 483 yards.

Though hardly one of Ross's elite designs, Ardsley was a fascinating example of weaving golf holes through prohibitive spaces, squeezing and shaping them as needed. Why would Ross take on such a task? The exorbitant influence of the club's wealthy membership, one guesses. But when Ardsley moved its operations further inland, Dr. Alister MacKenzie was retained for a 1928 redesign and the Ross layout was no longer.

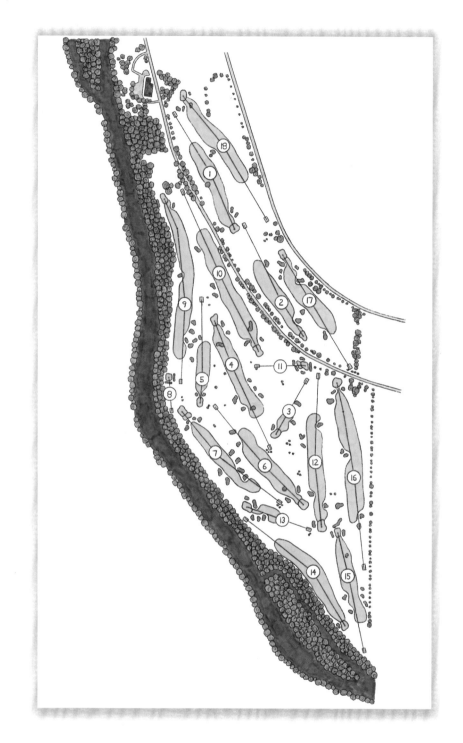

ARLINGTON																				
400	360	185	375	290	400	410	110	525	3055	505	150	450	205	425	340	510	360	439	3384	6439
4	4	3	4	4	4	4	3	5	35	5	3	5	3	4	4	5	4	4	37	72

ARLINGTON COUNTRY CLUB
COLUMBUS, OH

DONALD ROSS (1929)

Those familiar with the great body of Donald Ross's portfolio are well aware of the discrepancies between his most- and least-inspired work. At places such as Pinehurst and Seminole, the prolific Scotsman produced fascinating, world-class designs of timeless quality. At many lesser-known stops, however, he left layouts that were somewhat less exciting. For the researcher, who often must jump through hoops to locate a long-deceased track, such a range can often lead to disappointment. Thankfully, this does not prove true at the Arlington Country Club.

Born the Alladin Country Club in 1929, Arlington was located in the Grandview Heights neighborhood of Columbus, between the north banks of the Scioto River and today's Route 33. Immediately to its east lay Dublin Road Golf Course, a less ornate facility which has similarly vanished. To its west ran the northward course of the river. Because little documentation of the layout exists beyond aerial photos, we can only speculate as to the exact sequence of play. But considering the precise location of the clubhouse and the far greater likelihood of a Ross design ending with a strong par 4 than a 500+-yard par 5, the illustrated sequence is very likely accurate.

Arlington was a layout with a great deal of size packed into its relatively tight site, yet it also offered the sort of variety so frequently lacking in modern golf design. The par-3 eighth, perhaps 110 yards in length, was an obvious example, requiring just a pitch to a small green ringed by sand and the overhanging trees of the riverbank. The 150-yard 11th was another attractive one-shotter as was the 205-yard 13th, whose long-iron approach across an echeloned line of bunkers will certainly ring familiar to Ross aficionados.

Another important characteristic was Arlington's plethora of fairway bunkering, with 45 hazards in play and, on six separate occasions, at least four guarding a single driving area. The result, particularly at holes four and seven, were tee shots requiring a great deal of thought, particularly as wind conditions changed.

Arlington's terrain was low-lying, a condition highlighted by the flooded quarries which now occupy much of the site. A portion of the property is also crossed by the terminus of Interstate 670, which ends just east of the old Dublin Road course, at Grandview Avenue.

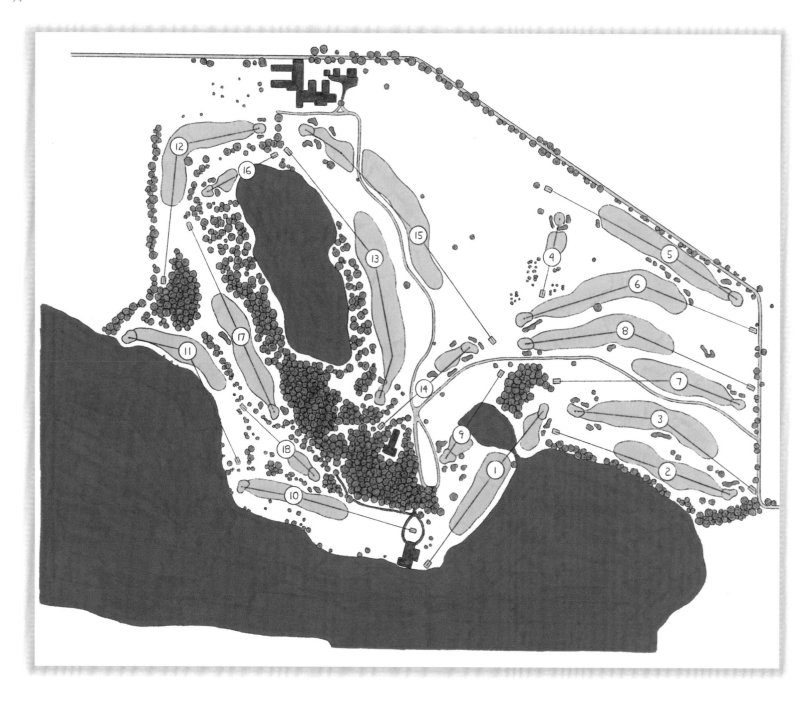

392	363	420	177	407	460	350	450	190	3209	350	375	417	565	230	550	147	390	210	3234	6443
4	4	4	3	4	5	4	4	3	35	4	4	4	5	3	5	3	4	3	35	70

AVIATION COUNTRY CLUB
PONTIAC, MI

⚜

HERBERT STRONG (1922)

*I*n recalling the early twentieth century's great automotive tycoons, the name of Walter Flanders is generally overlooked, lacking, as it does, much of the romance associated with such giants as Henry Ford and John F. Dodge. Yet the affluent Mr. Flanders was quite the successful manufacturer, affording him a grand, 850-acre estate on Green Lake, southwest of the Detroit suburb of Pontiac. Liquidated several years before Flanders' 1923 death, however, this property would ultimately be developed as a great but short-lived recreational facility, the Aviation Country Club.

Following the estate-turned-club model so frequent to the era, Aviation offered a wide variety of amenities including, not surprisingly, its own airplane runway. But like most such facilities, golf was intended as the club's mainstay, resulting in the hiring of Englishman Herbert Strong to build a most memorable course indeed. Strong, whose major works include Canterbury, Engineers, and the Ponte Vedra Club, responded with a tightly routed design featuring water on seven holes. Period reports have Strong calling Aviation his personal best and despite the commonplace of such testimonials, one look at this stylish layout suggests at least some legitimacy to the claim.

It should be noted that despite a prominent 1921 *Golf Illustrated* article citing a scarcity of man-made bunkers, the fact that the earliest available aerial (1937) postdates the club's closing likely means the omission of one or two hazards from the facing map. Similarly, a lack of definition in the photo's northeast quadrant makes the midsection of the front-nine routing somewhat murky.

Of course, it is really Aviation's inward half nine that captures our attention, beginning with one of the great par 4s of its day, the 375-yard 11th. Doglegging left along the edge of Green Lake, this bunkerless gem featured a plateau fairway and a green angled dangerously outward into the water. Also highly praised was the 550-yard 15th, where the player's drive had to carry low, heather-covered ground to reach another plateau fairway, setting up second and third shots across an access road and four bunkers.

Struggling against the Depression, the Aviation Country Club is believed to have closed during the mid-1930s, taking with it one of the more unique golf courses in the Midwest. Its land is today occupied primarily by residential development.

96

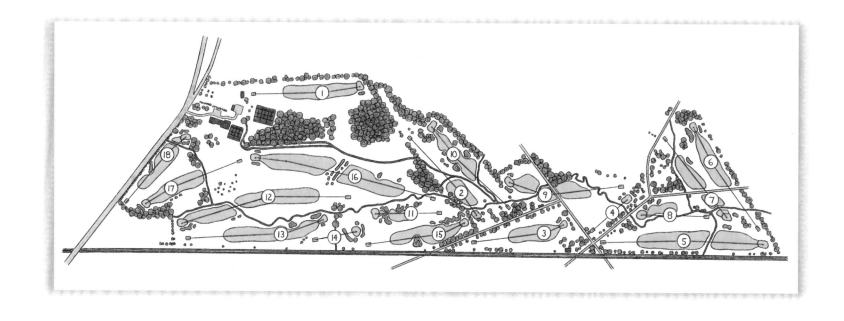

BAEDERWOOD																			
345	330	290	145	516	382	300	208	368	2884	345	204	525	440	140	315	598	345	278	3190	6074
4	4	4	3	5	4	4	3	4	35	4	3	5	4	3	4	5	4	4	36	71

BAEDERWOOD GOLF CLUB
JENKINTOWN, PA

⚜

CHARLES ALISON (1927)

*I*t was in September of 1903 that the Golf Association of Philadelphia sponsored an historic match between a team of elite locals and the visiting Oxford & Cambridge Golfing Society of Great Britain. The British squad, peopled by many of that nation's top collegiate players, defeated the Philadelphians handily on the old Huntington Valley course, with only a young A.W. Tillinghast and one other American able to manage so much as a tie of their individual matches.

The youngest member of the victorious British squad was one Charles H. Alison, divinity student, future World War I captain and eventual partner with H.S. Colt in one of golf's legendary architectural firms. By the early 1920s, Alison would be handling nearly all of the firm's American designs, creating numerous classic layouts including his defunct stateside master-piece Timber Point (see *The Missing Links*). Among Alison's less-chronicled projects, however, was one which proved even his pre-jet airplane world an exceedingly small place: the 1927 remodel of that very same Huntington Valley course upon which his team had triumphed nearly a quarter-century before.

By this time the old layout had been bought by the newly established Baederwood Golf Club, and Alison's job was to create a modern facility upon a narrow, road-bisected tract. What resulted was a surprisingly strong layout highlighted by a peculiar routing which managed to bring a single brook into play on 15 of 18 holes!

On the outward half, standouts included the second, fourth, and eighth, the latter pair being par 3s of distinction. Turning for home, the ninth and 10th required particularly accurate tee shots while the long 12th and 16th were obvious attention-getters. The 440-yard, par-4 13th was clearly a brute but the tiny 18th offered greater strategic interest, its preferred left side guarded by sand, out-of-bounds and, eventually, the creek.

Evidence exists to suggest that William Flynn may have touched up one or more of Baederwood's holes prior to 1930, and the property was sold off for residential development during the 1950s, well before unchecked equipment growth could render it too short for modern play. But perhaps this is just as well, for it is the growing obsolescence of just such innovative, fascinating courses that makes the game's modern evolution the great dollar-driven travesty that it is.

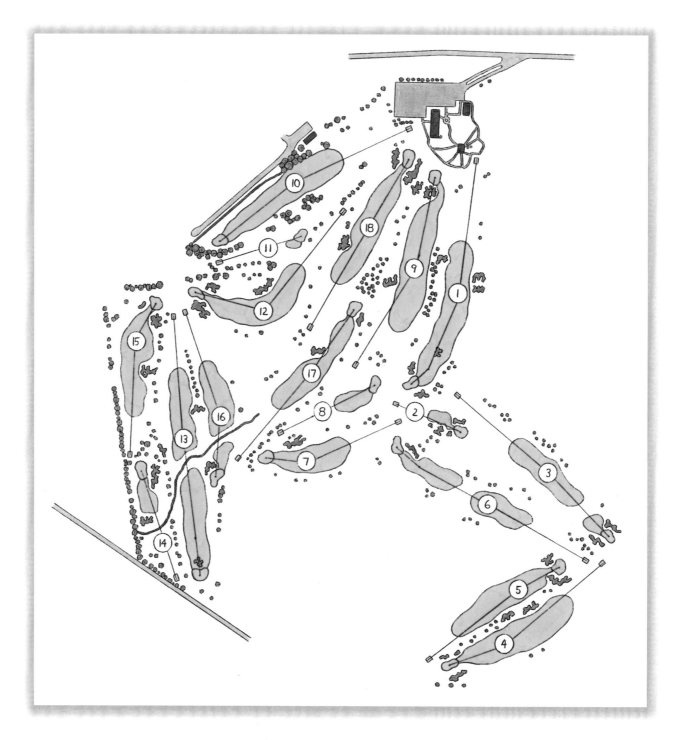

BALDWIN HILLS																			
475	145	420	385	340	470	300	235	425	3195	465	175	400	520	225	325	365	400	370	3245	6440
5	3	4	4	4	5	4	3	4	36	5	3	4	5	3	4	4	4	4	36	72

BALDWIN HILLS GOLF CLUB
CULVER CITY, CA

GEORGE THOMAS (1926)

Though nearly all of Captain George C. Thomas Jr.'s intricately strategic designs have been altered nearly beyond recognition, only two have disappeared from the golfing landscape altogether: the 36 holes which, for most of their existence, comprised the East and West courses of Los Angeles' Fox Hills Golf Club. The East course, which hosted the 1954 Los Angeles Open, is profiled in this book's sister volume *The Missing Links*. The West, which began life as an immediately adjacent facility called the Baldwin Hills Golf Club, steered largely clear of the tournament limelight and thus remains sadly overlooked among Captain Thomas's finer Southern California works.

Playing over the same hilly, canyon-dotted Culver City terrain as its sibling, Baldwin Hills began fairly modestly with only the third, a 420-yard par 4 played across two narrow barrancas, distinguishing itself early on. The 470-yard sixth traversed these same hazards and likely enticed many a bold player to try reaching its green in two, but it was not until the 235-yard eighth and 425-yard ninth that things really got going.

After routing the 10th and 11th through a small canyon, Thomas provided the layout's best stretch at holes 12 through 14. The 12th, a 400-yard par 4, dog-legged sharply right around a large fairway bunker that surely escapes the memory of most who played at Baldwin Hills—for it disappeared, likely due to economics, in the early 1930s. The 13th, at 520 yards, bore a clear similarity to Thomas's famous first at Riviera, with a small creek limiting the longer player's tee shot and a single bunker fronting a boomerang-like putting surface. But for sheer challenge, few Southern California holes were likely to match the 14th, a 225-yarder whose narrow green was sandwiched between out-of-bounds and one of the Captain's classic, meandering bunkers. With its tee angled flush against Centinela Avenue, this beast likely held its own with the legendary third at La Cumbre or the fourth at Riviera among Thomas's toughest one-shotters.

Though nothing whatever remains of the Fox Hills facility, drivers on Los Angeles' 405 freeway do move immediately adjacent to the site when passing Hillside Memorial Cemetery and the nostalgically named Fox Hills Mall.

For admirers of classic designs, fans of George Thomas and overcrowded L.A. golfers, a very great loss indeed.

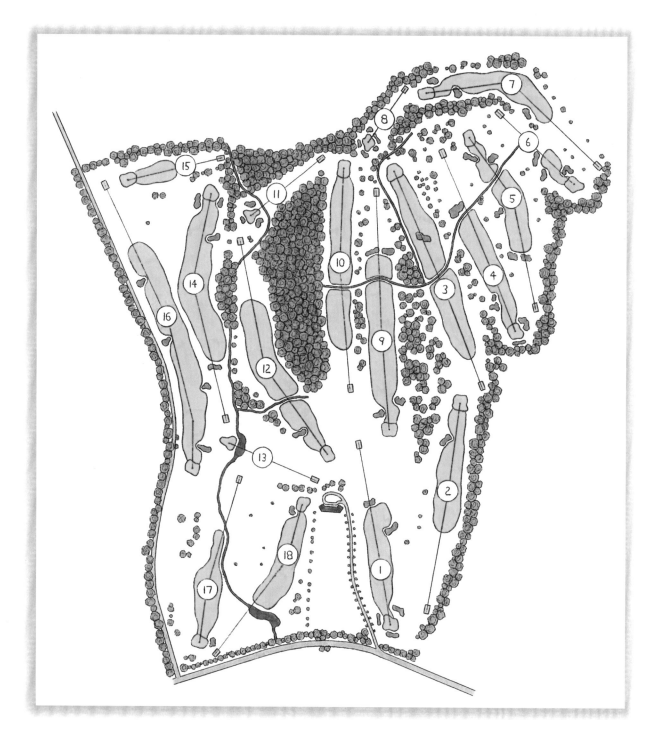

BANNOCKBURN																				
305	440	392	372	340	207	405	130	425	3016	462	170	445	160	378	183	580	184	348	2910	5926
4	5	4	4	4	3	4	3	4	35	5	3	5	3	4	3	5	3	4	35	70

BANNOCKBURN COUNTRY CLUB
GLEN ECHO, MD

DONALD ROSS (1924)

As with many Golden Age architects, Donald Ross has come to be associated with certain geographic areas. North Carolina, for example, where the transplanted Scot made his winter home at Pinehurst and managed to leave over 40 designs upon the state's landscape. Or New England, where countless Ross courses dot the map from the Connecticut coastline to the northernmost reaches of the White Mountains. Or Florida, where his work runs the gamut from ritzy, legendary Seminole to nearly anonymous inland munis. And perhaps we might add to this list, albeit in a small way, the rolling Maryland countryside that lies just north of Washington, D.C.

Ross's first documented entry into this neighborhood was his 1910 design of the venerable Chevy Chase Country Club, a layout plowed under by a 1922 C.H. Alison overhaul. Ross would also work at the Prince George's Country Club near Landover in 1921 (see page 166), Indian Spring Country Club in 1922 and Congressional, where he renovated Devereux Emmet's original 18 in 1930. There was, however, one more local project that is rather less-remembered: a 1924 redesign of Congressional's then-neighbor to the southeast, Bannockburn.

Bannockburn had begun life as a collaborative design effort between Englishman William Tucker and presidential dentist-turned-golf architect, Walter Harban. Little documentation exists as to the specifics of that layout, and the evidence suggests that Ross's alterations of it were quite thorough. The result was a golf course which despite a lack of length was considered quite challenging, with a number of tree-lined fairways and a small creek coming into play on five holes.

Curiously, Bannockburn featured seven bunkerless putting surfaces, certainly an oddity within the Ross portfolio. Also, the 185-yard 13th was another Ross rarity, a forced carry on a mid- to long-iron shot, played to a green closely guarded by water.

Comparing Ross's plans to later scorecards, it is apparent that several significant changes were made, primarily through the conversion of the 10th to a short par 5 and the 17th to a par 3. Regardless, aerial photos show a golf course clearly overgrown prior to the onset of World War II and it is doubtful that the club ever truly recovered from this Depression-related fall. Today the property houses that least-novel of post-golf developments, a residential neighborhood.

102

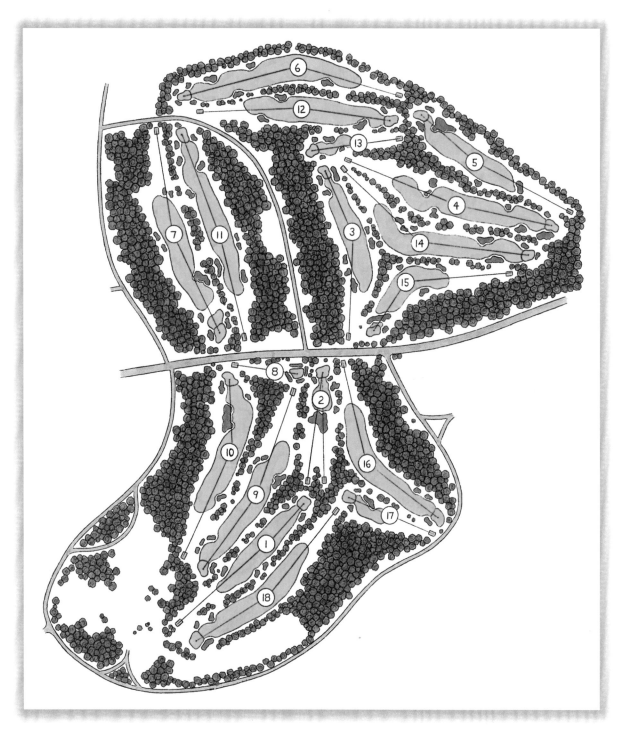

JAMES W. BARBER
PRIVATE GOLF COURSE
PINEHURST, NC

DONALD ROSS (1927)

James W. Barber was the sort of man upon whose back the game of golf prospered in America, and though we hardly group him with the C.B. Macdonalds and John Reids, it was through such relatively anonymous men as Barber that much of the gospel was spread.

Yet James Barber could not truly be called anonymous. Born in Liverpool, England, he emigrated to the United States circa-1880 to pursue a career in the shipping business. Graced with helpful connections in the UK, his Barber Steamship Lines would eventually become among the world's largest, servicing the six inhabited continents through a maze of affiliated and subsidiary concerns. A philanthropic man to the core, Barber built hospitals and cathedrals and generally made a positive presence of himself throughout his long and highly affluent life.

He began wintering in Pinehurst shortly after the turn of the century, becoming an early member of the area's famous Tin Whistles golfing group. Eventually, in 1927, Barber commissioned Donald Ross to lay out 18 holes on wooded terrain several miles northeast of town, near the Southern Pines reservoir. Accounts vary as to the purpose of this endeavor, though the best evidence suggests the creation of a private estate course which Barber eventually planned to sell off to developers. It is not certain that the entire 18 holes actually came to fruition, though published reports of 1928 did specifically make reference to the completed links. In any event the Depression, which arrived shortly thereafter, quickly succeeded in wiping out the entire proposition.

Regardless, Ross's design for Barber was serious business, measuring over 6,500 yards and featuring a strategic element generally found only among the architect's most prominent works. Built on typically rolling sandhills terrain, this layout may not have been Pinehurst No.2, but it surely was grander than any of Ross's four additional projects at the legendary resort. In fact it probably fell among the upper 10% of the celebrated architect's massive portfolio.

Today a variety of development exists upon the site, including the campus of Sandhills Community College and the modern Forest Creek Golf Club. Given the reverence with which Donald Ross's better designs are presently viewed, however, it is tantalizing indeed to consider how Mr. Barber's private layout might rate were it still among the living.

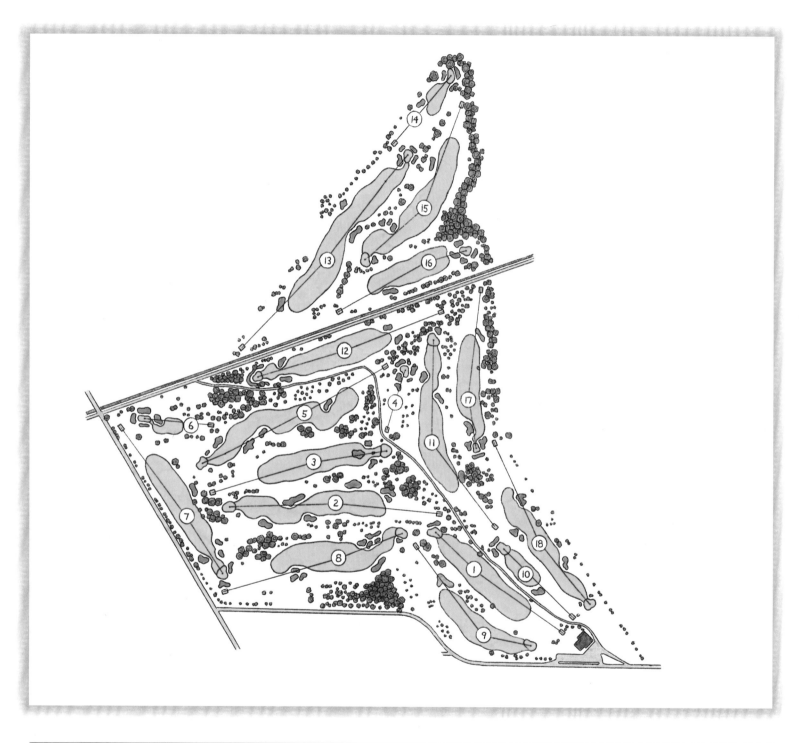

BRENTWOOD GOLF COURSE
JACKSONVILLE, FL

❧

DONALD ROSS (1923)

That great contemporary philosopher, songwriter Jimmy Buffett, once observed that "times change sailors these days," and in the case of Jacksonville's Brentwood Golf Course, that change has, over the course of 75 years, truly come full circle.

Brentwood was laid out in 1923 by Donald Ross and was, from day one, a public facility. It hosted the 1930 U.S. Amateur Public Links during its first decade and later would become a professional tour stop as regular host to the Jacksonville Open, an event favored by the Ben Hogans and Sam Sneads of the day.

Curiously, so well-known a layout went largely undocumented, thus a bit of uncertainty exists regarding certain aspects of its design. The hole sequence on the facing map, for example, is only an educated guess—though likely a very good one as a nine beginning with a long par 3 and closing with a stiff par 4 seems far more likely to have been the back than the front. Similarly, the volume of bunkering pictured (circa 1943) seems a bit wild for Ross, at least on a public layout where speed of play was surely a primary concern.

Following a short but distinctly absorbing outward half, the back nine was quite challenging, espe-cially holes 12 through 15. The 12th, at 420-yards, was particularly exacting, its long second played to a small green nearly ringed by a distinctly un-Ross-like bunker. Following the massive 13th and Redan-like 14th, the 400-yard 15th was another beauty, its total of four right-side fairway bunkers nudging the player leftward, toward the most difficult line of approach.

Beyond the possible post-Ross bunker alterations, the aforementioned change kicked into gear in the early 1970s when course operators refused to break a long-standing "Whites Only" policy, ultimately choos-ing to close down rather than integrate. Brentwood then languished for the better part of three decades, regressing into a wasteland of tires, refuse, and aban-doned automobiles before an inner-city redevelop-ment plan began to turn things around.

Presently part of the property serves as a First Tee facility, a city-, PGA Tour- and USGA-supported oper-ation designed to attract underprivileged kids to the game. How ironic then that Brentwood today endeav-ors to spawn the very golfers that it excluded – to the point of its own demise – for so many years.

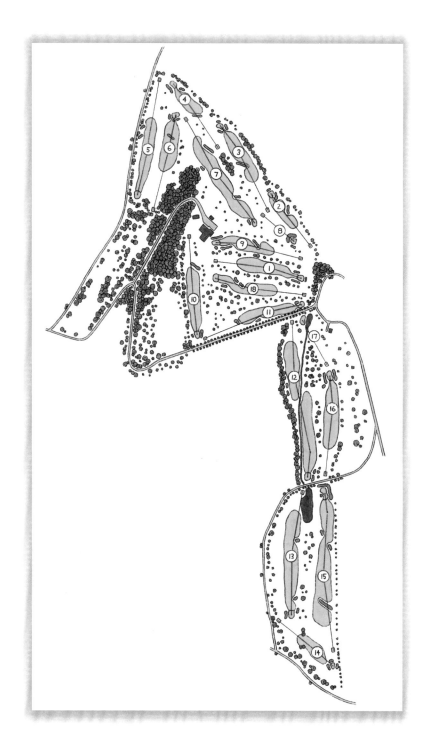

BRIAR HALL																				
335	255	348	274	428	364	440	145	334	2923	386	388	534	437	267	550	344	185	352	3443	6366
4	4	4	4	4	4	5	3	4	36	4	4	5	4	4	5	4	3	4	37	73

BRIAR HALL COUNTRY CLUB
BRIARCLIFF MANOR, NY

❧

DEVEREUX EMMET (1923)

*I*t is difficult to imagine a golf club firing a louder shot to trumpet its opening than did Briar Hall (nee Briarcliff Country Club) in 1923 when it signed up then-U.S. Open and PGA champion Gene Sarazen to serve as its first professional. A local product from nearby Harrison, Sarazen gave the resort instant national credibility—though with its mix of convenient location and affluent clientele, some degree of success seemed a given regardless.

Already in his 60s, architect Devereux Emmet was still at his peak in the early 1920s, and his comments on Briar Hall surely suggest that he considered it among his better designs. Most interesting, perhaps, was his assertion that this hilly, distinctly inland facility was designed to approximate the coastal links of Scotland. While we can take him at his word that the course was once dotted with artificial sand dunes (all extinct by the onset of World War II), the quasi-mountaintop upon which the layout opened and closed was hardly reminiscent of golf in the Old Country. Further, Emmet's assertion that the 353-yard ninth was "a duplicate" of the Gate hole at North Berwick seems particularly odd given its steeply uphill nature.

Not surprisingly, some of Briar Hall's best holes were built upon its flatter land, a narrow finger of which extended south, beyond Pine Road. The 12th and 13th come immediately to mind and they would survive, with the addition of several bunkers, for the entirety of the course's existence. The drive-and-pitch 14th, on the other hand, began life rather uniquely, offering the standard 155-yarder listed on the scorecard or an optional "19th," a parallel hole measuring a stiff 225 yards. This configuration was short-lived, however, as the entire ensemble was converted into a single short par 4 within a year of opening. The 550-yard 15th, a true behemoth featuring a Road Hole-like green complex, was altered later, sometime after the war.

Despite its auspicious beginnings, Briar Hall would eventually become better known for the severity of its terrain than as the year-round sporting center originally envisioned. After several decades operating in the shadows of Westchester County's more famous clubs, it was purchased in 1997 by Donald Trump for conversion to what Trump rather amusingly bills as "the finest golf course in New York State."

108

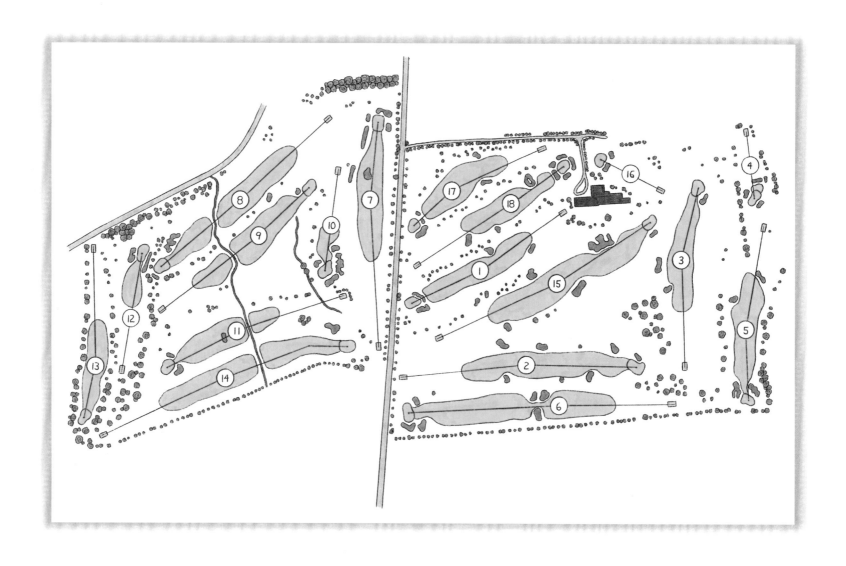

BROADMOOR COUNTRY CLUB
NEW ROCHELLE, NY

DEVEREUX EMMET & A. H. TULL (1929)

*F*ew agglomerations of classic golf facilities can match that which resides just six miles beyond New York City, in southern Westchester County. For here lies the Winged Foot Golf Club, a household name whose two A.W. Tillinghast-designed courses are justifiably famous the world over. Immediately adjacent sits Quaker Ridge, a similarly renowned layout, while barely a mile distant we find Wykagyl, a bit less publicized but still one of the finest courses in New York State. Throw in two more Tillinghast tracks along the perimeter (Larchmont's Bonnie Briar and Scarsdale's Saxon Woods) and you have a veritable greenbelt of thickly pedigreed Golden Age golf.

It may, however, come as a surprise to some locals (including, admittedly, your author, who grew up within walking distance) to discover that a sixth classic course once lay within this splendid nest: the Broadmoor Country Club.

Straddling Weaver Street at a point southeast of the Hutchinson River Parkway, Broadmoor lay adjacent to today's Cherry Lawn driving range, longtime home of noted instructor Chuck D'Amore. Opened in 1929, it may well have been the first true design collaboration of Devereux Emmet and A.H. Tull, the latter having just become a full partner in Emmet's firm that very year. Yet acknowledging Tull's undeniably growing role, it is curious to note that only three of Broadmoor's bunkers (on holes eight, 10 and 15) demonstrate his grand, free-flowing style. Such bunkering would soon be in evidence throughout such layouts as the Huntington Crescent Club and Greenacres, so perhaps their paucity at Broadmoor certifies this as predominantly an Emmet creation—perchance his last?

Broadmoor's best holes generally lay west of Weaver Street, for this land was blessed with both a creek and a broad, sweeping downgrade. The long par-4 eighth took advantage of both features, running downhill and across the brook to a green backed by a large, distinctly Tull-style bunker. The 336-yard 11th, with single fairway bunker dead-center, was another inviting downhill test.

The club's par 3s were also noteworthy, particularly the long, sandy 10th and the 240-yard 12th, the obligatory Emmet backbreaker which on this occasion was routed across the bottom of the downgrade. At only 120 yards, the tiny 16th then began yet another of the architect's favored tactics, a short but decidedly tricky set of finishers.

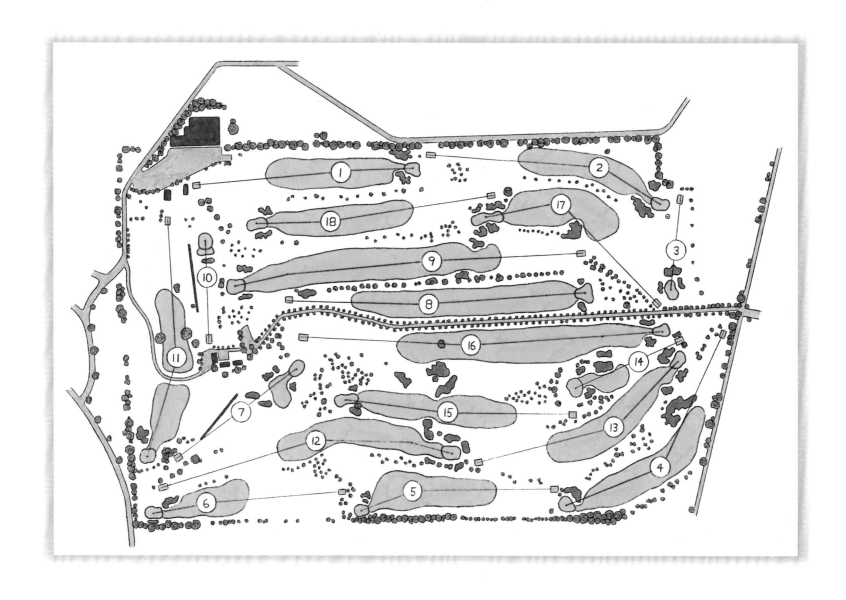

CALIFORNIA																				
344	385	149	408	332	327	242	520	560	3267	153	367	496	374	185	380	581	350	385	3271	6538
4	4	3	4	4	4	3	5	5	36	3	4	5	4	3	4	5	4	4	36	72

CALIFORNIA COUNTRY CLUB
CULVER CITY, CA

ARCHITECT UNKNOWN (1917)

Located just southwest of Hillcrest Country Club, upon land that is today known as Cheviot Hills, the California Country Club was perhaps the least-documented of the Los Angeles area's many Golden Age layouts. For even today, in an era when golf's architectural history enjoys unprecedented popularity, little is known of the course's design pedigree. It has been suggested that it was initially laid out by English transplant Norman MacBeth, and more generally accepted to have been renovated during the Depression by *Golf Illustrated* editor-turned-architect Max Behr. But aerial photos from the late 1930s indicate a wilder, rough-edged bunker style far more consistent with Southern California mainstay Billy Bell—a theory advanced by the presence of the 242-yard seventh hole, the sort of oversized par 3 nearly always present on a Bell design.

Whatever the specifics of its lineage, California's proximity both to opulent neighborhoods and movie studios made it a premier club in its day, a circumstance enhanced by its willingness to admit show business people at a time when Los Angeles Country Club and Bel-Air steadfastly refused to do so. This clientele changed somewhat following a World War II closing, though celebrities remained in profusion (along with

gamblers) until the ever-increasing value of the land forced the club's ultimate sale.

California is remembered as one of the region's hilliest courses, though in truth the majority of its out-lying holes were played across relatively flat or gently-rolling terrain. Its 6,538 yards were fairly long for the day, yet strangely only one par 4 (the 408-yard fourth) exceeded 400 yards. This quirk can largely be explained by the presence of two abnormally long par 5s, the 560-yard ninth, and the 581-yard 10th, though neither was particularly memorable. The seventh, however, which played across a large ravine, then between bunkers to a relatively small green, is certainly one of L.A.'s more lamented losses.

Were it still in existence today, California Country Club would make a fine classroom for budding golf course architects. Shoehorned into a tiny property distinguished by several prominent hills and two ravines, its creators succeeded impressively in finding locations for 18 interesting, playable holes. Not quite as significant a feat as George Thomas's spectacular canyon routing at nearby Bel-Air perhaps, but still one worthy of the aspiring designer's study.

112

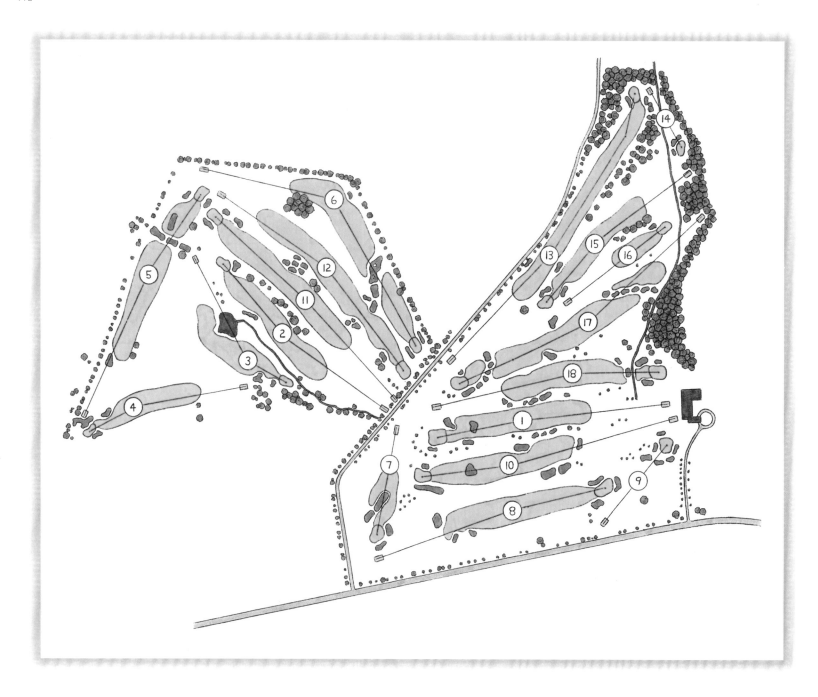

CANOE BROOK																				
401	394	268	297	431	513	193	431	162	3090	447	459	458	553	117	338	229	517	403	3521	6611
4	4	4	4	4	5	3	4	3	35	4	5	5	5	3	4	3	5	4	38	73

CANOE BROOK COUNTRY CLUB (NORTH)

SUMMIT, NJ

⚶

WALTER TRAVIS (1916)

As home to an unprecedented collection of classic Golden Age courses, the New York metropolitan area also boasts an inordinate number of venerated 36-hole facilities. Winged Foot, Baltusrol, Westchester, and Montclair all come quickly to mind as does one more, Canoe Brook. But Canoe Brook, a 100+ year-old club which straddles Morris Turnpike in the prosperous New Jersey suburb of Summit, must be considered something of an interloper on this list. For while the others all possess 36 genuine Golden Age holes, Canoe Brook does not, its present 7,066-yard North course being a distinctly modern affair bearing little resemblance to the early 18 which first put the club on the golfing map.

This original facility had its roots in a 1902 design by little-known architect Jack Vickery, a layout occupying land on either side of Canoe Brook Road. Though little photographic evidence exists to document Vickery's work, it became a footnote of history when, in 1916, the legendary Walter Travis was called in to redesign it. Travis, the three-time U.S. Amateur champion, was just beginning his architectural career, yet he succeeded in turning Canoe Brook into one of the area's finest period tests.

Travis's layout utilized much of the land occupied by the present North course, but also featured a stretch of seven holes which today lie buried beneath the adjacent Short Hills Mall. His design also offered a genuine oddity: a sequence of three consecutive par 5s. The last of these, the 553-yard 13th, was to become the course's number one handicap hole, its narrow fairway cutting between trees before turning, rather late in the game, into a small, bunkered green.

Another strong three-shotter was the 517-yard 17th. Here one's drive had to carry a line of six diagonal bunkers simply to get into play. Where things really got interesting, however, was on one's approach, where a similar rampart of sand affected both an aggressive second and any type of third.

In the late 1940s, the club traded the land across Canoe Brook Road for similar acreage on its eastern boundary. Former Devereux Emmet associate A.H. Tull added eight new holes there, beginning a long-term evolution which has left only the original corridors (and some hazarding) of holes one, 17, and 18 in play today.

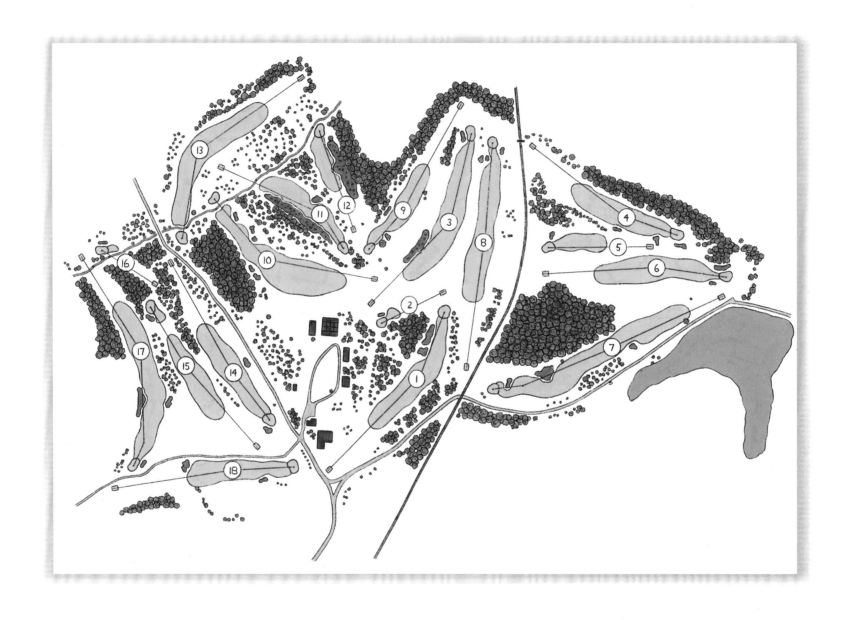

CAROLINA PINES																				
409	143	421	351	210	397	525	457	344	3257	408	314	226	454	385	362	139	476	368	3132	6389
4	3	4	4	3	4	5	5	4	36	4	4	3	5	4	4	3	5	4	36	72

CAROLINA PINES GOLF CLUB
RALEIGH, NC

⚶

DONALD ROSS (1932)

The ties of the renowned Donald Ross to the state of North Carolina are well documented, and are enough to make the native of Dornoch, Scotland perhaps the grandest figure in the state's golfing history. Wintering in Pinehurst for the last 47 years of his life, Ross built more courses in North Carolina than in any other state save Massachusetts, and his designs literally dot the landscape from the Great Smoky Mountains to the Atlantic.

Built in 1932, several years after most of his area best, Carolina Pines was located just north of today's Raleigh Golf Association course in an area listed on modern maps as Twin Lakes Estates. Set on the sort of gently rolling terrain that Ross explicitly preferred, it was created by local businessman Herbert A. Carlton as a 450-acre resort catering to a clientele of reasonable (though not necessarily affluent) means. Guests were housed at the Carolina Pines Hotel and the resort included the standard roster of recreational amenities, the most popular of which was golf.

Because the course was handcuffed by the Depression shortly after opening, only scorecards and post-closing aerials exist to document the layout's particulars. Thus while the facing map's routing appears exact, the positioning of hazards is likely only 90% accurate.

Though offering a handful of less-challenging holes, Carolina Pines also featured several really outstanding ones, particularly the 314-yard 11th and 226-yard 12th. Both appear to have featured the sort of sand-and-wire grass waste areas familiar to fans of Pinehurst No. 2, with the 11th allowing for a safe lay-up, a full drive or an all-out attempt to reach the putting surface.

Another prominent back-nine feature was the creek which fronted the putting surface of the 408-yard 10th, then crept behind the green at the dangerous 12th. This same hazard provided a fine strategic element at both the 454-yard 13th and the 139-yard 16th, the latter requiring a pitch to a tiny green guarded by trees, water and sand.

The Depression did indeed cripple the resort's operation, relegating the golf course to the slag heap well before the onset of World War II. The Carolina Pines Hotel survived into the 1950s, however, and remains in use today as a fraternity house for nearby North Carolina State University.

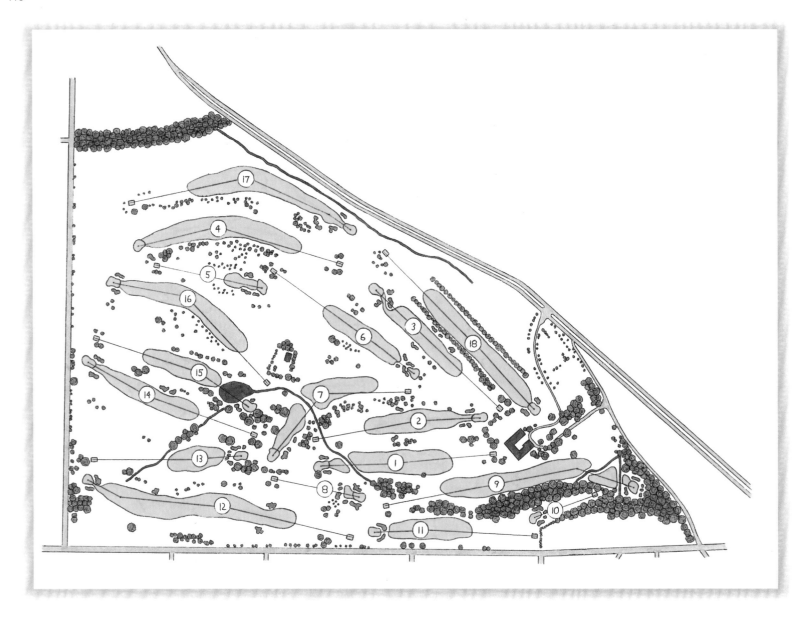

CEDARBROOK																			
355	345	350	425	230	340	345	180	510	3080	135	330	545	310	370	350	405	475	436	3356	6436
4	4	4	4	3	4	4	3	5	35	3	4	5	4	4	4	4	5	4	37	72

CEDARBROOK COUNTRY CLUB
CHELTENHAM, PA

✥

A. W. TILLINGHAST (1921) / DONALD ROSS (DATE UNKNOWN)

The names atop the masthead are certainly eye-catching, and it can safely be said that Cedarbrook Country Club, located in the north Philadelphia suburb of Cheltenham, was the rare course indeed that enjoyed the full-scale efforts of both A.W. Tillinghast and Donald Ross.

But one should not assume the magnitude of their labors to be equal. For while no photographic record of Tillie's design is known to remain, it is believed that Ross did little or no changing of the routing, instead concentrating his efforts upon adding length and some bunkering. It has been reported that alterations were made continually throughout the club's existence, but World War II-era aerial photos indicate a layout fairly consistent with Ross's version.

At 6,436 yards Cedarbrook was a moderately long course, though it can be legitimately argued that nearly all of its longest holes fell among its least fulfilling. One exception, however, might be the 510-yard ninth, a three-shotter bending slightly right, past trees and across two creeks. Unlike most par 5s, the real thinking here was done by the man who wasn't going for the green in two, as a laid-up second offered distinct choices: play for the small triangle of fairway between the creeks (leaving a simple pitch for one's third) or lay well back, to where a full iron shot would be required.

But it was with its shorter holes that Cedarbrook excelled, particularly on a pair of drive-and-pitch par 4s. At the 310-yard 13th, one drove across a brook to the course's widest fairway, leaving a pitch to a narrow putting surface bothered by six bunkers and overhanging trees. The 350-yard 15th was even more difficult, its second shot requiring a forced carry over the club's one lake to a green virtually surrounded by trouble.

Philadelphia, one of America's golfingest cities, has managed to retain more of its top Golden Age designs than nearly any other metropolis. And Cedarbrook certainly tried, thrice turning down postwar purchase overtures from Temple University before ultimately being forced to move when the Commonwealth of Pennsylvania condemned part of the property for highway construction in 1955.

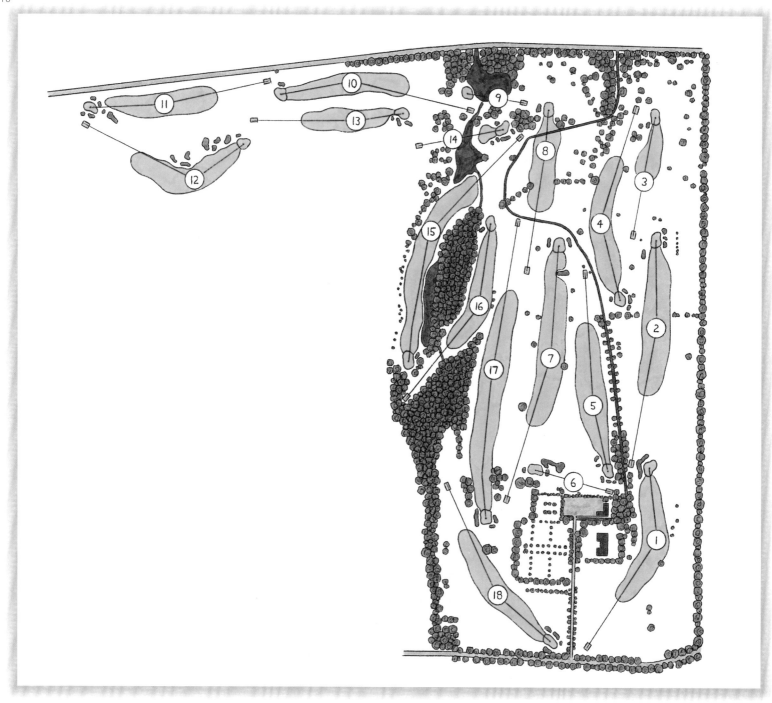

COLDSTREAM

370	430	235	378	375	148	520	310	110	2876	385	350	368	295	168	496	380	545	370	3357	6233
4	4	3	4	4	3	5	4	3	34	4	4	4	4	3	5	4	5	4	37	71

COLDSTREAM COUNTRY CLUB
EAST HEMPSTEAD, NY

⚜

DEVEREUX EMMET (1925)

*P*reviously we have noted a remarkable gathering of A.W. Tillinghast-designed courses in southern Westchester County, a collection perhaps matched only by San Francisco's Lake Merced-area cluster for proximity and quality. In terms of a single architect's dominance of a neighborhood, however, it is doubtful that anyplace could equal Long Island's intersection of Merrick Avenue and the Hempstead Turnpike where, in the shadow of today's Nassau Coliseum, Devereux Emmet once reigned as the undisputed king.

For here, upon mostly open countryside, Emmet crafted an amazing seven immediately adjacent 18s: the famous five at Salisbury Country Club (see page 170), a wonderful layout at the Meadowbrook Hunt Club (see *The Missing Links*) and, immediately south across Hempstead Turnpike, the Coldstream Country Club.

Of the seven, Coldstream was by far the least-documented, opening in 1925 and expiring only 15 years later, during World War II. Its presence was always noted among period golf guides and maps, of course, and its Emmet lineage has never been disputed. But beyond these basics, it lacked the sort of publicity frequently accorded so many Long Island clubs of the period, seldom hosting major tournaments or being profiled in national magazines.

Yet Coldstream was also a typically fascinating Emmet layout, featuring the architect's usual wide variety of holes laid out, once again, over a former country estate. Though the eastern body of the property was relatively featureless, its north-central section included a prominent water hazard utilized on three of the course's best holes. The first of these, the 110-yard ninth, was easily Coldstream's shortest but its waterside green offered very little margin for error. The 168-yard 14th, another attractive one-shotter, ultimately re-crossed the hazard, and was followed by the 496-yard 15th, a dangerous-but-reachable par 5 featuring water down nearly its entire left side.

Also worth noting were holes 10-13, for the treeless land upon which they were situated was almost certainly not a part of the original estate. As such, these holes more resemble the wide-open Salisbury in design style, though the heavily bunkered 11th and fine dogleg 12th appear to have been of some real account.

Today the Coldstream site has been commercially developed and divided by roadways, with the Meadowbrook Parkway approximating the original estate's western boundary and Glenn Curtiss Boulevard slashing through the property's midsection.

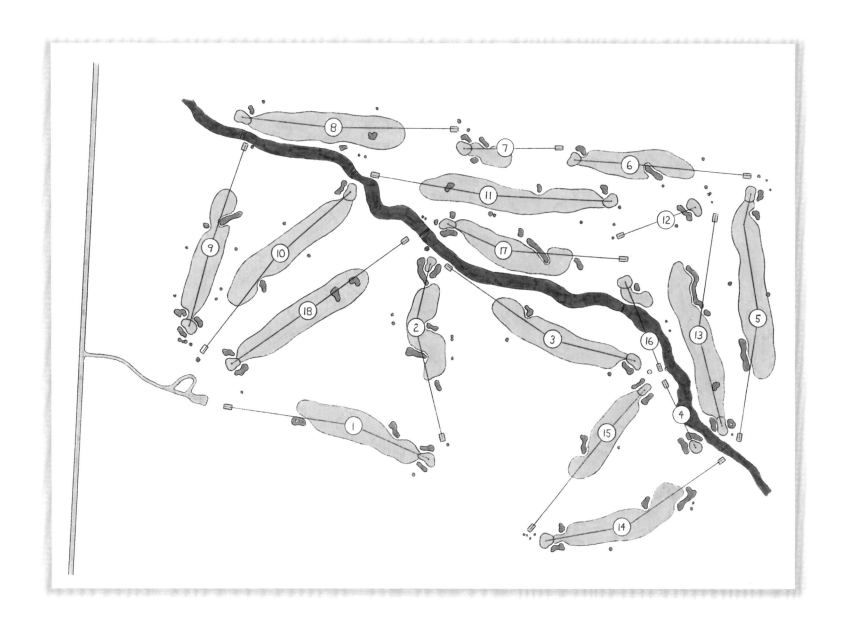

120

COLONY																			
425	355	430	145	490	350	200	430	385	3210	440	490	160	420	400	360	185	375	425	3255	6465
4	4	4	3	5	4	3	4	4	35	4	5	3	4	4	4	3	4	4	35	70

COLONY GOLF CLUB
ALGONAC, MI

CHARLES ALISON (1926)

*I*n a generally murky field, it can reliably be stated that few lost American golf courses were as mysterious and intriguing as the Colony Golf Club. Located on reclaimed marshland some 30 miles northeast of Detroit, it was conceived in the mid-1920s as the centerpiece of a real estate development along the eastern shore of Lake St. Clair's Anchor Bay. There, upon native terrain that could only just be called terra firma, a series of 75-foot wide canals were dredged, displaced dirt was stacked to create a dike, and the site was drained and reshaped into a demanding 18-hole golf course. The question historians ask more than 75 years later is, by whom?

Published records on both sides of the Atlantic have credited Englishman Charles Alison with building, in 1923, a "Colony Country Club" in Algonac, New York. With no such location being traceable within the borders of the Empire State, however, one immediately turns to this same-named course in Algonac, Michigan, particularly given the presence of a Detroit branch office of the Colt & Alison firm during the 1920s.

At this point it becomes a matter of style; specifically, does Colony look like an Alison design? To this we can answer a confident yes, particularly when examining the large-scale greenside bunkering of holes two and four, or the angled fairway hazards at the second and 14th.

The second, at 355 yards, was certainly worthy of the connoisseur's attention but the third, with its challenge to flirt with the more dangerous left side off the tee, was also quite good. The 145-yard fourth then played to a small green guarded by both the canal and two very large bunkers, closing an exciting stretch.

The 430-yard eighth was another strategic gem, its front-right greenside bunker suggesting a drive aimed along the banks of the water. More long par 4s would follow at the 10th, 13th and 14th before the 185-yard 16th, the layout's final par 3, brought the canal more directly into play.

An open, wind-affected layout, Colony was reportedly played by both Walter Hagen and Gene Sarazen before being converted to a farm during World War II. It reopened to golfers only briefly after the cessation of hostilities before ultimately being abandoned, and the site remains essentially undeveloped today.

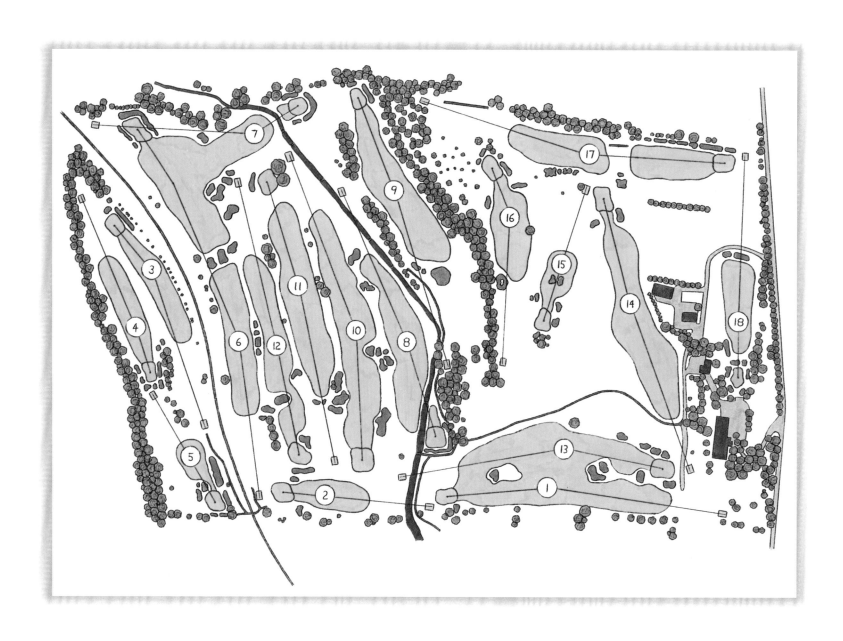

FAIRVIEW																				
394	214	289	267	167	548	298	343	386	2906	424	384	377	367	389	191	264	418	298	3112	6018
4	3	4	4	3	5	4	4	4	35	4	4	4	4	4	3	4	5	4	36	71

FAIRVIEW COUNTRY CLUB
ELMSFORD, NY

❦

DONALD ROSS (1912)

Now located across the state line in Greenwich, Connecticut, Fairview Country Club will shortly be coming upon its 100th anniversary, having originally been founded in Bronxville, New York in 1904. It has utilized four separate golfing facilities over the years and it is the third of these – which was in play from 1912 through 1968 – that attracts our interest.

Located on Saw Mill River Road in Elmsford, version number three featured a converted English Tudor mansion for a clubhouse and Donald Ross's first New York metropolitan area design, an offbeat layout which included five sub-300-yard par 4s, crossing fairways and the traversing of a railway line among its idiosyncrasies.

Despite its relative shortness, Fairview did offer some memorable holes, not the least of which was the 298-yard seventh—and not just because its tee shot was played directly over the top of the preceding green.

Most famous – or perhaps infamous – was the club's ninth, only 386 yards but with a steeply uphill approach that induced far more fives than threes. If this challenge unfairly added a stroke to one's card, however, the 17th surely offered the chance to make amends, for its gully-crossing 418 yards would actually remain a par 5 well into the 1930s.

Perhaps one reason why this layout has been largely forgotten is that during its heyday it was known far more for the remarkable stable of players produced by its caddie ranks. For few indeed are the clubs that can claim two U.S. Open winners (Johnny Farrell and Tony Manero), two PGA champions (Tom Creavy and Jim Turnesa) and a two-time U.S. Amateur winner (William Turnesa). Fairview also played host to numerous local events, most notably the 1930 Met Open (won by 1925 U.S. Open champion Willie MacFarlane) and the 1959 Met Amateur.

So historic a past proved of little consequence, however, when by the late 1960s, increasing commercialization and freeway construction threatened the quiet Elmsford countryside. With a shrewd eye toward the future (and likely aware that their already-altered Ross layout might soon prove too short for the modern game), the club elected to sell off its existing land and move east to Greenwich. There it commissioned a new layout, a 1968 Robert Trent Jones Sr. track which it plays on to this day.

280	395	245	380	320	170	500	370	490	3150	370	445	140	390	445	335	415	175	545	3260	6410
4	4	3	4	4	3	5	4	5	36	4	5	3	4	4	3	4	3	5	35	71

FLINTRIDGE COUNTRY CLUB
FLINTRIDGE, CA

❧

ARCHITECT UNKNOWN (1920)

*B*y delving through the many books and magazines chronicling golf's Golden Age, the avid historian can find lists, articles and photographs galore highlighting the era's countless fine courses. Consequently, few are the genuinely excellent layouts whose pedigree remains undocumented, whose obviously talented designer has been deprived of credit justly earned. But beyond question, one such anonymous jewel was the old Flintridge Country Club.

Of course, Flintridge may have been the work of a prestigious architect, we simply don't know. But if one accepts its widely published year of birth as 1920, it precedes any known project by Billy Bell or Max Behr, leaving only Willie Watson as a viable option among early, high-profile California builders.

Beyond such questions of credit, however, lies the fact that Flintridge, at 6,410 yards, par 71, likely stands as the most overlooked course in the history of Southern California golf. Located in the foothills of the San Gabriel Mountains, just southwest of today's Jet Propulsion Laboratory, the club was opened as part of a 1,700-acre subdivision developed by U.S. Senator Frank Flint. With a small residential neighborhood separating its nines, Flintridge was also one of the region's first real estate-oriented layouts.

The course's primary feature was a creek-filled barranca which influenced play on six holes, beginning with the 380-yard fourth. But Flintridge's finest hole was very likely the seventh, a 500-yard par 5 of heroic proportions. Here, after a long downhill drive, one faced a dangerous second, with the ball placed closest to the barranca leaving the best angle of attack for the short third.

On the back nine the barranca influenced two more outstanding holes. The 415-yard 16th required a long drive across the abyss to set up a mid-iron to a narrow, well-bunkered green while at the 175-yard 17th, the putting surface was fronted by the hazard and flanked by bunkers and overhanging trees.

Though Senator Flint's nearby resort hotel still stands (long ago converted to the Sacred Heart Academy), the Country Club itself followed the usual California Depression/war-era slide into oblivion. The barranca (as the concrete-walled Flint Canyon Channel) and the residential streets that divided the two nines are still clearly visible today, nearly run over by the 210 Freeway which cuts directly across the heart of the former Country Club property.

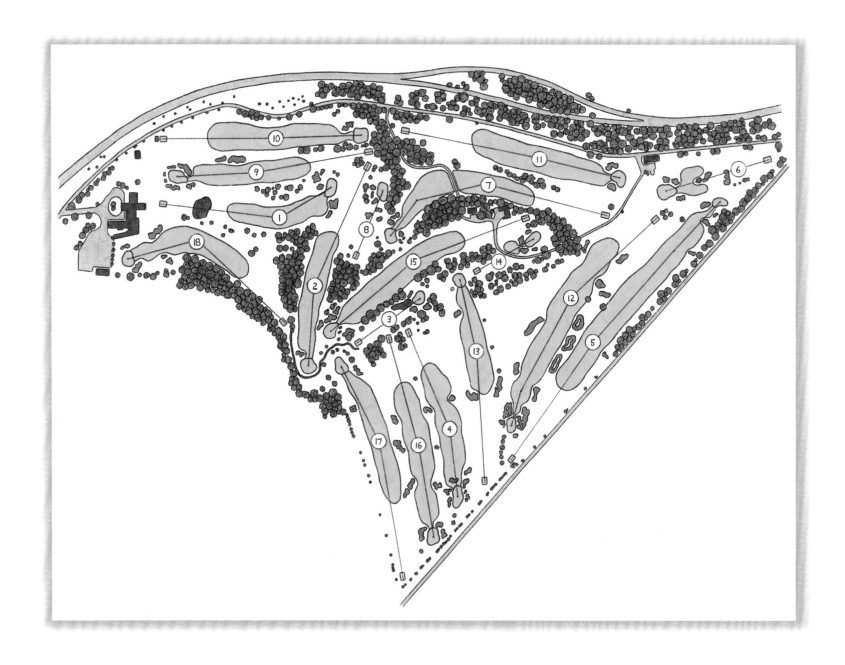

GLEN OAKS (Approximate)																			
340	410	150	340	620	220	475	135	390	3080	400	435	500	385	130	460	395	430	385	3520	6600
4	4	3	4	5	3	5	3	4	35	4	4	5	4	3	5	4	4	4	37	72

GLEN OAKS COUNTRY CLUB
GLEN OAKS, NY

❧

WILFRED "PIPE" FOLLETT (1925)

The Lido, Bayside, Deepdale, Fresh Meadow, Oakland...

The list of lost courses that once existed near the Queens/Nassau County line rivals nearly any gathering of courses – extant or gone – imaginable. Surrounded by such gems then, it is hardly surprising that Glen Oaks, which was located just across today's Northern State Parkway from the original Deepdale property, went largely overlooked.

Much of this is perhaps due to having been designed by one Wilfred "Pipe" Follett, hardly a bellwether name in a neighborhood of Macdonalds, MacKenzies, Tillinghasts, and Raynors. Yet Follett, a native of England and an Oxford graduate, was himself a man of some real golfing distinction. For prior to trying his hand in the design field, he followed Max Behr and preceded A.W. Tillinghast in one of the era's plum jobs, editor of *Golf Illustrated* magazine.

Such status likely had much to do with Follett's initial foray into architecture, helping the well-connected Devereux Emmet to design the nearby Queens Valley Golf Club in 1923. Glen Oaks would come two years later and though it appears to have been Follett's first solo effort, it succeeded in showing a good deal of style and polish.

Perhaps taking a cue from Emmet, Follett built nearly 100 bunkers over Glen Oaks' hilly terrain, and it was this feature which surely lingered longest in the golfer's memory. Glen Oaks also demonstrated Follett's apparent taste for the short par 3, with three one-shotters measuring 150 yards or less. In each case the target was patently small, especially at the 135-yard eighth and the water-fronted third. Follett also demonstrated a marked fondness for trees as many of his doglegs were heavily overhung, several to an almost unprecedented degree.

Though it survived both the Depression and World War II, precious little documentation exists regarding the hole yardages or sequence of play of the Glen Oaks layout. Still, published reports of a back-tee yardage of 6,600 and a high-quality 1942 aerial photo have allowed a very accurate scaling of distances. Similarly, deductive reasoning suggests this sequence of play as by far the most likely.

Golf is still played at Glen Oaks on an entirely new Francis Duane layout, a pseudo-executive track built to service the high-rise North Shore Towers which are today the centerpiece of the property.

GRASSY SPRAIN																				
380	470	140	505	320	350	490	415	440	3510	515	380	245	400	175	320	400	115	452	3002	6512
4	5	3	5	4	4	5	4	4	38	5	4	3	4	3	4	4	3	5	35	73

GRASSY SPRAIN COUNTRY CLUB
YONKERS, NY

⚶

DEVEREUX EMMET (1921)

*T*hough destined to survive less than 20 years, and shoehorned into an almost impossibly difficult parcel of land, the Grassy Sprain Country Club enjoyed a flashy, high-profile existence. Located in Yonkers along Tuckahoe Road, its L-shaped property was split not only by Central Avenue but also a New York City aqueduct and Grassy Sprain Brook, the latter (and its tributaries) materially affecting play on eight holes. The layout was designed in 1921 by that champion of undersized New York-area golf course sites, Devereux Emmet, and was widely considered among the best of the veteran architect's 85+ projects—no small accomplishment considering the strangely fractured nature of the land.

As a tournament venue, Grassy Sprain enjoyed success as host of the 1925 Metropolitan Open, then a highly prestigious national event won by local hero Gene Sarazen. Further, it counted among its members former NCAA, U.S. and British Amateur champion Jess Sweetser and another high-profile amateur of the day, John G. Anderson. It was also the occasional stomping grounds of the legendary gambler A.C. "Titanic" Thompson, who is reported to have once won a $20,000 wager by stiffing a do-or-die approach at the par-3 17th.

Grassy Sprain's front nine ran primarily east of Central Avenue, before crossing it for holes eight and nine. A tributary of Grassy Sprain Brook menaced the earliest holes, particularly fronting the green of the short par-5 second and guarding both the dogleg and green of the 320-yard fifth in a manner not dissimilar to Augusta National's famous 13th.

The 380-yard 11th required a precise approach to a very narrow green guarded by sand and water, but the inward half reached its zenith at the famous 12th, known throughout the metropolitan area as "Robber's Roost." Stretching 245 yards from the tips, it was a terribly difficult downhill par 3, played through a grove of large elm trees to a green flanked by sand and, slightly to the right, Grassy Sprain Brook.

Thompson's lightning bolt at the 17th (which has alternately been reported as taking place at the last) is certainly the stuff of legends. But it was perhaps because of such shenanigans that Grassy Sprain was constantly losing members to Westchester County's many more established clubs. Consequently, it was ultimately sold off to developers in 1938.

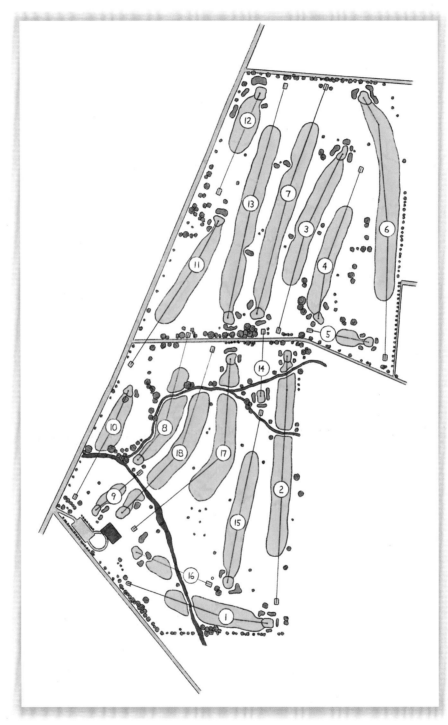

HILLCREST																				
326	513	420	337	135	585	557	283	138	3294	289	374	240	530	140	379	165	447	430	2994	6288
4	5	4	4	3	5	5	4	3	37	4	4	4	5	3	4	3	5	4	36	73

HILLCREST COUNTRY CLUB
CINCINNATI, OH

WILLIAM LANGFORD (1925)

Located at the northeast corner of Seymour and Reading Roads, diagonally across from today's Woodward High School, the Hillcrest Country Club ranked among the better courses in southern Ohio during golf's Golden Age—rather comparable, one guesses, to Donald Ross's nearby Maketewah Country Club, though certainly well below Seth Raynor's original design at the Camargo Club.

Built in 1925 by the prolific William Langford, Hillcrest was routed upon a rather small patch of land bisected nearly in the middle by Losantiville Avenue. Yet the property could hardly be called ill-suited or featureless, for the rolling terrain was tree-dotted and much of its southern half was affected by a small creek, which the architect brought into play on at least 10 occasions. Interestingly, the final product differed from many Langford layouts in that it had fewer bunkers, narrower fairways and, most noticeably, smaller greens. There is little evidence, however, to suggest that these putting surfaces were not severe in their elevation and contour, both hallmarks of a traditional Langford design.

Hillcrest's outward half was distinguished first by the presence of three par 5s, two of which came in succession and stretched comfortably beyond 550 yards. But perhaps not surprisingly, the most engaging of the three was the shortest, the 513-yard second, where the creek had to be carried whether one was going for the green in two or laying up. Also exceptional was the 283-yard eighth, a petite charmer whose fairway and green both nestled along the banks of the hazard.

The 10th hole was similarly short but featured a heavy dose of strategy. For at 289 yards, it was dominated by a single bunker placed front and center of a wide, A-shaped green. Thus the player was offered two preferred angles of approach: from the left side of the fairway, close to neighboring Reading Road, or from the right, an area reached by fading one's drive around a large tree. A third option, of course, was simply to try and hammer a driver all the way home.

Also notable were the 240-yard, *par-4* 12th (likely a par 3 in later years) and the 447-yard 17th, a creek-crossing par 5 which, had the course survived, would surely have been converted to a two-shotter, resulting in a stiff pair of par-4 finishers.

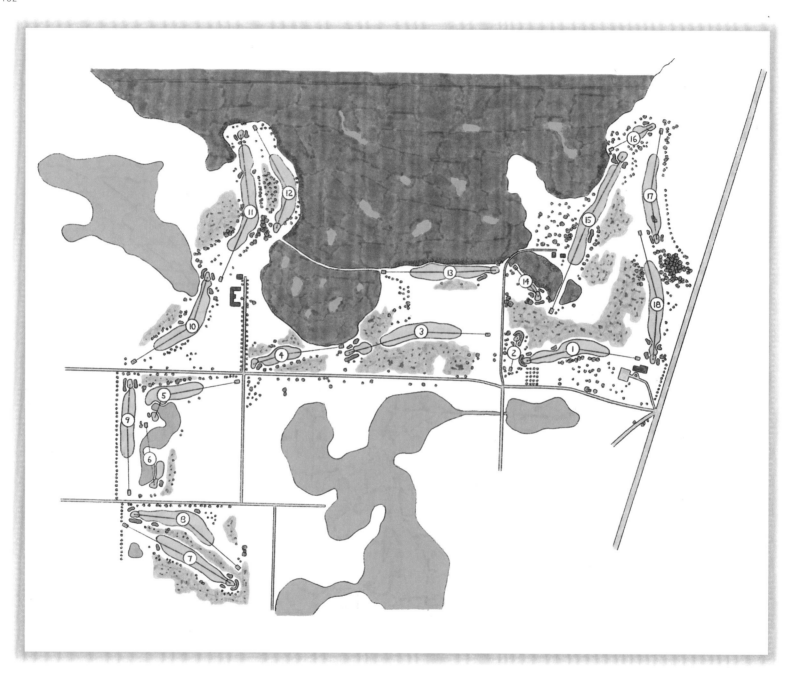

HOLLY HILL																				
410	130	490	338	347	198	440	450	384	3187	400	496	380	415	140	600	170	395	440	3436	6623
4	3	5	4	4	3	4	4	4	35	4	5	4	4	3	5	3	4	4	36	71

HOLLY HILL GOLF & COUNTRY CLUB
DAVENPORT, FL

❦

WAYNE STILES & JOHN VAN KLEEK (DATE UNKNOWN)

The architectural firm of Wayne Stiles & John Van Kleek is one which, comparatively speaking, has been rather overlooked in the annals of golf design. Stiles, a trained landscape architect, branched into the golf business relatively early, being credited with nine-hole courses in Brattleboro, Vermont and Nashua, New Hampshire in 1916. He had a good 15 projects under his belt by 1924 when he formed a partnership with the Cornell-educated Van Kleek, opening offices in Boston, New York, and St. Petersburg, Florida. Over the next seven years the firm would be responsible for more than 20 courses, the majority located in central Florida or New England and most of which remain in play, relatively intact, today.

Of those which have expired the grandest, by far, was Holly Hill, a late-1920s design which genuinely was a bit ahead of its time. For Holly Hill was a big layout, not simply in its 6,623-yard, par-71 measurements but also in its routing, a wide-ranging sequence that screamed of future real estate development. Within this routing it made full use of the available natural features, incorporating ample stretches of Florida's native sandy terrain, two lakes, and a large area of everglades-like swamp.

It began tamely enough, at least in terms of distance, though the first four holes all offered natural sand hazards of a Lawrence-of-Arabia-like stature. Things really picked up at the fifth and sixth, where forced carries were required over water. At the 347-yard, dogleg-left fifth, it came in the form of a mid- to short-iron second. At the sixth it was a nearly 200-yard blast across the length of the lake, though an alternate tee was available at a more modest 158.

The 10th green flirted with the waters of Lake Mary, a suitable warm-up for holes 12-15, all of which were routed along the edges of the glades. Offering shades of early C.B. Macdonald, this stretch benefited the slicer tremendously, for in each case the trouble lurked mostly along the left, while a rightward miss often left room for recovery. Though at 600 yards, the 15th stood literally in a class by itself.

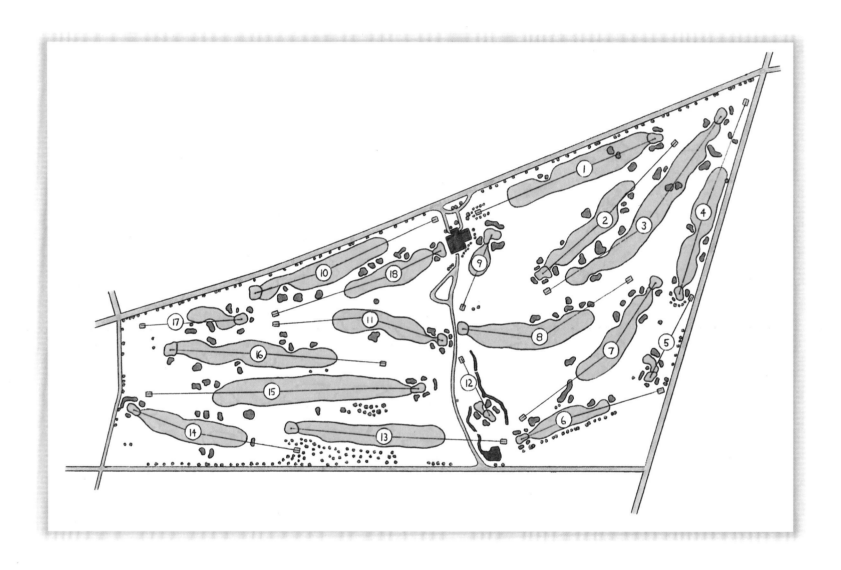

HOMESTEAD																				
388	371	520	401	185	316	415	365	152	3113	398	342	138	456	350	552	430	202	362	3230	6343
4	4	5	4	3	4	4	4	3	35	4	4	3	5	4	5	5	3	4	37	72

HOMESTEAD COUNTRY CLUB
SPRING LAKE, NJ

⚬∧⚬

DONALD ROSS (1920)

In the early 1920s, a number of successful Jersey Shore golf resorts underwent dramatic facelifts, their ancient courses replaced with more modern layouts authored by some of the top architects of the Golden Age. A number of these classic designs remain in play today including Hollywood Golf Club, Deal Golf & Country Club, and Spring Lake Golf Club, the latter a George Thomas creation subsequently modified by A.W. Tillinghast. Missing from the scene, however, is a course which was located immediately across the street from Spring Lake, the Homestead Country Club.

Opened in 1920, Homestead was one of Donald Ross's earliest jobs in the Garden State, predating even his classic design at Plainfield Country Club by a full year. Situated just over a mile from the Atlantic, its oddly shaped tract was blessed with the sort of gently rolling terrain so familiar to British seaside golf. It is perhaps not surprising then that Ross's bunkering at Homestead seemed more random than usual, often resembling the naturally created (and thus not always centrally positioned) hazarding of his homeland. This was particularly true on the outward half, a relatively short nine dotted by more than 70 bunkers!

The back nine was slightly more forgiving, rising gently toward the inland end of the property. Following the out-of-bounds-lined 10th, it featured two relatively short, precise tests at the 11th and 12th, each played to a small green virtually surrounded by sand. Things then opened up considerably down the homestretch, particularly at the par-5 13th, 15th, and 16th, the first and last of which would surely play as long, downwind par 4s today. This same sea breeze would stiffen the 202-yard 17th considerably, of course, leaving the 18th, at a relatively unmolested 362 yards, to provide the player one final opportunity for birdie.

Though Ross's design is indeed long gone, golf is still played on the Homestead site on a short, modern layout routed through a series of real estate subdivisions. While offering one or two putting surfaces positioned atop Ross's originals, the present layout has nothing whatsoever in common with its illustrious predecessor. Thus, as is so often the case, someone made a great deal of money developing the property—but destroyed perhaps their finest long-term marketing tool in the process.

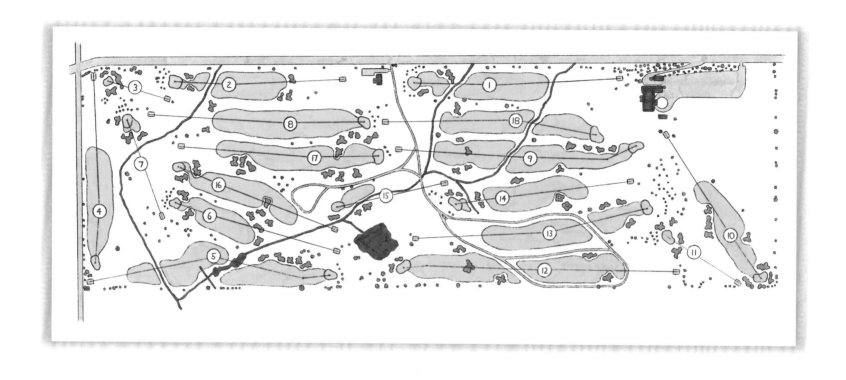

INGLEWOOD																			
400	325	125	359	477	326	195	430	506	3143	335	170	537	465	341	215	327	382	413	3185	6328
4	4	3	4	5	4	3	4	5	36	4	3	5	4	4	3	4	4	4	35	71

INGLEWOOD COUNTRY CLUB
INGLEWOOD, CA

DESIGNER UNKNOWN (CIRCA 1925)

*I*t is one thing to glance back today, nearly 75 years after the fact, and overlook a lower-profile course from golf's Golden Age, particularly when the layout in question has long since vanished from the landscape. It is quite another, however, when the various maps and guidebooks of the period make such an omission, as was the case for many years with the old Inglewood Country Club.

Located on the south side of Manchester Avenue between the Inglewood Park Cemetery and Hollywood Park racetrack, the Country Club could not have been more centrally positioned. Aerial photographs of the area confirm the layout's presence by the mid-1920s, yet it was omitted from the 1929 publicity materials of the Junior Chamber of Commerce, the 1926 Albert Thurston golf map of Los Angeles and, most notably, the *American Annual Golf Guide*—which managed to omit it annually, without fail, for the life of the publication.

So was Inglewood just a simple, nondescript layout?

As the course hosted the 1955 Los Angeles Open (won by Gene Littler with a respectable eight-under-par 276 total) we can pretty well assume otherwise. In fact, though squeezed onto a small rectangular tract,

Inglewood was a tricky, heavily bunkered layout which, quite obviously, was capable of challenging better players. Older area golfers often recall its later years when, like so many public facilities, it slipped into some degree of disrepair. Indeed, by 1955, numerous bunkers were gone, the strategically important creek had been largely filled in and the construction of several buildings had taken place well within the boundaries of the course. No wonder, then, that few people were screaming bloody murder when the time arrived for Inglewood's demise.

Interestingly, no architect of record has ever been determined for Inglewood's original design. The usual array of Southern California suspects (Willie Watson, Billy Bell, J.D. Dunn, and Max Behr) can all be considered inconclusively, though it should be noted that the earliest aerial photographs reveal a bunkering style fairly consistent with Bell's work at nearby Sunset Fields.

Whatever the case, Inglewood was certainly overlooked for many a year, though Los Angeles sports fans of recent vintage should have little difficulty recalling its location.

The Great Western Forum, after all, sits flush upon what used to be the front nine.

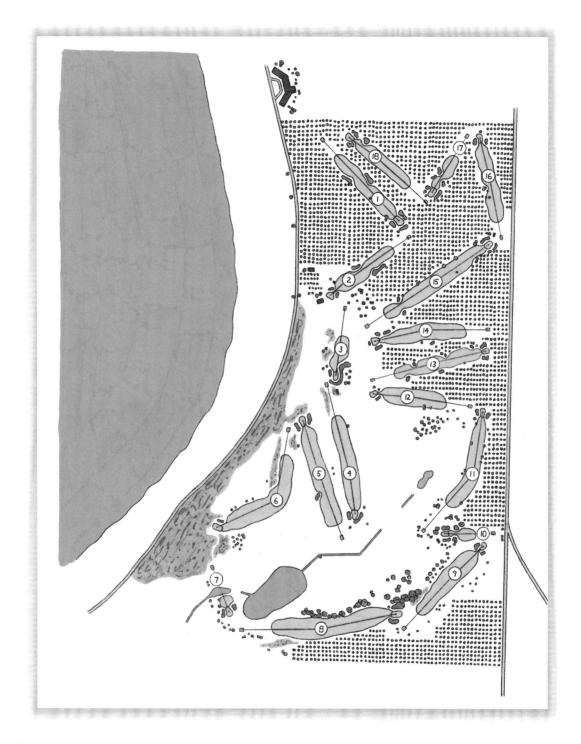

KENILWORTH LODGE (Approximate)																				
372	346	222	443	390	452	159	532	408	3324	151	434	337	381	372	478	363	220	346	3082	6406
4	4	3	4	4	5	3	5	4	36	3	4	4	4	4	5	4	3	4	35	71

KENILWORTH LODGE COUNTRY CLUB

SEBRING, FL

WAYNE STILES & JOHN VAN KLEEK (DATE UNKNOWN)

ven the serious student of Golden Age architecture may find it difficult to get a handle on the work of Wayne Stiles and John Van Kleek, for many stylistic differences pervade their portfolio. These differences were probably best represented by their bunker shaping, which seemed to vary between an artistic, classic look and an almost rigid, geometric one—a difference which may reside simply in which partner handled the lion's share of a given project.

But regardless of the "who did whats," most historians would agree that the firm's finest layouts were Florida's Pasadena Yacht & Country Club (where they reportedly had help from the legendary Walter Hagen), the Taconic Golf Club in Massachusetts and perhaps their lost course at Holly Hill (page 132). Beyond these three, the pecking order gets cloudier, though somewhere near the top would likely stand another Florida creation, the Kenilworth Lodge Country Club of Sebring.

The Kenilworth course was built for a hostelry which remains in service today, located near the shores of Lake Jackson. Routed through both dense citrus groves and open, sand-strewn terrain, it was a long and challenging layout—perhaps overly so for its older, winter-season clientele. A close look reveals that the architects seemed acutely aware of where the difficulty lay, for the eight holes that were lined on both sides by the endless rows of citrus were, with only one exception, among the club's shortest.

Perhaps not coincidentally, Kenilworth's best stretch lay within its "open" holes, beginning with the 222-yard, par-3 third. The par-5 sixth was also of real merit, its 452 yards easily reachable in two, provided one had the guts to cut off at least some of the sandy waste that filled the dogleg corner. Following the short seventh, the 532-yard eighth was another strong three-shotter, running between trees and more citrus groves to a very well-bunkered green.

While the Kenilworth Lodge is now listed on the National Register of Historic Places, the cost of maintaining the golf course became prohibitive in the early 1970s. A large segment of the tract still remains undeveloped as of this writing, though one assumes the plot to have a distinctly commercial future.

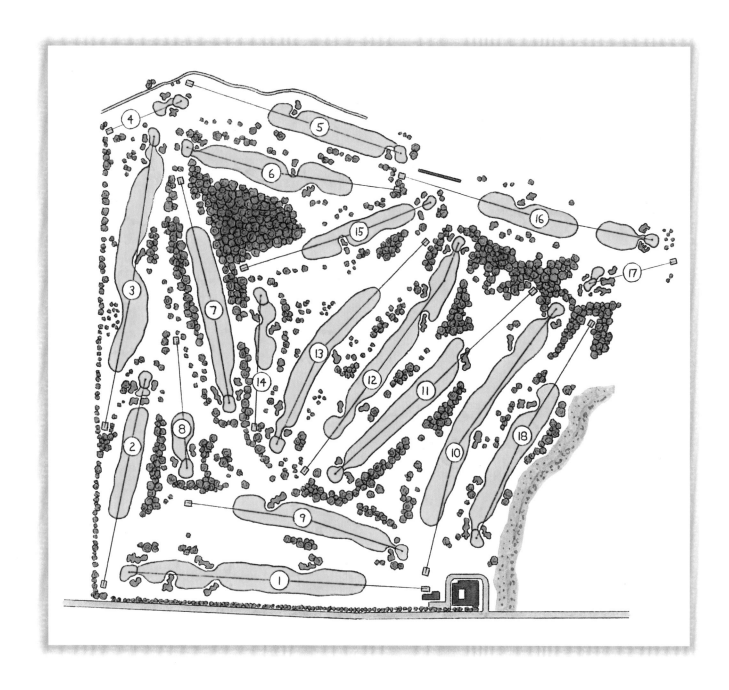

LAKE MERCED																				
527	355	525	145	390	380	440	225	380	3367	505	435	480	440	230	335	444	165	425	3459	6826
5	4	5	3	4	4	4	3	4	36	5	4	5	4	3	4	4	3	4	36	72

LAKE MERCED GOLF & COUNTRY CLUB

DALY CITY, CA

❧

DR. ALISTER MacKENZIE (1929)

Within golf architectural circles, the state of California and Dr. Alister MacKenzie have become nearly synonymous, with names like Cypress Point, the Valley Club of Montecito, and Pasatiempo coming instantly to mind atop the doctor's Golden State resume. Dig deeper and the architectural devotee might cite the Meadow Club, Green Hills, Haggin Oaks, or even the scant remains of a once-great layout at Pacifica's Sharp Park. Less often, however, does one hear the still-extant name of Lake Merced.

MacKenzie was hired by Lake Merced in 1928, at roughly the same time as his redesign of Claremont Country Club, just across San Francisco Bay. His mandate was not to completely overhaul local architect William Lock's original 1923 layout but rather to fine-tune it; to remodel bunkers and green approaches with an eye towards improved strategy and lower maintenance bills. The result was an attractive, highly strategic layout played over hilly terrain, framed by a younger generation of the verdant northern California foliage that so beautifully defines the area today.

Though filled with strong holes, Lake Merced's three finishers likely represented the course's best run. The 16th, a full-blooded par 4 at 444 yards, required first a drive over a modest ravine, then a pinpoint approach across a second depression to a tiny, hillside green. Following the often-photographed 165-yard 17th, the 18th was a 425-yarder routed along the edge of another ravine. Here the angled green distinctly favored a right-side approach, the ideal tee shot for which mandated the carrying of a pair of prominent fairway bunkers.

It should be noted that even prior to its modern destruction, the Lake Merced layout was altered significantly. Aside from general lengthening (from 6,450 yards in 1936 to 6,826 by 1954) the third hole was remodeled from a mid-length par 4 to a 525-yard par 5 prior to World War II, while the 13th was reversed, reduced from 475 yards to a very tough 440-yard two-shotter. Several obvious bunkering alterations took place as well.

The demise of MacKenzie's layout came in the early 1960s when the club lost acreage to the construction of the 280 Freeway. California architect Robert Muir Graves was hired for a major reconstruction, the result being a tough but nondescript course which was ultimately replaced by today's Rees Jones version.

142

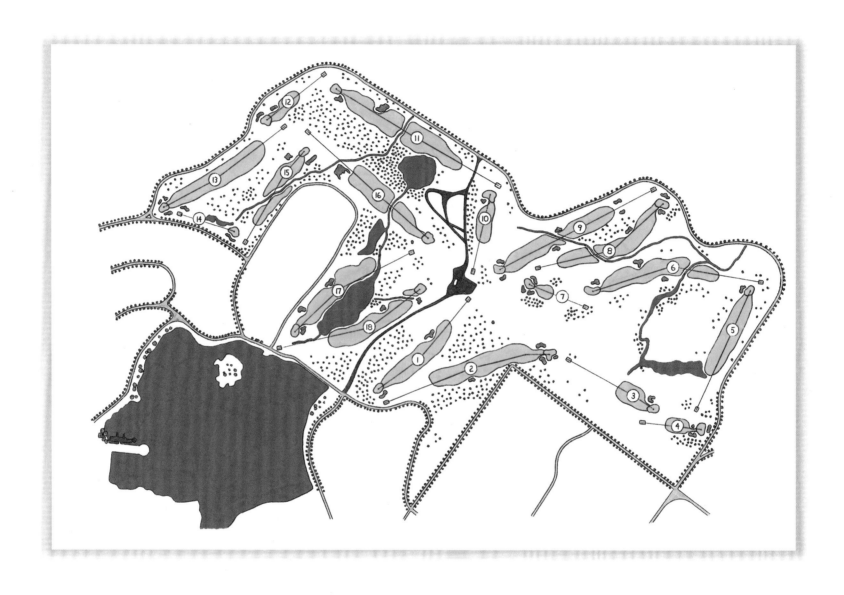

LAKE NORCONIAN (Approximate)																			
385	515	300	190	380	520	180	425	525	3420	230	565	220	435	165	330	430	425	463	3263	6683
4	5	4	3	4	5	3	4	5	37	3	5	3	4	3	4	4	4	5	35	72

LAKE NORCONIAN CLUB
NORCO, CA

JOHN D. DUNN (1928)

Few among American golf pioneers enjoyed a wider range of influence, both quantitatively and geographically, than John Duncan Dunn. A product of one of Scotland's legendary golfing families, J.D. had already laid out several courses around Europe prior to emigrating to the United States in 1894, at age 20. Following stints with two sporting goods companies, he became the first professional at the Ardsley Country Club, an ultra-ritzy place whose original 1896 course had been built by his uncle Willie. By 1900 Dunn had become in-house golf architect for the Florida West Coast Railway. Then, following World War I, he moved to Los Angeles where, while working at the Los Angeles Country Club, he built at least 12 Golden State designs.

A number of these layouts were constructed in the mountains and deserts to the east of Los Angeles, and were only of modest length and challenge. A prominent exception, however, was the Lake Norconian Club.

The brainchild of Rex B. Clark, founder of the town of Norco, the Lake Norconian Club was, in its day, one of America's genuinely elite resorts. Catering to a Hollywood clientele, its property featured a grand,

Spanish-style hotel, an air strip, hot sulphur wells and a man-made lake of 65 acres. Little mention is made in historical records of residential development, but aerial photos of the property during its very brief heyday indicate several geometrically spaced roads leading to nowhere—a pretty sure sign.

The rapid onset of the Depression following the club's 1928 opening left the course largely undocumented. Indeed, since it expired even before a clubhouse could be built, the precise sequence of play (as well as exact hole yardages) remains uncertain. Still, as old aerial photos illustrate clearly where the clubhouse was intended to go, we can safely wager that the 10th was far more likely a long par 3 than the first, and build our sequence from there.

Ruined by the Depression, the entire property was sold to the federal government on December 8th, 1941 – the very day the nation went to war – and converted into a naval hospital. The splendid main hotel building remains in service as the California Rehabilitation Center, a medium-security drug facility which has catered to several noted celebrities.

144

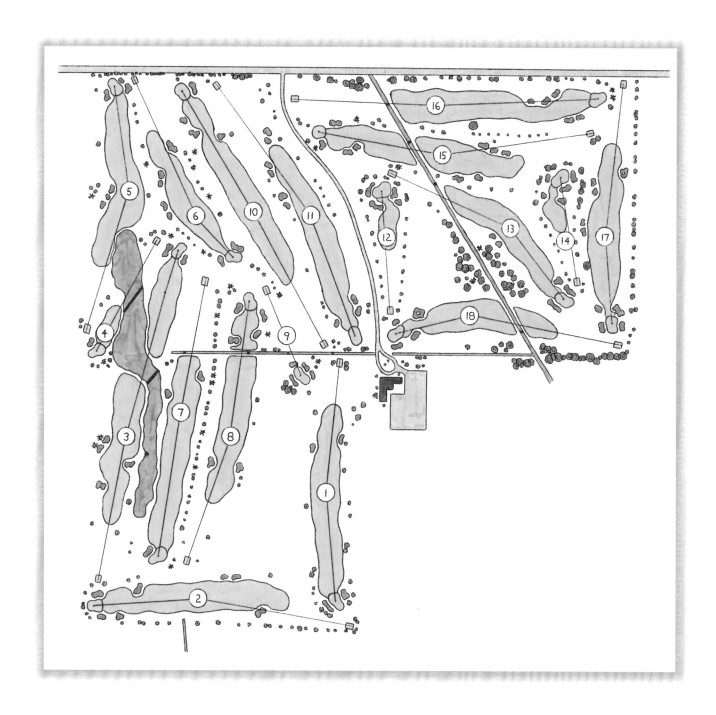

MELBOURNE COUNTRY CLUB
MELBOURNE, FL

⚛

DONALD ROSS (1926)

*I*t has long been said that as the flattest state in the Union, Florida represents America's poorest setting for good golf. With the exception of a few exceptional coastal locations, the thinking goes, the terrain is simply too dull to yield many interesting golfing features, and the constant need for drainage guarantees the presence of numerous man-made lakes. Thus architect Tom Doak speaks for many observers when he writes: "There are more than 1,000 golf courses in Florida today. I'll take Seminole; you can have the other 999."

However...

With all due respect to Doak's essentially accurate contemporary observation, a look back at some of the Sunshine State's best prewar designs in their original form paints a rather different picture. For over the years, much good work by men like Donald Ross, William Flynn, and William Langford has, through poor maintenance, real estate development, or sheer ignorance, either disappeared or been altered beyond recognition.

A fine example of the latter was Ross's Melbourne Country Club layout, a 6,405-yard track which opened during the great hurricane year of 1926. Located on the site of today's Melbourne Municipal Golf Course, just two miles from the Intracoastal Waterway, this par-71

design featured water—in the form of one lake and Crane Creek—in play on 10 holes. A good-sized layout for the day, it relied far more upon traditional strategic elements (e.g., the wonderful angles of the 514-yard third) and Ross's intricate green contouring than the sand and water overkill so frequent in present-day Florida golf.

Tracing the evolution of the Melbourne layout has proved difficult, particularly since one published source attributed a 1926 Melbourne, Florida design to Indiana-based architect William Diddel. But Ross's original plans still exist, and while some pre–World War II alterations deviated from them noticeably, photographic evidence from that period reveals that the vast majority of holes still adhered to Ross's specs. Following substantial remodeling by William Amick in the 1960s, however, virtually nothing remains of that early design, with the clubhouse now situated toward the property's northwest corner and numerous water hazards added.

Today's Melbourne Municipal Golf Course may well fit into Tom Doak's "other 999." But during the 1920s it was a pleasant and strategic layout of some genuine merit.

Commonplace then, a rarity now.

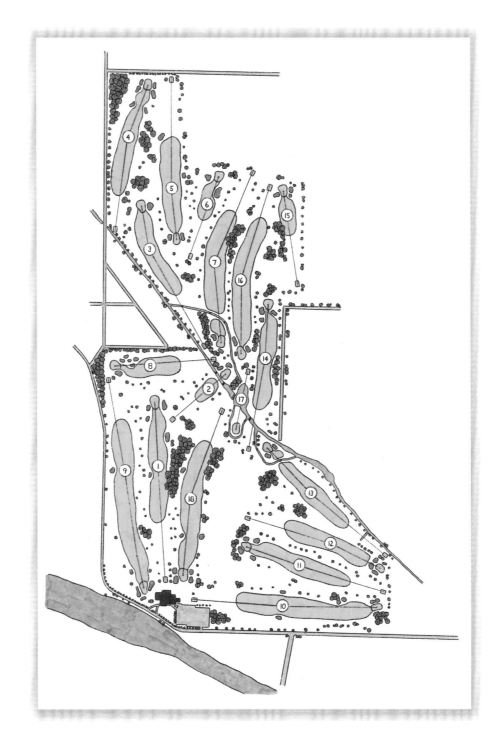

MIAMI																				
410	173	387	370	406	210	452	237	528	3173	453	372	335	370	341	234	451	143	428	3127	6300
4	3	4	4	4	3	5	3	5	35	5	4	4	4	4	3	5	3	4	36	71

MIAMI COUNTRY CLUB
MIAMI, FL

❧

DONALD ROSS (1919)

By most credible accounts, Donald Ross built or remodeled approximately 40 golf courses in the state of Florida, roughly 10% of his overall verifiable career output. This prolific run began in 1915 with a renovation of nine holes and the construction of 27 new ones at the Belleair Country Club in Clearwater and ended, in grand style, with the Seminole Golf Club, in Juno Beach, in 1929. Not surprisingly, so large a body of work included designs of various sizes and styles. What might surprise, however, is that one of the most advanced and modern was actually accomplished rather early: the Miami Country Club, which was completed in 1919.

Located near Northwest 20th Street, on the north shore of the Miami River, the Country Club layout actually began life in association with Henry Flagler's Florida East Coast Railway, built for guests of the company's nearby Royal Palm Hotel. As golf's rapid growth soon necessitated an upgraded facility, Ross was brought aboard in 1918, ultimately remodeling half of the existing track and joining it with nine new holes. Such was a common practice for the Scotsman, but in this case the result was one of his period's best.

Originally featuring more than 90 bunkers (at least 25 of which would grow over prior to World War II), it became a frequent winter tournament venue, hosting such legends as Harry Vardon, Walter Travis, Jerry Travers, and Willie Park Jr.

Water figured prominently into the Miami routing, particularly at the 370-yard 13th where a creek fully encircled the entire green complex. The purist might suggest that as the water was well-removed from the putting surface, this could not truly be called an island green. Fair enough. But at the 143-yard 17th, Ross rendered the question moot by creating one of the earliest American versions of the real thing. Though a modestly short ball would likely end up dry, anything missed left, right, or long surely went down with the ship.

Rooted in resort or public-access golf, the Country Club briefly went private in the late 1920s before the Depression returned it harshly to the public domain. Ultimately a victim of increased real estate values, it has since been replaced by a section of the Dolphin Expressway, two hospitals, and the Miami Civic Center.

148

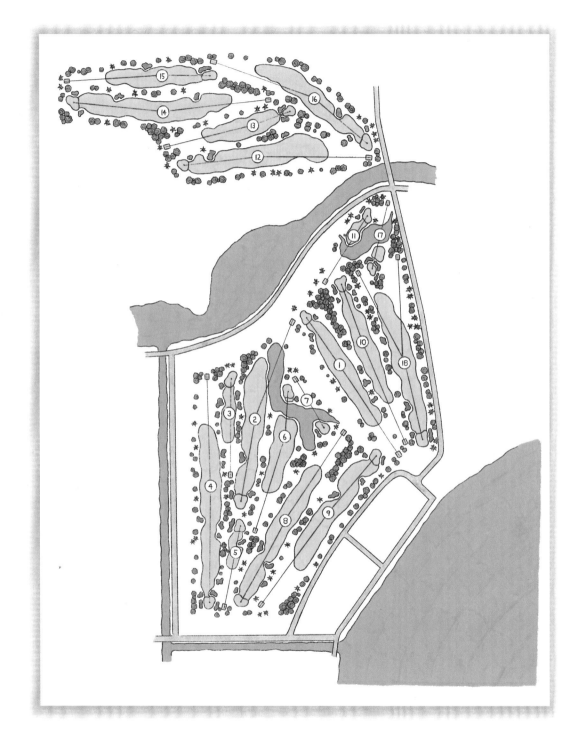

MIAMI SHORES COUNTRY CLUB
MIAMI, FL

DONALD ROSS (1926)

*F*or many lost courses, the fall into extinction has been more a matter of bad timing than bad design, a chronological misfortune of coming into existence in proximity to a period of economic upheaval, wartime, or natural disaster. Yet among all of those whose timing led to a premature demise, it is unlikely that any were shorter-lived – and thus more completely overlooked – than Donald Ross's layout at Miami Shores.

Indeed a great deal of research has been required simply to confirm that this facility did, in fact, actually exist. That Ross drew up plans for the bayfront property located just north of today's Broad Causeway and east of Biscayne Boulevard, was an undisputed matter of record. That no golfing guidebook or magazine of the period ever made mention of such a club, however, was equally factual, suggesting that perhaps the course had, for any number of reasons, never come to fruition. But a detailed 1926 map of Miami confirms such a development in just the suggested location and a 1927 edition of the *Automobile Green Book* ratifies its existence as an active entity.

For a little while.

There can be no doubt that this 6,394-yard layout expired either in the "Hundred Year Hurricane" of 1926 or as an immediate casualty of the Depression. Whichever the case, it was, while it lasted, a crafty little course which packed a surprising amount of length into so small a property. Perhaps the most demanding hole was the 446-yard, par-4 second, its drive played over a pond, though the approach to the 340-yard sixth certainly offered less margin for error. The 141-yard seventh and 197-yard 11th were similarly dangerous, their greens perched closer to water's edge than was generally the Ross style.

At the 430-yard par-4 18th, the educated eye may spot several similarities to Ross's original closer at Seminole (later altered by Dick Wilson) including length, squarish green, cross-hazard well short and alternate tees. In comparing these similarities, it is worthwhile to note that the Miami Shores finisher came first, by three years.

In the repetitive world of modern South Florida golf, Miami Shores would certainly represent a neat addition were it still in existence—Robert "Red" Lawrence's nearby Miami Shores Golf Course being related in name only.

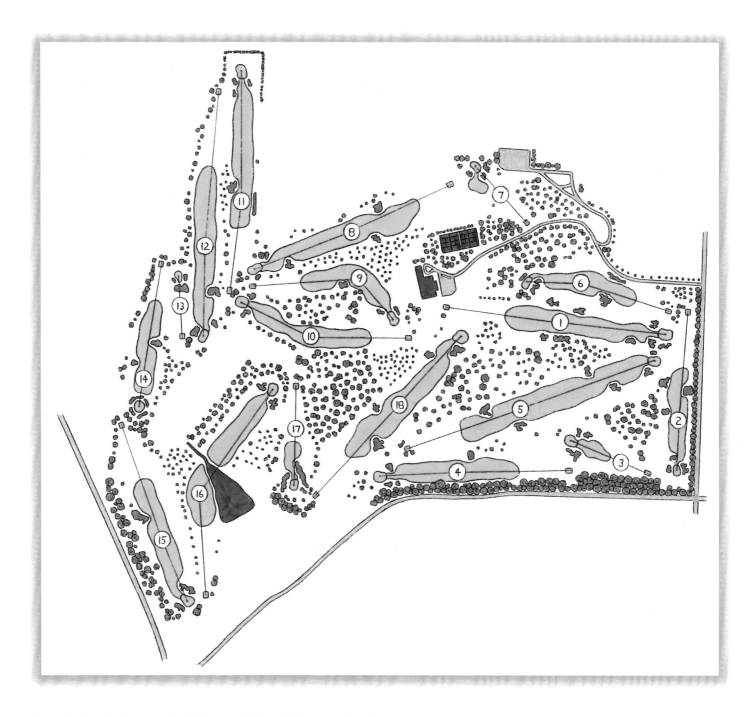

MIDWICK																				
453	321	181	388	541	286	154	413	410	3147	380	430	460	124	295	363	467	207	436	3162	6309
4	4	3	4	5	4	3	4	4	35	4	4	5	3	4	4	5	3	4	36	71

MIDWICK COUNTRY CLUB
MONTEREY PARK, CA

❧

BILLY BELL (1927)

Located in Monterey Park just south of today's 10 Freeway, Midwick was, at the time of its 1912 opening, the ritziest of all Southern California country clubs. A grand piece of acreage bordering Atlantic Boulevard to the east and Hellman Avenue to the north, Midwick featured a Norman MacBeth-designed golf course, a world-class tennis club, and polo facilities deemed good enough to host several equestrian events during the 1932 Los Angeles Olympics (Riviera hosted the rest).

But as technology changed the game of golf, MacBeth's links fell out of favor and by the late 1920s, local designer Billy Bell was called in for a full renovation. What resulted was clearly one of Bell's very best layouts, a 6,309-yard track featuring great variety, five par 4s well in excess of 400 yards, and an excellent set of finishers. It also served to highlight Bell's trademark style of rough-edged bunkering, a technique executed so well at Midwick that the architect chose a photo of the club's seventh green for his period advertisements.

On so uniformly strong a layout, selecting top holes is no easy task, but the 453-yard, par-4 first, the long fifth, the drive-and-pitch sixth and the aforementioned seventh certainly all provided a very high standard of play. The back nine was a neat mix of long and short, with the 11th and 12th requiring power, the 13th and 14th a marked degree of finesse and the closers (measuring 467, 207 and 436 yards respectively) something more on the level of brute force.

Also noteworthy was the rebuilding of holes nine and 10 circa-1930, a job possibly performed by Bell himself. Consequently the versions pictured in the facing map (taken from a 1933 aerial) are out of sync with the 1927 scorecard numbers. They are, however, the versions that would last.

As more and more of Los Angeles's wealth found its way to the city's west side, and affluent golfers flocked to newer facilities like Riviera and Bel-Air, Midwick's fortunes began to slide. The hardships of wartime were the final blow and in 1941 the property was sold off for eventual subdivision. In a nod to sentimentality, the streets of today's residential neighborhoods carry names like Sarazen and Baltusrol Drives as a faint reminder of what was.

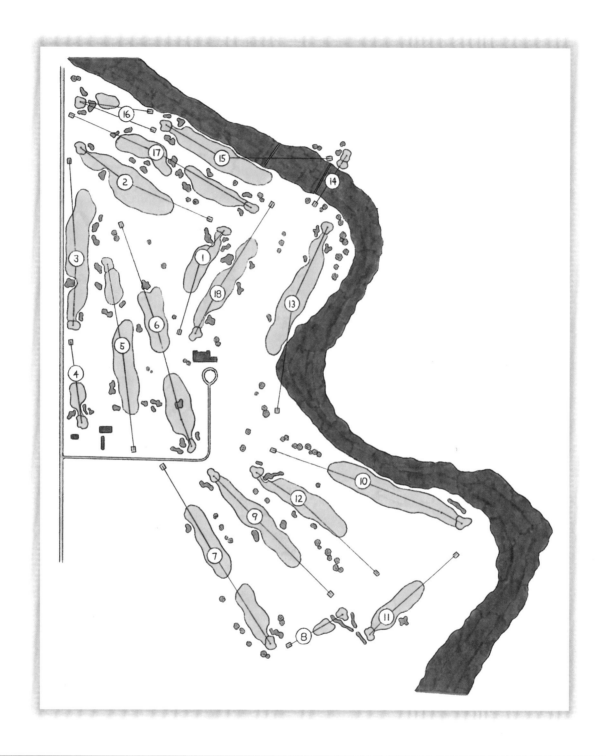

MILWAUKEE																				
267	392	396	196	433	552	485	150	409	3280	486	279	375	458	145	419	204	508	362	3236	6516
4	4	4	3	4	5	5	3	4	36	5	4	4	4	3	4	3	5	4	36	72

MILWAUKEE COUNTRY CLUB
MILWAUKEE, WI

WALTER TRAVIS (1924)

*I*n a game where enormous changes in equipment make the cross-generational comparison of players an exercise in pure subjectivity, one fact is indisputable: Mr. Walter Travis, native of Maldon, Australia, was the first true superstar of American golf.

Having emigrated to New York at the age of 23, Travis didn't even begin playing the game until he was 35—a remarkably late start given the average lifespan of the day. But within three years he had made up for lost time, winning the first of his three U.S. Amateur titles in 1900 on his home course, the Garden City Golf Club. Also becoming the first foreign-born winner of a British national title (the 1904 Amateur at Royal St. George's), Travis would earn the title of golf's "Grand Old Man" by remaining competitive on the national level until well into his 50s.

His legacy to the game was far more than trophies, however, as Travis was the founder and editor of *The American Golfer* magazine and, in due course, an architect of real standing.

Like many of today's top designers, the Old Man did a fair amount of redesign work, one example being his 1924 job for the Milwaukee Country Club, a well-established organization dating back to 1895. The layout which Travis reworked was a technologically outdated affair built in 1911, primarily by the club's professional, Alex Robertson. At age 62 and in wavering health, Travis never visited the club but his detailed plans were carried out by on-site construction men, resulting in a more modern and strategic layout.

An open, essentially treeless course, Travis's design is surely best remembered for holes 13-15, all of which prominently featured the Milwaukee River. The 415-yard 15th was clearly the titan of the bunch, owing primarily to a 200-yard carry from the back tees. A testing hole in any era, the lone knock against it might have been a relative lack of strategy—that is, the daring drive played closest to the water gained little appreciable advantage over that played safely left.

Perhaps not surprisingly, club membership was not entirely delighted by such difficult holes and wasted little time in making changes. In 1928, C.H. Alison was retained for a complete makeover, leaving Milwaukee Country Club as the shortest-lived design of Walter Travis's career.

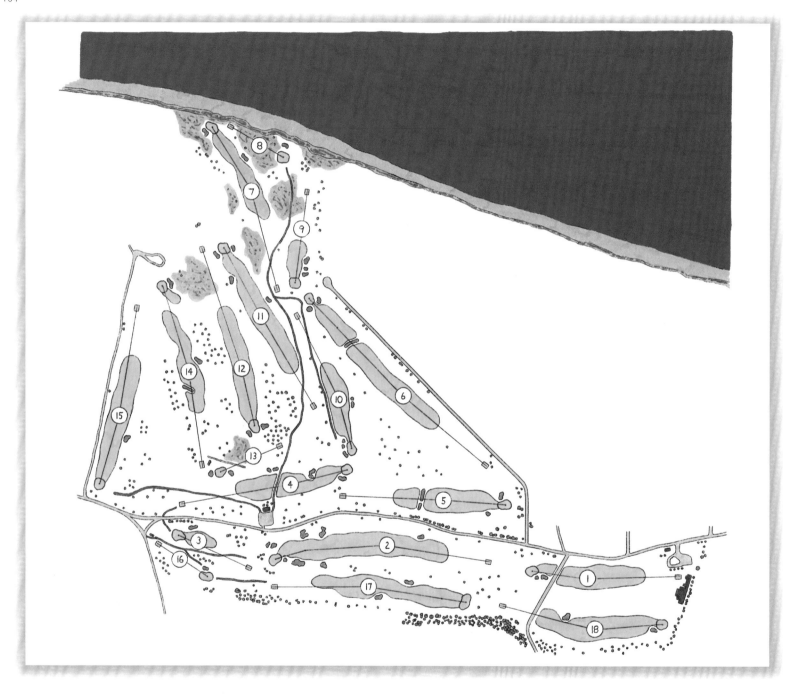

NANTUCKET																				
315	497	170	378	370	540	380	138	217	3005	314	408	410	152	380	400	132	449	366	3011	6016
4	5	3	4	4	5	4	3	3	35	4	4	4	3	4	4	3	4	4	34	69

NANTUCKET GOLF CLUB
NANTUCKET, MA

❧

DONALD ROSS (1917)

Like Overhills, Brentwood or Boca Raton, the Nantucket Golf Club is another facility for which the specifics of Donald Ross's involvement are difficult to determine. Traditional sources credit Ross with having built nine holes here in 1917. Local historical records cite golf being played over nine holes on the site as early as 1897, later expanding to 18—all without any mention of Ross. However a map housed at North Carolina's Tufts Archives marked "Nantucket Golf Course, Donald J. Ross Architect" clearly illustrates 18 holes which are, routing-wise, a perfect match for the layout as it appeared in 1927. Conclusion? That Ross was surely involved here, perhaps to the tune of remodeling the old nine and adding a new one.

Or so it seems.

Whatever the precise answer, early aerial photographs show Nantucket to have been one of America's more natural courses, its holes marching to and fro across vast expanses of sandy coastal terrain. Because such a landscape can make it difficult for an aerial to delineate natural sand from man-made bunkers, the hazard placement on the facing map may not be 100% accurate. Of course the differences are a bit less impor-

tant on this sort of tract, so our margin for error must adjust accordingly.

Following an opening six of good length and challenge, the front nine closed with a wonderful three-hole detour through the dunes to the island's northern bluffs. While the 380-yard seventh was probably the best of this threesome, the 138-yard oceanfront eighth was surely the most spectacular, and the 217-yard ninth the most difficult.

Rather unique on the inward half was the 152-yard 13th where photos appear to indicate an old stone wall – shades of the famous Pit at North Berwick! – closely guarding the bunkered putting surface. The finishers then returned home parallel to the openers and, though appearing rather bland from above, were surely enhanced by Ross's trademark green contouring.

The Nantucket Golf Club was apparently clobbered by the Depression, area historical accounts next mentioning golf in 1949 with the construction of a new nine-hole public course. Failing to attract a substantial number of players, this layout closed within a few years and the land was ultimately donated to the Nantucket Conservation Foundation in 1976.

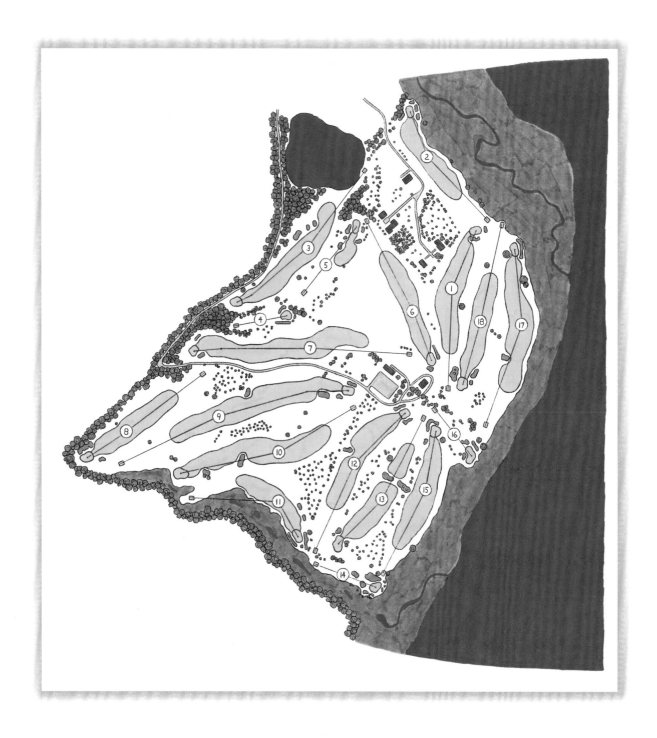

NORTHPORT																				
380	350	450	120	225	370	530	340	570	3335	448	300	403	375	150	360	125	425	400	2986	6321
4	4	5	3	3	4	5	4	5	37	5	4	4	4	3	4	3	5	4	36	73

NORTHPORT COUNTRY CLUB
NORTHPORT, NY

DEVEREUX EMMET (1921)

The year 1921 was, by any measure, a good one for Devereux Emmet who expanded his reputation with the opening of seven new courses of real repute. Indeed Pelham (page 216) and Pomonok (see *The Missing Links*) would gain lasting fame as sites of the 1923 and 1939 PGA Championships, while Grassy Sprain (page 128) would host Gene Sarazen's prestigious Metropolitan Open win in 1925. A fourth course, the McGregor Golf Links, was impressive enough to have its routing reprinted in George Thomas's *Golf Architecture in America*, and today's heavily altered Rye (NY) and Hartford (CT) Golf Clubs were also well received—but what of course number seven?

All but forgotten from that Emmet Class of '21 is the long-deceased Northport Country Club, a challenging track situated on a stretch of marshy coastline some five miles northeast of Huntington. Though perhaps not on par with Long Island's world-renowned elite, Northport featured a number of truly striking holes, beginning with the 350-yard second, a gentle dogleg-right whose green complex extended well out into the marshland. At the opposite end of the prop-

erty the 300-yard 11th was even more impressive. Though the marsh may have been drier this far inland, the tee shot remained a serious test of judgment, tempting the aggressive player to go very near – or directly at – the narrow, tightly bunkered putting surface.

Perhaps equally memorable was the 150-yard 14th, a photographer's dream with its well-bunkered green sitting out on a promontory, backed first by the marsh, then the open waters of Long Island Sound. The 125-yard 16th occupied a similar setting but its angled putting surface sat much closer to the hazard line. Here pin placement made all the difference.

As late at the 1930s, the 425-yard 17th was played as a par 5, a legitimate commentary, one suspects, on its general degree of difficulty. Running entirely along the edge of the marsh, and potentially stretched to 440+ yards, it would today be one of the finest and most talked-about par 4s on the East Coast.

Golf is still played on the Northport site in the form of the modern Crab Meadow Golf Club, a 1965 William Mitchell design bearing little resemblance to its predecessor, which vanished circa World War II.

158

OAK RIDGE COUNTRY CLUB
TUCKAHOE, NY

⚘

WALTER TRAVIS (1923)

As an architect, Walter Travis has frequently been portrayed as an advocate of the penal school of design, the idea being that as one of the most accurate tee-to-green players in history, he created layouts predisposed toward his own strengths. A notoriously short hitter, Travis is also believed to have favored more diminutive courses, as well as deep bunkers and heavily contoured greens. These last two alleged preferences do, in fact, appear accurate, at least so far as photographs of his more famous green complexes indicate. One look at Tuckahoe's old Oak Ridge layout, however, should quell any penal and short-course rumors completely.

To begin with, at 6,350 yards with a par of 70, Oak Ridge was a fairly long layout for its day. Its two par 5s ran in excess of 500 yards, one par 3 measured 232 (longer than Travis himself likely could drive it) and there were par 4s listed at 428, 431, and an especially demanding 450. More importantly, Oak Ridge's 110+ bunkers were scattered all across the landscape, positioned at odd angles, readily defining differing avenues of play. Such variety, combined with some very wide fairways, made the layout more resemble a British links than anything remotely penal.

By a mile.

With the exception of the 140-yard second, Oak Ridge initially required power, especially at the 534-yard third and 406-yard fourth, the latter carving its way past a dozen scattered bunkers. There followed a brief brush with water at the sixth and seventh, then something of a respite at the eighth before the challenge picked up in earnest at the turn.

For at 450 yards, the ninth may well have been the club's toughest hole, yet it was also among its most strategic. Built beyond the reach of the average player's two best, it instead provided several lay-up options in preparation for one's third, all affected by a diagonal line of four bunkers running from 300 to 360 yards out.

Rather curiously, Travis's chosen routing for Oak Ridge relegated the closers to a faintly monotonous back-and-forth procession. Still, the 356-yard 18th provided both an engaging tee shot and a green angled dangerously around a prominent bunker—just the sort of precision finish that a deadly iron player like Travis would covet.

160

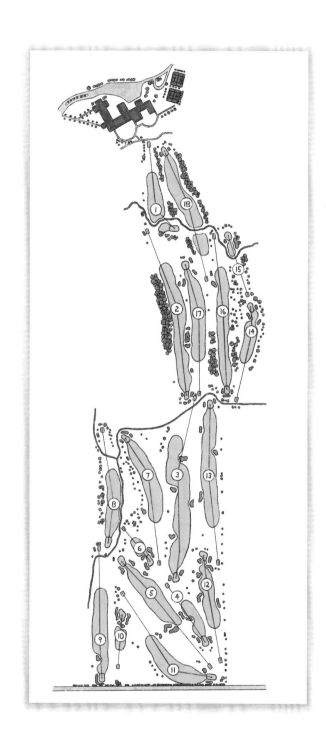

OLYMPIA FIELDS (No.2) (Approximate)																			
290	520	540	215	415	130	395	350	380	3235	150	400	325	480	290	190	480	400	420	3135	6370
4	5	5	3	4	3	4	4	4	36	3	4	4	5	4	3	5	4	4	36	72

OLYMPIA FIELDS COUNTRY CLUB (NO. 2)

OLYMPIA FIELDS, IL

⚜

WILLIE WATSON (1918)

"Golf for golf's sake" is how Charles Beach, founder of the Olympia Fields Country Club, initially described his planned establishment. There would be multiple courses to be sure, but to Beach's way of thinking the entire undertaking was far more about golf than the spectrum of other club activities occupying America's plentiful post-World War I leisure time. Ancillary facilities? The need for accommodations would be met by constructing a handful of simple log cabins. Dining? A central cafeteria would suffice. A locker room? Well, a place to change one's shoes and store clothing maybe, but had anything more ever been required back in Scotland?

That Beach's low-key approach was soon scrapped in favor of unparalleled opulence is mostly a testament to the club's unexpectedly immediate popularity. For the rapidly growing membership agreed early on to fill their 750-acre neighborhood with an unprecedented four courses, each intended as a full-sized layout of the highest caliber. While this alone would prove unique among American private clubs, it was Olympia Fields' non-golf amenities – a school, fire station, private railway depot, and, oh yes, the world's largest clubhouse – that are most frequently recalled.

The club's first course, the Number One, was designed by expatriate Scotsman Tom Bendelow and remains largely intact as the present-day South course.

Another Scottish émigré, Willie Watson, was responsible for the Number Two course which opened in 1918. Though Watson enjoys rather a stronger reputation than Bendelow among the architectural *cognoscenti*, there is little to suggest that his 6,330-yard, par-72 effort in any way exceeded his countryman's, though Number Two's generally flatter terrain may have offered fewer possibilities with which to work.

It should be noted that both the Numbers Two and Three layouts are illustrated here as they existed late in life, just prior to the onset of World War II. Though almost entirely consistent with their original routings, numerous minor alterations had been made both by club professional Jack Daray and, during his 1922 planning of the Number Four course, the great Willie Park. That both layouts were lengthened and generally improved over this period (and thus appear in their "best" form) is widely accepted. As no scorecards from the period are known to exist, however, the yardages listed here represent only a highly educated approximation.

162

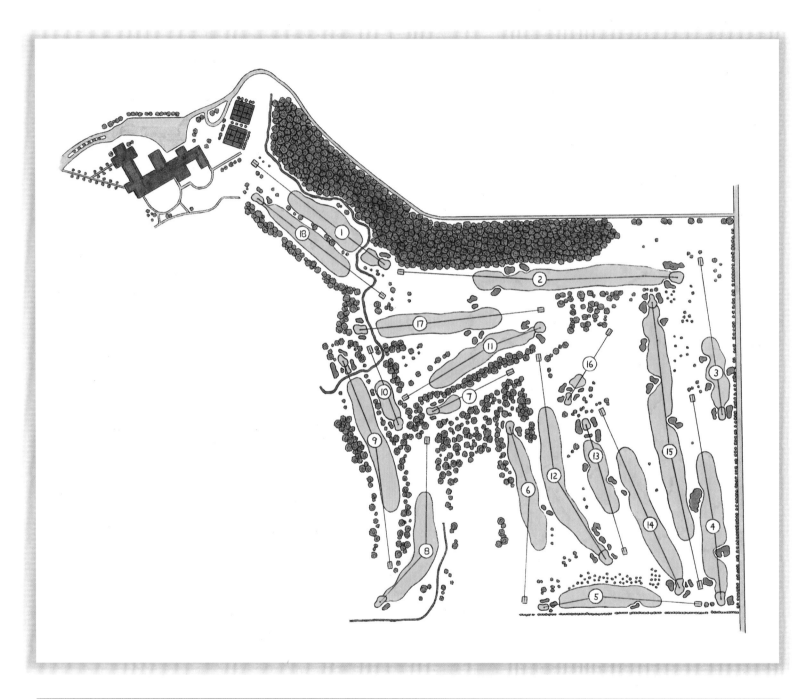

OLYMPIA FIELDS COUNTRY CLUB (NO. 3)

OLYMPIA FIELDS, IL

WILLIE WATSON & TOM BENDELOW (1920)

Two years after opening the Number Two, Olympia Fields again expanded. Perhaps undecided as to whose work they preferred among their existing 36 holes, the membership arranged for Tom Bendelow and Willie Watson to collaborate on the Number Three course, initially a 6,418-yard, par-70 layout which opened in 1920.

A notably difficult track from the beginning, Number Three was well reviewed in its early years, praised both for the variety of its terrain and the specific design of its holes. The membership, however, was apparently not satisfied. For despite (or perhaps because of) par not being broken for several years after its opening, club pro Jack Daray was directed to make significant alterations to Number Three during the latter part of the 1920s. The result, essentially, is the layout presented here.

Number three's best stretch of holes fell in its midsection, where numbers six through 11 traversed rolling, wooded terrain. Following a precise iron shot at the 180-yard seventh, the dogleg-right eighth presented a classically strategic equation: drive close to the right-side treeline and open up the optimum angle of approach or play safely left, avoiding the forest but adding distance and a greenside bunker to one's approach. But this was just a warm-up for the tremendously difficult ninth, a 430-yard par 4 which first required a long tee shot to a narrow, tree-lined fairway. From there the player was left with a very taxing approach across Butterfield Creek to a spindly green flanked by four bunkers. In its day, this may well have been the entire complex's most challenging hole.

Olympia Fields existed as the world's only 72-hole private club for over 20 years before the combination of accumulated debt (the club had assumed a $500,000 mortgage on the clubhouse) and the general effects of the Depression and World War II forced its financial hand. Unable to cover its obligations, the membership elected to assure long-term survival by selling off courses Number Two and Three to developers, leaving, with a modest amount of reworking, Numbers One and Four as today's acclaimed South and North layouts. The latter, designed by the aforementioned Willie Park, will shortly return to the golfing limelight as host of the 2003 U.S. Open.

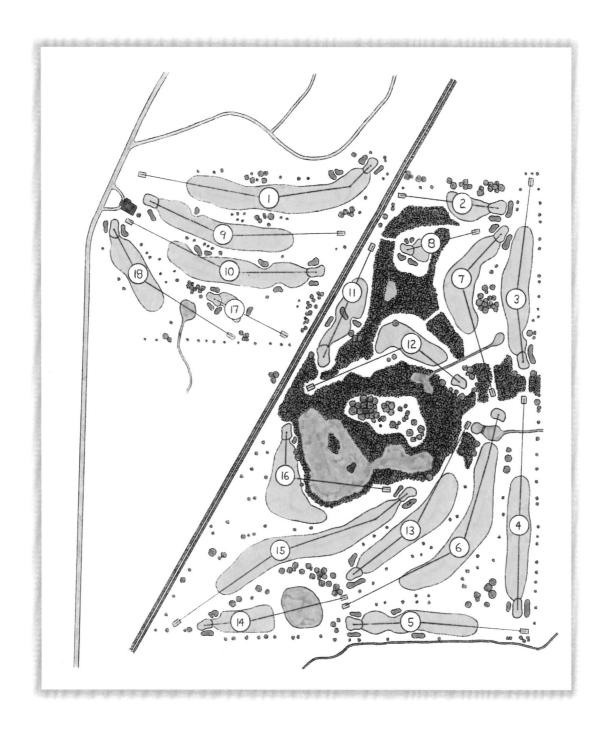

PALMETTO																			
490	200	360	415	350	545	345	150	405	3260	410	245	380	335	300	535	325	160	360	3050	6310
5	3	4	4	4	5	4	3	4	36	4	3	4	4	4	5	4	3	4	35	71

PALMETTO COUNTRY CLUB
PALMETTO, FL

WAYNE STILES & JOHN VAN KLEEK (DATE UNKNOWN)

For the St. Petersburg-based design firm of Stiles & Van Kleek, the accessibility of a potential golf course site was surely of great importance. For in an era of distinctly less reliable automobiles, visits to Central Florida outposts like Sebring and Lake Wales might well have seemed akin to Speke's journey to the source of the Nile.

In this context, the Palmetto Country Club project must have looked an attractive proposition, situated, as it was, just a few miles southeast of Tampa on the main drag of U.S. Highway 41. The land allocated for the club's golf course, however, was a bit less welcoming, its midsection sliced by the tracks of the Atlantic Coast Line Railroad and largely occupied by a grand expanse of swamp- and lake-filled wilderness.

The resultant course was a mix of challenging, highly memorable holes with others of a more mundane nature. This mundane side was well apparent during stretches of the front nine, where only the 545-yard sixth offered any great inspiration. But things picked up quickly at the 245-yard, one-shot 11th, a par-bending brute which required a driver of all but the very longest hitters. Some leeway was provided by the relatively short position of the three cross-bunkers as well as the size of the putting surface (easily the club's largest). But in the end, the 11th's length and position – pinched between the tracks and the swamp-filled overgrowth – surely made par a coveted score.

The 380-yard 12th was a sharp dogleg-right, requiring nearly 150 yards of carry to reach a generous fairway. From there one's second was played over a creek to a narrow green hemmed in on three sides by the morass. The 300-yard 14th required a similar tee shot to carry a lake, before things turned for home with the 535-yard 15th.

But surely no hole impressed quite like the 325-yard 16th, a bonafide thriller in the finest strategic tradition. Doglegging nearly 90° around the swamp, this captivating drive-and-pitch allowed the more aggressive player to bite off as much as he dared, with the direct line requiring nearly 250 yards of carry.

All told then, Palmetto may be only a modest loss, but its best holes would surely interest any fan of classic golf design.

166

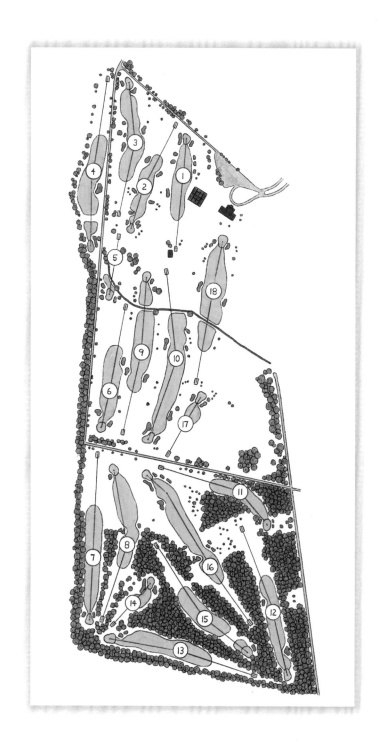

PRINCE GEORGE'S																				
315	323	370	485	173	354	473	443	445	3381	498	366	439	428	162	403	516	181	394	3387	6768
4	4	4	5	3	4	4	4	4	36	5	4	4	4	3	4	5	3	4	36	72

PRINCE GEORGE'S COUNTRY CLUB
LANDOVER, MD

✶

DONALD ROSS (1921)

*I*f ever a lost course's architectural credit has been inaccurate, this must surely be the time. For while nobody disputes that Donald Ross originally worked here in 1921, a very strong body of evidence exists to suggest an early (and thorough) makeover by William Flynn—and it is Flynn's style more than Ross's that is apparent when examining both the strategy and scale of the prewar layout.

Located just south of the intersection of Route 50 and Landover Road, Prince George's (alternately known, during much of the Depression, as the Beaver Dam Country Club) occupied an oddly shaped tract which at one time included a third nine in its northeast corner. As no record exists of Ross having built 27 holes, we might cautiously attach Flynn's name to this extra loop as well, though it would be completely subdivided by the early 1950s.

Regardless, the surviving 18 was one strong layout, a full-sized test which stood up quite nicely among the nation's elite prewar championship courses. Hyperbole? Historical hype? Certainly not, at least once the player faced the heavily wooded southern section of the property beginning on the seventh tee.

At 473 yards, the par-4 seventh was colossal for its day, cutting a narrow swath through the forest to a small, tightly bunkered green. The 443-yard eighth was even tougher, its fairway pinched tightly between bunkers in a style patently dissimilar to the more forgiving Ross norm. Finally the 445-yard ninth crossed sand, a brook, and prominently placed trees before reaching its small putting surface. Truly a powerhouse threesome—and with the course's overall par of 72, not one of these was originally built as a par 5!

Following the 498-yard 10th, things returned to the forest once more, first with the extremely tight 11th, then at the long 12th and 13th. The par-3 14th bore more than a passing resemblance to a Redan while a prominent break in the 15th fairway suggests a modest ravine crossing before the green.

Though the Prince George's name currently survives at a nearby public facility, the loss of this, the original, is substantial. For with some requisite added length, its combination of toughness and character would likely have launched it right past a U.S. Open-sterilized Congressional as the connoisseur's choice among Capital-area classics.

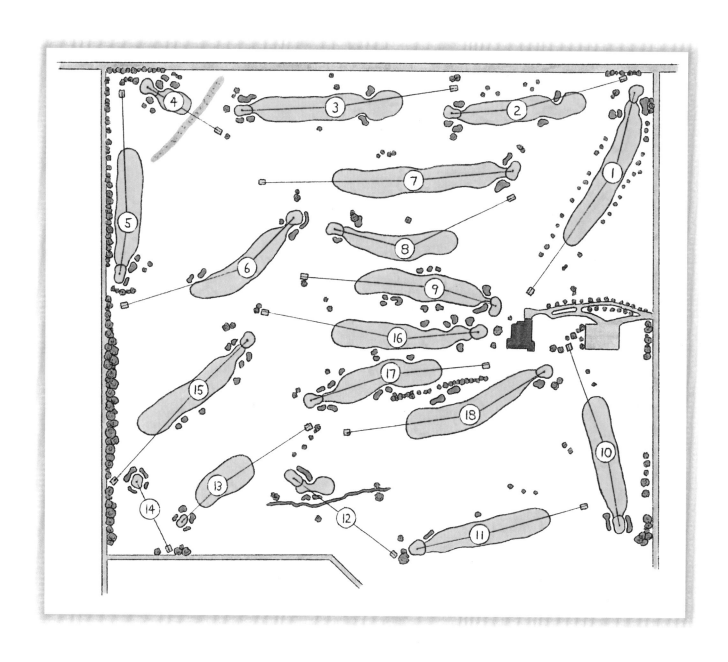

RANCHO																			
448	355	428	167	358	385	520	365	385	3411	374	350	205	330	155	375	440	375	425	3029	6440
4	4	4	3	4	4	5	4	4	36	4	4	3	4	3	4	4	4	4	34	70

RANCHO GOLF CLUB
LOS ANGELES, CA

✺

HERBERT FOWLER (1922)

For countless Los Angelenos, the game of golf – in its public-course form, at any rate – is synonymous with one venue: grand old Rancho Park. Located along Pico Boulevard on the northern edge of affluent Cheviot Hills, this venerable municipal layout ranks perennially among the busiest in the world, exceeding 100,000 rounds played annually. A long and challenging enough track, it has also seen its share of memorable moments in tournament play, listing Ken Venturi, Doug Ford, Charles Sifford, and Arnold Palmer among those who have won the PGA Tour's prestigious Los Angeles Open upon its fairways.

Given such history, it often comes as a surprise, even to old-time Angelenos, to discover that Rancho is not a product of the Golden Age at all but rather a 1947 collaboration between Billy Bell and greenkeeper-turned-architect William Johnson. The land upon which it sits, however, has hosted golf since 1922, and it's here that our story gets interesting.

Contemporary volumes have suggested Max Behr as the builder of the original Rancho Golf Club, which was owned, incidentally, by downtown's famous Ambassador Hotel. But period magazine accounts tell a different story, instead crediting the work to the dis-tinguished British architect Herbert Fowler. Fowler, whose old-world design exploits are legendary, operated fairly extensively throughout California in the early 1920s, listing Los Angeles Country Club's North course (where club member George Thomas supervised construction) as his marquee layout. As that project was completed in 1921, it seems obvious that the visiting Englishman squeezed in the design of Rancho – which lies barely a mile distant – on the same trip. In any event, as one glance at the facing map will indicate, his original Rancho facility bore zero resemblance to the Bell/Johnson postwar track which was later to follow.

Rancho's clubhouse was built off of Motor Avenue and occupied the site of today's Cheviot Hills Park & Recreation Center. The course itself was laid out in two separate loops, and those familiar with the modern configuration will have little difficulty mentally superimposing Fowler's layout over the extant terrain.

While history does not record the reason or precise date of the first Rancho's closing, 1938 aerial photos clearly illustrate a property torn up in preparation for future development. The Depression then, seems the most likely culprit.

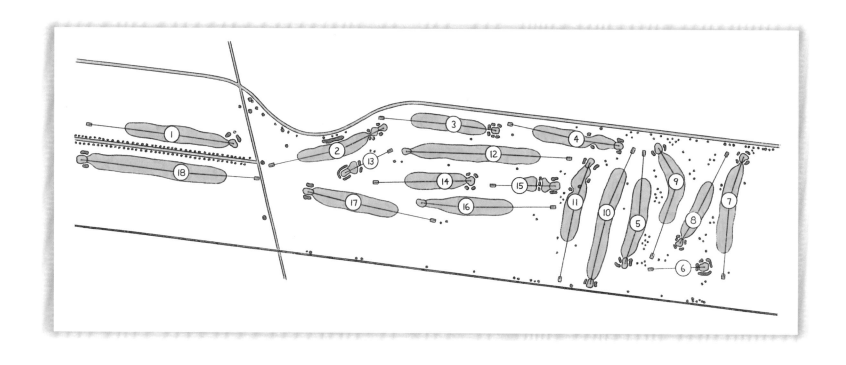

SALISBURY (No.3)																				
453	379	340	359	356	149	389	320	365	3110	432	368	510	160	371	205	439	390	600	3475	6585
5	4	4	4	4	3	4	4	4	36	4	4	5	3	4	3	4	4	5	36	72

SALISBURY COUNTRY CLUB (NO. 3)

EAST MEADOW, NY

⚘

DEVEREUX EMMET (1923)

Given the massive amount of land necessary for the construction of a five-course golf facility, it seems surprising that such an operation could exist – in the form of the famous Bethpage State Park – so close to land-expensive New York City. Bethpage, of course, was the brainchild of powerful New York State Parks Commissioner Robert Moses, and thus enjoyed (and needed) the full clout of a government agency to be brought to fruition. But several miles closer to the Big Apple, another long-forgotten 90-hole facility was developed earlier, and with private funds: the Salisbury Country Club.

Located on land that encompasses today's sprawling Eisenhower Park, Salisbury was developed primarily by the owner of the nearby Garden City Hotel, Mr. J.J. Lannin. Having purchased what would eventually be known as the No.1 course in 1918, Lannin proceeded to bankroll the construction of four more Devereux Emmet-designed layouts between 1922 and 1925. Of the five courses, No.4 was widely considered the best and as such, generally operated with No.3 as a private facility, leaving hotel guests and the public to play over the remaining 54 holes.

Salisbury is perhaps best remembered for hosting the third of Walter Hagen's four consecutive PGA Championships, on the No.4 course in 1926. But that same season the No.3 also made history, hosting a Metropolitan Open won by MacDonald Smith in spectacular fashion over Gene Sarazen. Still tied after two 18-hole play-off rounds, Smith finally bested Sarazen in round seven, winning after a record-setting 126 holes!

Curiously, despite their international reputation, Salisbury's courses (save the historic No.4) do not appear to have been among Emmet's very best. But No.3, which sat between the Long Island Railroad tracks and today's evocatively named Salisbury Park Drive, did at least offer a solid challenge, its mid-length par 4s generally featuring tightly bunkered greens, its one-shotters all of some interest. It is also worth mentioning that No. 3 grew substantially during the mid-1920s, though it is unclear whether holes were actually redesigned or perhaps traded out in a resequencing upon the arrival of course No. 5 in 1925.

Following Depression-era financial problems, only the No. 4 course remains in play today, with a pair of modern Trent Jones Sr. designs having replaced the other four Salisbury layouts in 1951.

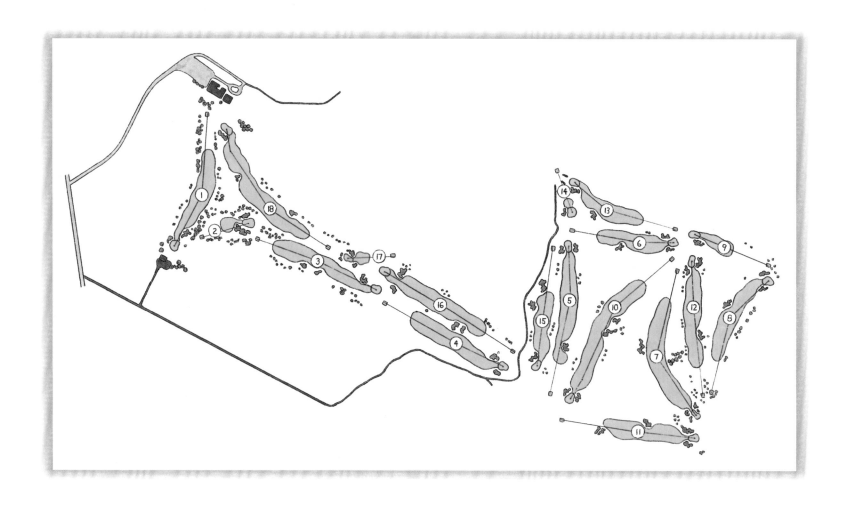

SUNSET FIELDS (North)																				
395	148	400	390	405	325	505	370	225	3163	470	410	400	345	125	365	430	130	480	3155	6318
4	3	4	4	4	4	5	4	3	35	5	4	4	4	3	4	4	3	5	36	71

SUNSET FIELDS GOLF CLUB (NORTH)
LOS ANGELES, CA

BILLY BELL (1928)

For those familiar with the broad body of Billy Bell's architectural work, there has always been debate regarding the depth of his overall talent. This is not intended as a slight really, for it is clear that a number of his courses, often built for municipal purposes, were never intended as landmark works. Yet others clearly did carry more lofty expectations, so it is this latter group by which we must judge.

What confuses the picture is Bell's close professional connection with the great George Thomas, resulting in the captain's frequently being consulted on Bell designs that might otherwise have been considered solo. At El Caballero, Palos Verdes, and Castlewood, for example, we know that Thomas had documented input. At several other of Bell's best, we can only examine the earliest photos, size up the bunkering and playing strategies, and wonder.

Sunset Fields, the largest of Bell's solo undertakings, was just such a facility. Located off Crenshaw Boulevard north of Stocker Street (on land currently housing a residential neighborhood and the Crenshaw Plaza Mall), it was a 36-hole operation surely intended to be on par with Thomas's two courses at nearby Fox Hills.

Though over 200 yards shorter than its sister layout, the North course was likely the better Sunset Fields track, particularly in its 11 outlying holes where a significantly greater degree of elbow room was enjoyed. A narrow out-and-back routing was required to gain access to this terrain and offered a fairly solid beginning. Once afield, however, things really picked up at the 505-yard seventh, a sweeping dogleg-left which was surely reachable in two but featured a tiny green smothered by four bunkers. Distance was less an issue at the 370-yard eighth, but here an angled green suggested a drive played dangerously close to a left-side fairway bunker. At 225 yards, the ninth, with sand left and out-of-bounds right, completed the run.

Coming down the stretch the 440-yard 16th was an obvious challenge while the 17th, at only 130 yards, represented the favored Bell ploy of a tiny, all-or-nothing par 3 placed just before the finish. The 18th, a distinctly reachable par 5, offered a final chance at birdie provided one carefully measured their approach to the narrow, sand-fronted putting surface.

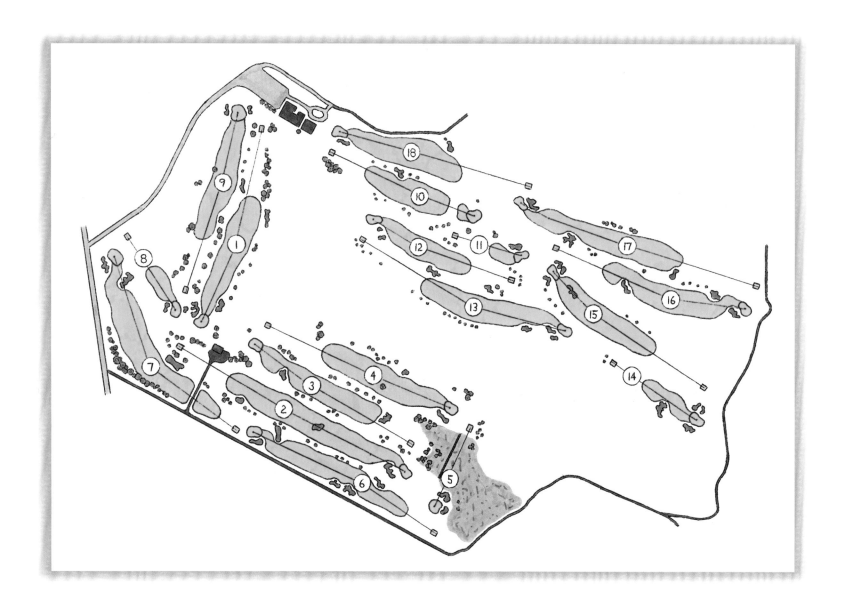

SUNSET FIELDS (South)																			
415	535	395	420	160	440	460	175	385	3385	350	150	320	480	200	370	390	500	410	3170	6555
4	5	4	4	3	4	5	3	4	36	4	3	4	5	3	4	4	5	4	36	72

SUNSET FIELDS GOLF CLUB (SOUTH)
LOS ANGELES, CA

☙

BILLY BELL (1927)

An interesting footnote to Billy Bell's work at Sunset Fields is that despite published reports to the contrary, the North and South courses were not built simultaneously. The South in fact came first, opening in 1927, and was fully operational at least one year before land was ever broken on the North. The latter likely came on line in either 1928 or '29, and was absolutely in play by the early part of the 1930s.

As mentioned previously, the South was easily the longer layout despite its relatively cramped routing. It also featured the most appealing hole on either course, the 160-yard fifth where a forced carry was required across 100 yards of barranca. Perhaps in a concession to the presumably more modest skills of the public-course golfer, Bell resisted the temptation to perch the green close to the hazard, instead providing two bunkers as a generous buffer zone. No such leeway was provided at the sixth, however, a 440-yard par 4 featuring a narrow, tightly-bunkered fairway and equally demanding green.

Perhaps the most historical hole on the golf course was the par-3 11th. Measuring only 150 yards, the South's shortest hole was, according to period arti-cles, a Redan replica—hardly an oddity for its day but certainly a rare occurrence among Billy Bell's solo designs. Of course, those same printed accounts suggested that there were additional replicas sprinkled across the layout, a statement not easily supported by a close examination of early photos.

The South's best stretch may well have been its finishers, beginning with the 200-yard 14th where a tightly-bunkered green left little room for error on one's long-iron or wooden approach. Following two sound par 4s came the 500-yard 17th, a just-long-enough par 5 with a sprawling left-side bunker placed precisely where a laid-up second would otherwise be aimed. Similarly, the 410-yard 18th asked for an approach played from the right side, requiring the ideal tee ball to skirt both out-of-bounds and one nicely positioned bunker.

As an afterthought, we must consider that in recent years, Los Angeles has frequently been cited as offering the fewest public golf holes per capita of any major city in America. When one considers the loss of 72 holes at Sunset Fields and Fox Hills, it's easy to understand why.

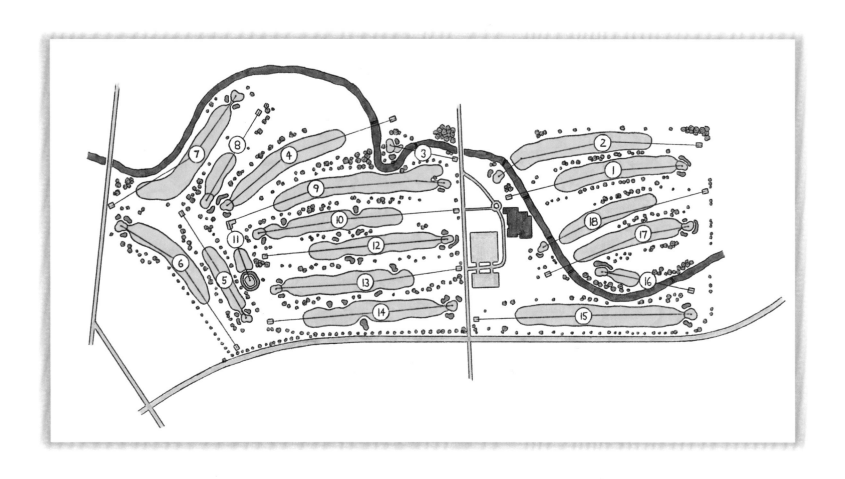

TAM O'SHANTER																				
415	495	160	445	300	445	415	250	520	3445	475	150	440	445	445	515	215	375	410	3470	6915
4	5	3	4	4	4	4	3	5	36	5	3	4	4	4	5	3	4	4	36	72

TAM O'SHANTER COUNTRY CLUB
NILES, IL

CHARLES WAGSTAFF (1925)

Tam O'Shanter's place in golf history was forever cemented on August 9, 1953 when it hosted, for the 10th time, Mr. George S. May's World Championship of Golf. A nationally prominent event which, due to its massive purse, annually assembled one of golf's strongest fields, the 1953 edition carried an even greater importance as it was the first golf tournament of any type to be televised nationally. As play wound down to the 72nd hole, Virginian Lew Worsham found himself needing a birdie three to tie Chandler Harper's 279 total and force a play-off. Facing a 104-yard pitching wedge on his approach, Worsham proceeded instead to hole out for a two, capturing the victory and then-unheard-of first prize of $25,000.

Architecturally speaking, Tam O'Shanter was built in 1925 by Indiana native Charles Wagstaff, a Midwestern designer with rather a limited résumé. Routed over relatively bland terrain, it utilized the North Branch of the Chicago River on nine holes but was, it seems, designed more for toughness than strategy and aesthetics. As such, Wagstaff's work was noticeably modified over the years, enough so that while the routing remained essentially unchanged, the above-mentioned tournaments were played over a layout whose bunkering in particular bore little resemblance to the original. What's presented here, then, is something of a hybrid, with yardages drawn from 1954 but hazarding situated as it was prior to World War II.

Among the front nine's standout holes were the 495-yard second (a classic do-or-die par 5), the watery third, and the 415-yard seventh, whose drive challenged one to flirt dangerously with the sweeping curve of the creek.

Standing out on the inward half was the 11th, a 150-yarder originally played to a green completely ringed with sand. This doughnut aspect was altered out of existence by the 1950s, however, resulting in a considerably less attractive test. The length of holes 12-14 was certainly challenging enough as was the 18th, home to Worsham's 1953 heroics, but more generally a difficult, water-fronted finisher.

By the early 1970s, more than a decade after George May's death, his heirs sold the property to prospective developers. Traces of several original hole corridors still exist, though, on a nine-hole public course which occupies the northern reaches of the old property.

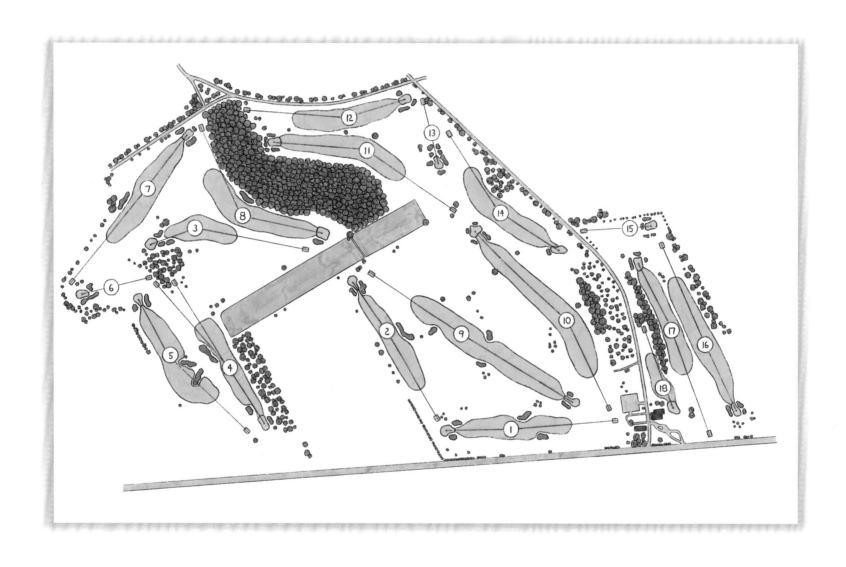

TREDYFFRIN																				
400	340	360	390	370	165	420	390	530	3365	500	440	370	155	365	135	420	412	190	2987	6352
4	4	4	4	4	3	4	4	5	36	5	4	4	3	4	3	4	3	4	34	70

TREDYFFRIN COUNTRY CLUB
PAOLI, PA

❧

ALEX FINDLAY (1917)

Born aboard a steamer in the North Sea, Alex Findlay emigrated to the United States from Montrose, Scotland in the early 1880s, soon to become one of the true pioneers of American golf. Initially he managed a friend's ranch in Nebraska where he introduced the game and laid out a rudimentary course. Later he became director of golf planning for Henry Flagler's Florida East Coast Railway, then was associated with the Wright & Ditson and Wanamaker sporting goods companies. Along the way, he found time to become a most prolific architect, building over 100 courses while also playing over 2,400. Though frequently cited for his unsuccessful attempt at convincing the Vatican to build a six-hole layout during a 1926 visit, he might also be remembered for serving as Harry Vardon's manager during the Greyhound's famous 1900 American tour.

Perhaps because he was not a player of championship caliber, Findlay's primary legacy is his body of design work, an inordinate percentage of which has been altered beyond recognition or plowed up entirely. In fairness, there is little to suggest that Findlay was particularly gifted as an architect, and many of his layouts were replaced by stalwart Golden Age designs. Tredyffrin, however, appears to have been a conspicuous exception.

Opened in 1917, near the corner of Lancaster Avenue and Route 252 in the Philadelphia suburb of Paoli, Tredyffrin was, by any measure, a far cry from rudimentary. In fact, measuring 6,352 yards with a par of only 70, it was really rather a stern test for its day. The back nine was probably the layout's better half, offering a testing drive at the 440-yard 11th, then a true target par 3 at the 155-yard, bunker-ringed 13th. The 14th, doglegging left around a thick stand of trees, was another fine strategic test, requiring a carefully drawn tee shot in order to minimize the impact of a front-right greenside bunker.

Curiously, Tredyffrin's 18th was a par 3, and a relatively nondescript one at that. Given its inconsistency with the rest of the layout, one is left to wonder if perhaps some alteration took place between Findlay's time and 1938, the year of the layout presented here.

Like so many American clubs, wartime doomed Tredyffrin, leaving the property to be sold to developers in 1944.

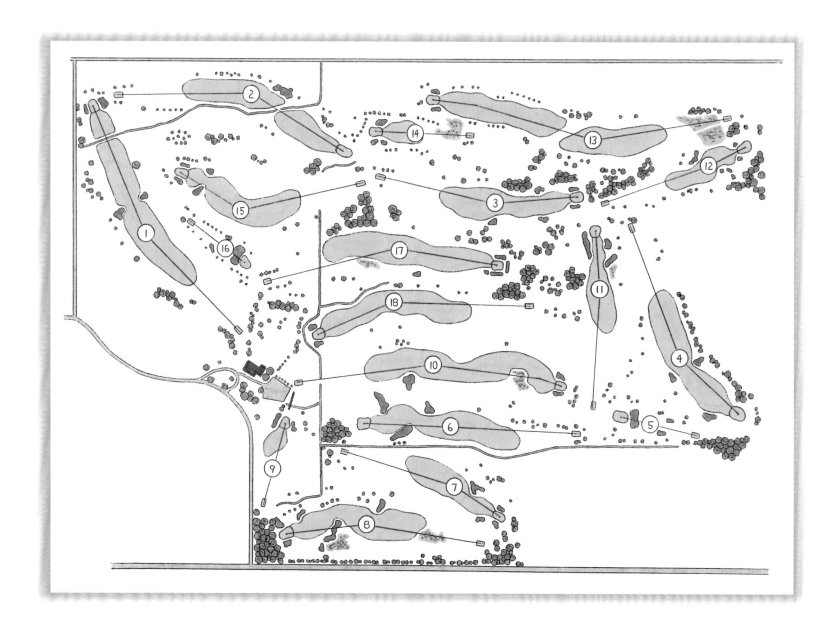

WEST PALM BEACH

495	445	370	400	150	400	315	370	155	3100	495	315	280	550	180	355	130	440	406	3151	6251
5	4	4	4	3	4	4	4	3	35	5	4	4	5	3	4	3	4	4	36	71

WEST PALM BEACH COUNTRY CLUB
WEST PALM BEACH, FL

WILLIAM LANGFORD (1921)

Located on a predictably flat stretch of real estate which now, buried beneath Palm Beach International Airport, has grown considerably flatter, the original West Palm Beach Country Club was both a groundbreaker and a bit of a mystery.

For the groundbreaking, we need look no further than its location, a half-barren patch nearly three miles west of Lake Worth. This qualifies as groundbreaking because if we accept the *American Annual Golf Guide's* published date of establishment (1921) as accurate, then West Palm would be the first of the Gold Coast's classic courses to be constructed substantially inland, away from the cooling coastal breezes of the Gulfstream.

Regarding the mystery, this lies mostly in the course's design being attributed to William Langford— a credit which likely is correct but also curious, as 1921 falls two years earlier than the architect's previously accepted Florida debut.

But these are only secondary concerns because in the main, West Palm offered a number of stellar holes, many of which were dotted by some of architecture's earliest attempts at enhancing a flat landscape with artificial mounding. The 445-yard second, with a narrow creek guarding the driving area, was a fine example, as was the 400-yard sixth, whose putting surface was bordered on three sides by mounds, creating something of a punchbowl.

The 495-yard 10th was an excellent par 5, with a large patch of sandy waste occupying the ideal landing area for one's second. Next came a pair of Langford staples, the short, nearly driveable 11th and 12th. The latter was especially reachable for longer hitters, but required a dead-straight shot to avoid conventional bunkers to the right and sandy waste to the left.

Though the 550-yard 13th was the course's longest hole, the par-4 17th and 18th were surely more challenging. At 440 yards, the 17th required a big tee shot to carry a right-side waste area, leaving a long iron to a small, tightly bunkered green. The 406-yard finisher then trooped back to the clubhouse, its fairway guarded left by mounds and right by a creek. Interestingly, this man-made hazard appears to have been routed deliberately behind the green instead of crossing in front of it, as would surely be the more demanding case today.

182

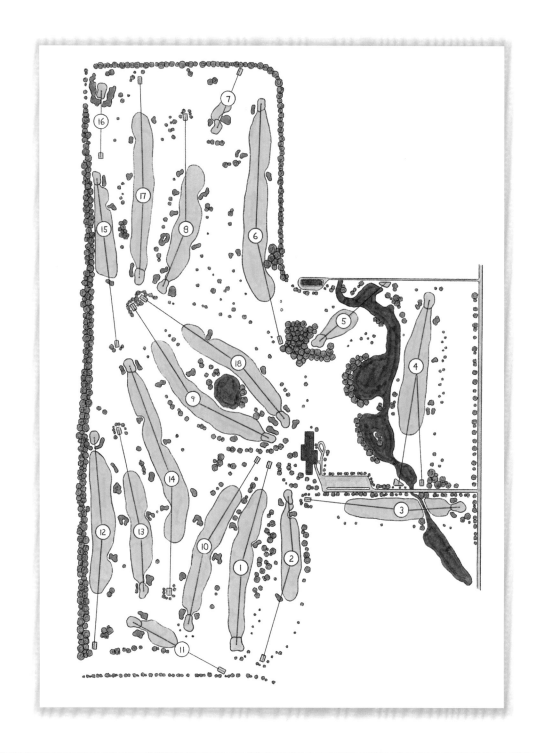

400	355	345	412	185	510	140	365	420	3132	373	205	475	355	500	365	145	438	402	3258	6390
4	4	4	4	3	5	3	4	4	35	4	3	5	4	5	4	3	4	4	36	71

WESTWARD HO GOLF CLUB
MELROSE PARK, IL

FRANK ADAMS & STUART GARDNER (1923)

Though not always operating at the same location, the Westward Ho Golf Club was one of America's oldest, counting itself among the 10 founding members of the Western Golf Association in 1899. During that same year the club moved to their second site, an 18-hole facility in Galewood built by a contemporary of Charles Blair Macdonald's, Englishman H.J. Tweedie. Tweedie's Westward Ho design would survive for 24 years before the club moved to its third and final location, a large acreage at the corner of Wolf and North Avenues in suburban Melrose Park. There a pair of local professionals, Frank Adams and Stuart Gardner, fashioned a 6,390-yard, par-71 course which would, for nearly 35 years, occupy a prominent place in Chicagoland golf.

Curiously, Adams and Gardner made only limited use of the property's potentially major water hazards—though the lake which separated the ninth and 18th holes would be far more in play today than either man might ever have imagined. They were considerably more generous in their use of sand, however, sprinkling more than 70 bunkers across the flat Midwestern landscape.

The club's most memorable holes were the 412-yard fourth – the closest thing it had to a true water hole – and the 145-yard 16th, a disproportionately bunkered par 3 with little margin for error. Both the ninth and 18th were strong par 4s and, like many of Westward Ho's holes, left plenty of room for lengthening had the club survived into the modern era.

Looking back, Westward Ho is probably best remembered for a pair of vastly different competitive events. In 1935, the club hosted a one-day Ryder Cup-like match between six local stars and a team of visiting Japanese professionals. The Japanese players lost handily but impressed their hosts with their desire to copy the American swings and mannerisms, blazing a trail for the Isao Aokis and Jumbo Ozakis to follow.

Twelve years later, the club would host the Chicago Victory National Golf Championship, an outgrowth of the prewar Chicago Open designed to raise money for veterans hospitals and other military charities. In what would turn out to be the last Chicago Victory event, the 1947 winner was Ben Hogan, giving Westward Ho a legacy it would carry for the 10 years that remained until its demise.

184

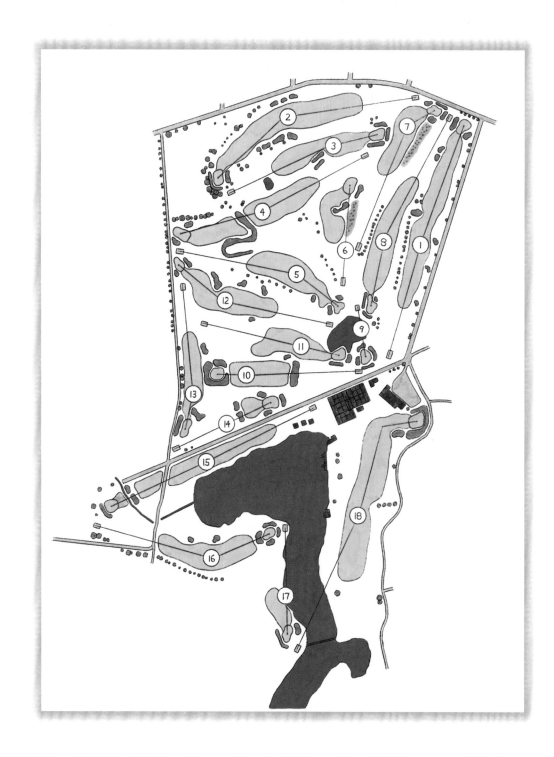

WOODMERE																				
457	440	320	400	344	215	305	400	105	2986	289	285	350	290	215	460	370	215	540	3014	6000
5	4	4	4	4	3	4	4	3	35	4	4	4	4	3	5	4	3	5	36	71

WOODMERE COUNTRY CLUB
WOODMERE, NY

❧

JACK PIRIE (1910) / GILBERT NICHOLLS (DATE UNKNOWN)

A short drive southeast of Kennedy International Airport lies a collection of Golden Age golf courses which, given the development of the surrounding area, seem something of an anachronism. Strung out from Lawrence to Hewlett Harbor, they flank the myriad sloughs and channels north of Long Beach, dotting ultra-valuable land with their short, character-filled layouts. Three of these courses, the Lawrence Village Golf Club, the Rockaway Hunting Club, and the Seawane Club, retain elements of their prewar designs to this day. But the fourth, the Woodmere Country Club, has been thoroughly altered.

Golf at Woodmere dates back to 1910 when a little-known architect named Jack Pirie built a 5,750-yard, par-70 layout on a tiny patch of land, some of which had previously belonged to the neighboring Rockaway Hunting Club. Published reports indicate that Gilbert Nicholls, twice a U.S. Open runner-up, was later retained to make changes to Pirie's layout. Though scant records exist to document his work, evidence suggests that it took place during the Depression and was confined primarily to the back nine.

Despite beginning with four short par 4s, this revised nine eventually opened up nicely, with the finishers carving an adventurous path around the waters of Woodmere Channel. The 460-yard 15th began this stretch, its fairway pinched between today's Keene Lane and the channel. The 17th, a dramatic par 3, required a long iron or wood across the water to reach a deep, narrow green.

Originally a par 4, the revised 18th appears to have been a rather grand par 5—this conclusion being based upon both the configuration of the green complex and the apparent presence of a tee adjacent to the 17th green in old photos. Additionally, so long a closer would be necessary to reach the then-published specs (in the *American Annual Golf Guide*) of 6,000 yards, par 71.

Parenthetically, the hole most remembered from the Pirie/Nicholls layout actually lay upon the front nine, the 400-yard fourth, where a snake-like fairway bunker was nearly 20 feet deep and the green featured three distinct levels.

With land to the club's west becoming available after the war, Trent Jones Sr. was hired to build a new 18 along more spacious lines—a nod to the realities of modern golf, perhaps, but a great disappointment just the same.

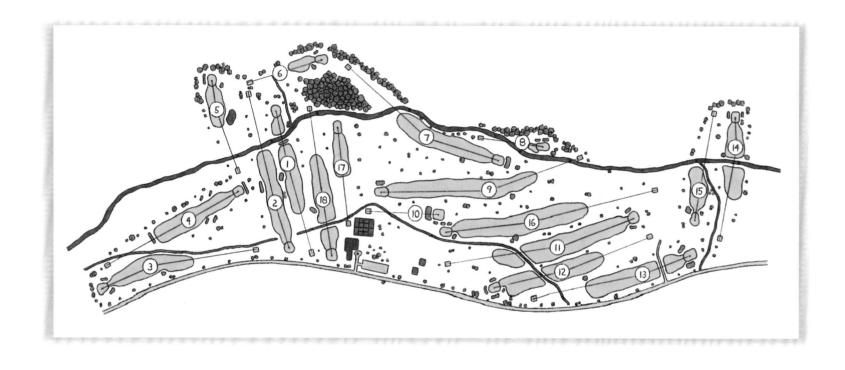

WOODSTOCK																				
315	360	373	332	215	185	415	160	545	2900	165	445	385	375	270	240	490	205	325	2900	5800
4	4	4	4	4	3	4	3	5	35	3	4	4	4	4	4	5	3	4	35	70

WOODSTOCK COUNTRY CLUB
WOODSTOCK, VT

WAYNE STILES (1925)

*I*n few sections of this country did golf enjoy a greater explosion of early popularity than New England, where countless nineteenth-century resort hotels dotted the region's scenic mountains and coastlines. One such seasonal center lay in Woodstock, Vermont, a town well established as a summer tourist destination by the early 1890s. In 1896 a decidedly rudimentary nine holes was put into play, soon to be upgraded by the peripatetic Alex Findlay. Another British émigré, William Tucker, would build an entirely new nine in 1906, then remodel that layout onto much of the land still utilized by Woodstock golfers today.

Golf in the classic, Golden Age sense, arrived in 1925 with the hiring of Wayne Stiles (sans partner John Van Kleek) to build the resort's first 18-hole course and it is this facility, which survived for 37 years, that is presented here.

Stiles's Woodstock layout was decidedly scenic and interesting, occupying a beautiful Green Mountain valley bisected by Kedron Brook and a smaller creek, the two combining to affect play on all 18 holes. Of course at only 5,800 yards, Woodstock was hardly a full-sized test even then, and would surely struggle to exist today without substantial lengthening. Yet it does serve to illustrate a bit of the old-fashioned design style so prevalent in early New England while also featuring a handful of memorable holes.

First among these was the 373-yard third, a dangerous par 4 requiring a very straight drive between a creek, a single bunker and, a bit farther left, today's Route 106. The 445-yard seventh was much longer and likely a bit tougher, owing to an extremely demanding drive to a fairway bending right-to-left around the brook. The 160-yard eighth then crossed the hazard, its narrow green pinched between sand and water and fronted by a set of terribly old-fashioned chocolate drop mounds.

The Stiles layout remained in play until 1961 when Laurance Rockefeller purchased the property for inclusion in his chain of high-profile RockResorts. Deeming the golf course substandard for contemporary play, he brought in Trent Jones Sr. who completely modified the site into today's 6,001-yard, par-69 layout. Only one Stiles hole, the old eighth, remains intact as the present fifth. It still plays directly across Kedron Brook—but without the chocolate drops.

LOST NINES

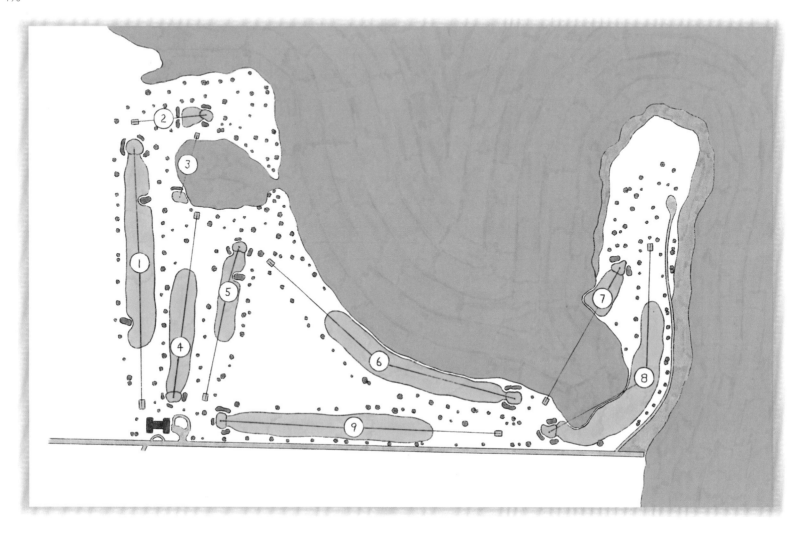

COFFEE POT GOLF COURSE

St. Petersburg, FL

ARCHITECT & DATE UNKNOWN 2,920 YARDS / PAR 36

Pinched between Coffee Pot and Smacks Bayous, along the western shores of Tampa Bay, the short-lived Coffee Pot Golf Course was noteworthy both for several spectacular holes and some vague evidence suggesting A. W. Tillinghast as its designer. For the most part, the holes – particularly numbers six through eight – speak for themselves. As for Tillie's involvement, we'll likely never know for sure.

COFFEE POT									
425	165	110	305	260	500	270	410	475	2920
4	3	3	4	4	5	4	4	5	36

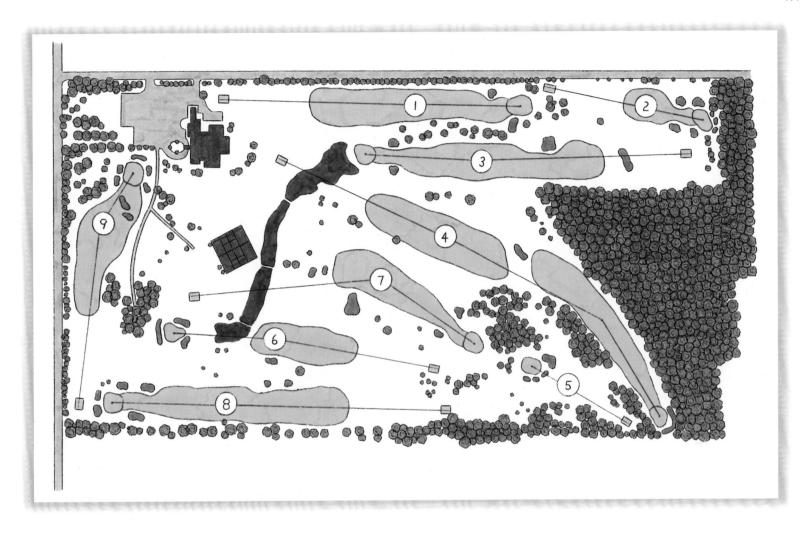

COLONIE COUNTRY CLUB

Albany, NY

CHARLES ALISON (1923) 3,009 YARDS / PAR 35

Located at the intersection of Wolf Road and Central Avenue, the old Colonie Country Club loop likely was built – or perhaps rebuilt – by Charles Alison. Though past research might well have confused this with Michigan's lost Colony Golf Club (page 120), several holes will look rather familiar to Alison fans. For skeptics, compare the 567-yard fourth to Old Oaks 567-yard first (page 197).

COLONIE									
347	200	373	567	143	332	362	400	285	3009
4	3	4	5	3	4	4	4	4	35

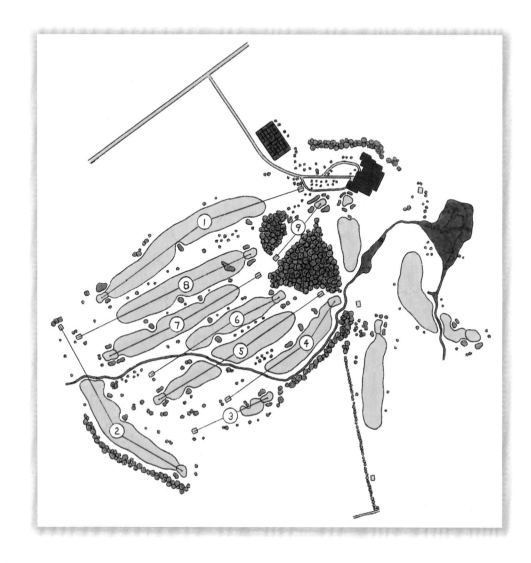

CONGRESSIONAL COUNTRY CLUB

Bethesda, MD

DEVEREUX EMMET (1924) 3,496 YARDS / PAR 37

Long before multiple "Open Doctors" conspired to create today's "championship" layout, Congressional began life as an old-style Devereux Emmet design, the back nine of which remains in play as part of the club's present Gold course. Emmet's track was intended to interest and challenge the club's influential membership. The modern design is about "defending par" during U.S. Open rounds—exactly eight of which have been played in the last 40 years.

CONGRESSIONAL									
567	460	195	368	480	365	424	465	172	3496
5	4	3	4	5	4	4	5	3	37

FT. GEORGE ISLAND GOLF CLUB

Ft. George Island, FL

DONALD ROSS (1927) +/-3,335 YARDS / PAR 36

    Ft. George certainly enjoyed a most attractive location: a seemingly remote island in the Intracoastal Waterway that was, in actuality, rather close to downtown Jacksonville. Some accounts list the course's architect as a local named Maurice Fatio, more claim Donald Ross. Whatever the case, the jungle layout was briefly expanded to 18 holes during the modern era, the overgrown remains of which are still visible in aerial photographs.

FT. GEORGE									
380	475	360	180	400	430	530	140	440	3335
4	5	4	3	4	4	5	3	4	36

HANOVER COUNTRY CLUB

Hanover, NH

RALPH BARTON (1931) 2,940 YARDS / PAR 36

Favorite son Ralph Barton built this addition to Dartmouth College's existing 18 in 1931, in spots showing his roots as a Macdonald/Raynor disciple. Beginning and ending in the ravine to the left of today's 18th fairway, this occasionally awkward loop is probably best remembered for its tree-lined, double-dogleg ninth. It was gradually left to seed in the years following World War II.

HANOVER									
315	330	120	290	340	170	540	345	490	2940
4	4	3	4	4	3	5	4	5	36

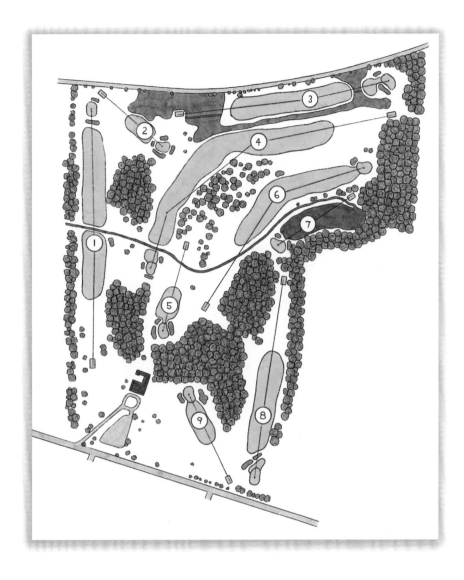

INGLESIDE COUNTRY CLUB

Atlanta, GA

A.W. TILLINGHAST (DATE UNKNOWN) 2,866 YARDS / PAR 33

    This Tillinghast-designed nine witnessed substantial change during its lifetime, including the filling of the swampy area surrounding the third hole during or shortly after the World War I. Though hardly a Winged Foot or Baltusrol, it featured several challenging holes including the all-or-nothing par-3 seventh, which surely racked up its share of big numbers.

INGLESIDE									
460	149	385	590	158	425	165	356	178	2866
4	3	4	5	3	4	3	4	3	33

KELSEY CITY GOLF CLUB

West Palm Beach, FL

WILLIAM LANGFORD (1924) 3,135 YARDS / PAR 36

This William Langford nine, built for resort developer Harry Kelsey, was short-lived and woefully undocumented. Located west of Route 1 and south of Northlake Avenue, it wandered through thick Florida scrub, making use of native sand on several holes, including both par 3s. Interestingly, it appears that no clubhouse was ever built, though a clearing near the ninth green clearly suggested its intended location.

KELSEY CITY (Approximate)									
425	380	170	350	525	130	405	290	460	3135
4	4	3	4	5	3	4	4	5	36

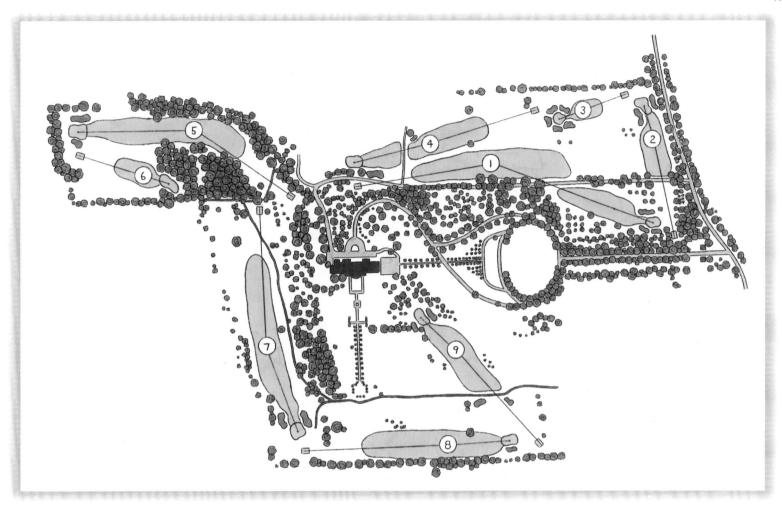

OLD OAKS COUNTRY CLUB (WEST)

Purchase, NY

CHARLES ALISON (1926) 3,005 YARDS / PAR 35

Charles Alison enjoys the credit for the lost third nine of this stately Westchester club, though he worked off an initial routing drawn by A.W. Tillinghast. Completed before its still-extant sister 18, the West ran counterclockwise around the old William Reed estate, whose entry roads and tree-lined promenades remained highly visible throughout. The loop was abandoned in the early 1970s following construction of Interstate 684.

OLD OAKS (WEST)									
567	251	136	359	418	164	412	380	318	3005
5	4	3	4	4	3	4	4	4	35

ST. LUCIE RIVER COUNTRY CLUB

Port Sewall, FL

WILLIAM LANGFORD (1924) 3,205 YARDS / PAR 36

Located just east of Stuart, between the Navy's Witham Field and Hell Gate Point, the St. Lucie River Country Club joins Kelsey City as a second lost Langford nine along Florida's affluent East Coast. Featuring several strategically interesting holes (particularly numbers two and four), it lies buried beneath the present Martin County Golf & Country Club, a 1980s Ron Garl design.

ST LUCIE RIVER									
390	420	195	515	130	375	400	280	500	3205
4	4	3	5	3	4	4	4	5	36

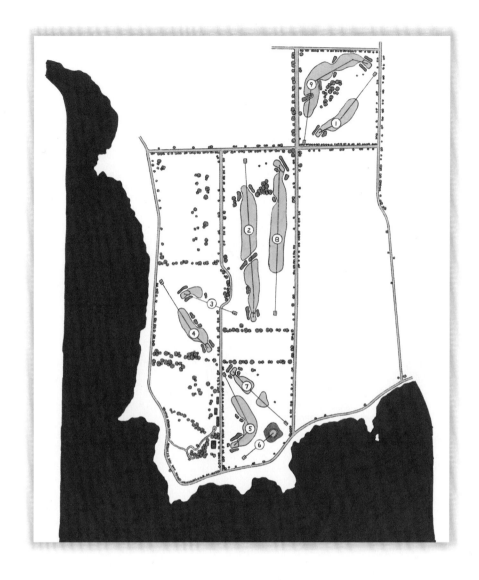

T. SUFFERN TAILOR'S OCEAN LINKS

Newport, RI

SETH RAYNOR (1920) 3,034 YARDS / PAR 37

Located immediately adjacent to the famous Newport Country Club, T. Suffern Tailor's private nine was a genuine Macdonald/Raynor track featuring several of the usual replica holes. Perhaps most famous for hosting the famed Gold Mashie tournament (an amateur event won by such luminaries as Francis Ouimet and Jesse Guilford), the course was sold by Tailor's widow following his death in 1931.

OCEAN LINKS									
310	545	191	305	315	140	258	510	460	3034
4	6	3	4	4	3	4	5	4	37

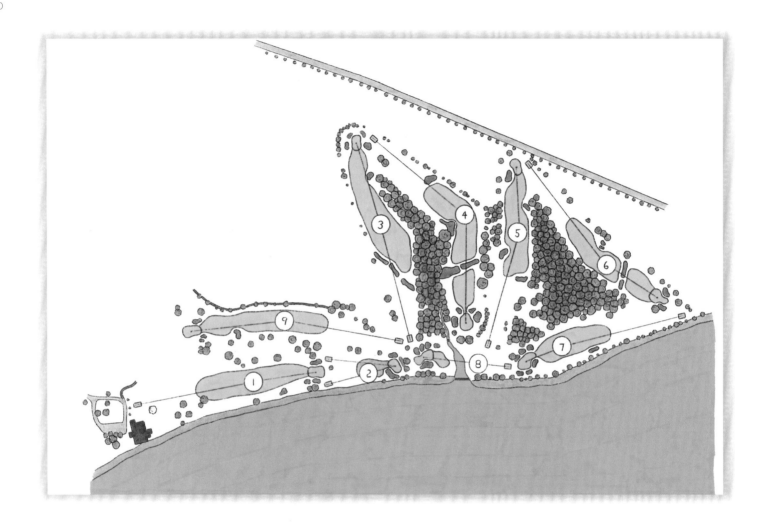

WAIALAE COUNTRY CLUB

Honolulu, HI

Seth Raynor (1926) Front Nine: 3,223 yards / Par 36

Waialae, annual site of the PGA Tour's Hawaiian Open, actually retains only ten of its original Seth Raynor holes, with the front nine (played as the back during tournament week) having long ago been sacrificed to land development and course modernization. But the lone true survivor is a good one: the 187-yard Redan eighth, which remains highly visible on television, as the tournament's often-pivotal 71st hole, each January.

WAIALAE									
390	160	428	460	380	400	360	190	455	3223
4	3	4	5	4	4	4	3	5	36

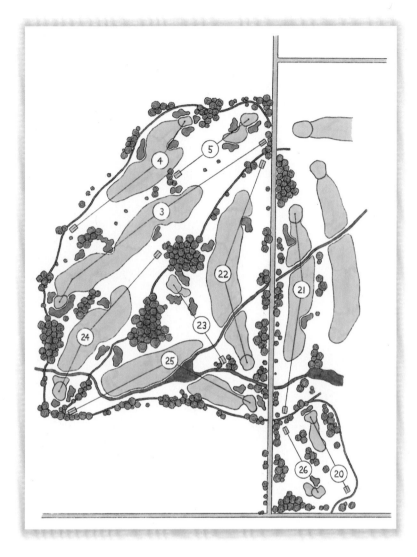

WAKONDA CLUB

Des Moines, IA

WILLIAM LANGFORD (1922) OUTLYING 10 HOLES

    William Langford actually built 27 holes at Wakonda, 10 of which are defunct. Eight of the departed lay across Park Avenue and three of these (labeled 3, 4, and 5 on the above map) were originally part of the primary 18. To fill their shoes, the present course uses the first and last holes of the extra nine as its first and third. The modern par-3 second, which replaced holes 20 and 26, was added to make 18 holes.

WAKONDA									
#3	#4	#5	#20	#21	#22	#23	#24	#25	#26
480	287	177	150	380	380	170	317	403	123
5	4	3	3	4	4	3	4	4	3

LOST HOLES OF
FAMOUS COURSES

BEL-AIR COUNTRY CLUB

Los Angeles, CA

HOLES 9-12

Bel-Air's fabulous foursome does still exist, but the removal of nearly all of George Thomas's marvelously creative features has sanitized them beyond repair. The ninth, originally a go-for-it-or-not drive-and-pitch across a dry wash, has been lengthened and sterilized, its options (and excitement) all removed. With four bunkers added, the famous Swinging Bridge 10th remains at least somewhat intact but the par-4 11th, whose original alternate fairway is long gone, surely isn't. This optional driving area, reached via a blind tee shot over a jungle-covered ridge, offered a much easier line of approach, providing the hole with nearly all of its former strategy. And finally there's #12, the Mae West hole, whose green was guarded at its front by two enormous mounds. Here a safe tee shot left a semiblind approach over the left mound, whereas a drive played close to the right-side canyon wall opened the ideal line of approach. The flattening of the mounds in 1961 (part of an overall Dick Wilson renovation) simply ruined one of golf's all-time most creative holes.

Lost yardages: #9-290, #10-200, #11-377, #12-379

Bel-Air, Circa 1930

Bel-Air, Modern

COLONIAL
COUNTRY CLUB

Ft. Worth, TX

HOLES 3-5 AND 8

Known as the "Horrible Horseshoe," Colonial's holes three through five are not in fact original, having been added by Perry Maxwell in preparation for the 1941 U.S. Open. At number three, Maxwell only created a new green complex in the vicinity of the old fourth tee, lengthening the hole nearly 40 yards. The fourth and fifth were entirely replaced, however, with today's versions (which both, incidentally, began life bunker-free) adding a bit of length to the layout. Of far greater loss was the wonderful eighth, a perilous one-shotter called "the toughest par 3 I ever saw," by no less than Byron Nelson. Angled across a corner of the Trinity River, this hole was completely rebuilt in 1968 when flood-control issues mandated a re-routing of the waterway.

Lost yardages: #3-434, #4-148, #5 367, #8-198

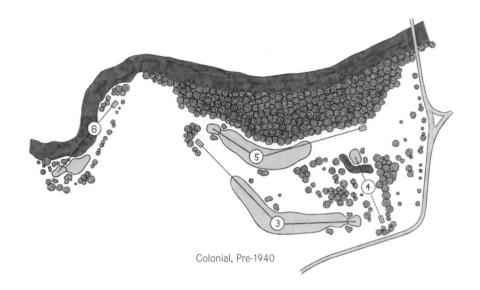

Colonial, Pre-1940

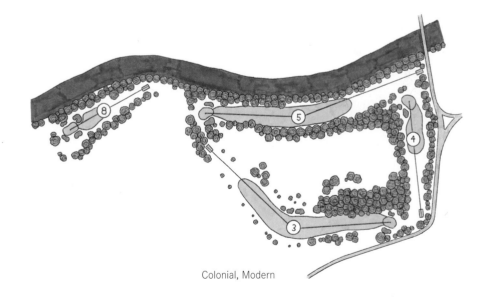

Colonial, Modern

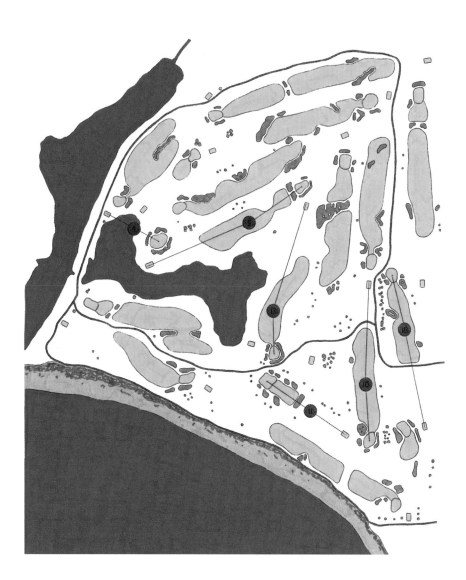

COUNTRY CLUB
OF FAIRFIELD

Fairfield, CT

HOLES 4,5,10,11,13, AND 18

Seth Raynor's 1920 design for the seaside Country Club of Fairfield was an ambitious one, requiring the dredging of landfill off the Long Island coast and its shipping, via barge, across Long Island Sound. The resultant layout (seen here as it appeared in 1934) still has 12 original holes in play, though several of the lost holes were vintage Macdonald/Raynor classics. The fourth, played across a man-made pond was a replica of the Short hole and met its demise when A.W. Tillinghast moved the green right, to the water's edge. The fifth was a rendition of the famous Alps (based on the 17th at Prestwick) and the 11th the obligatory Biarritz—classic Golden Age holes whose untimely removal are a source of regret to connoisseurs everywhere.

Lost yardages: #4-150, #5-415, #10-367, #11-230, #13-350, #18-360

GRIFFITH PARK GOLF COURSE (HARDING)

Los Angeles, CA

HOLES 4-11

Much discussed but seldom seen by architectural afi-cionados is George Thomas's original 1923 work at Griffith Park, a good deal of whose routing remains in play today. On the Harding course, holes four through 11 are long defunct (though the present ninth vaguely approximates the old eighth), replaced with a series of back-and-forth holes of limited interest. The barranca-filled riverbed through which they ran is all grass now, removing all the excitement of Thomas's rugged challenge.

Lost yardages: #4-305, #5-388, #6-392, #7-133, #8-430, #9-368, #10-377, #11-370

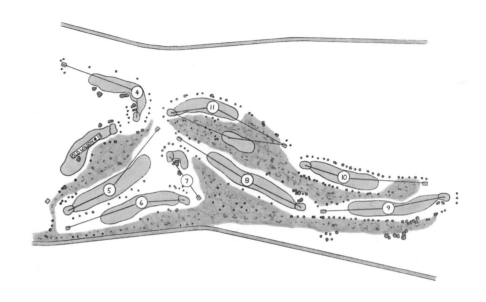

GRIFFITH PARK GOLF COURSE (WILSON)

Los Angeles, CA

HOLES 7-12

Six holes are gone from today's more demanding Wilson course, most of which occupied the same dried riverbed as those lost from the Harding. Holes seven through nine have been partially replaced by athletic fields with the drive-and-pitch eighth probably being the greatest loss. Holes 11 and 12, which neatly skirted the sandy waste, are covered by parts of the present layout's ninth and 10th.

Lost yardages: #7-394, #8-295, #9-400, #10-200, #11-285, #12-389

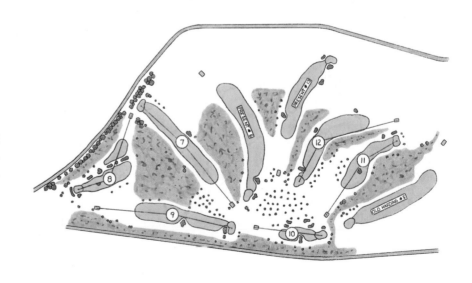

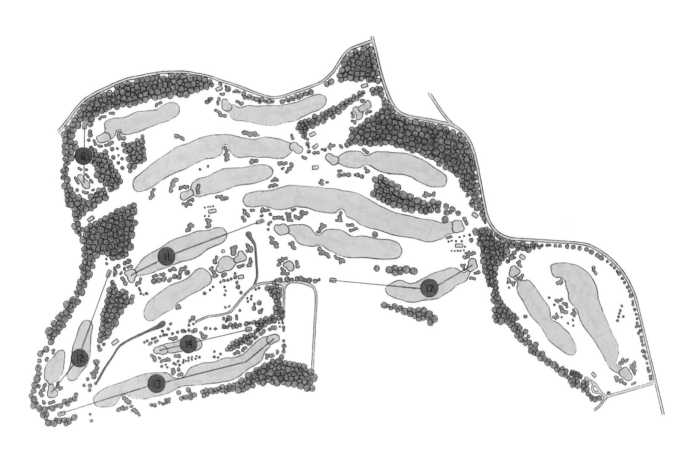

HUNTINGTON CRESCENT CLUB (EAST)

Huntington, NY

HOLES 6,11-14, AND 17

Though outliving its illustrious sister layout (see page 36) by roughly half a century, the Huntington Crescent Club's East course is far from 100% intact. Perhaps the most significant loss was the tiny sixth, little more than a pitch but one played across a deep ravine to a narrow, well-bunkered putting surface. The old 11th today features an entirely new green complex nearly 100 yards beyond the original, while the split-fairway 12th, par-5 13th, and very difficult one-shot 14th have completely vanished. The drive-and-pitch 17th is gone as well, though its green site is utilized for the current 17th, a par 3 which approaches from a different direction.

Lost yardages: #6-135, #11-325, #12-310, #13-525, #14-225, #17-335

INVERNESS CLUB

Toledo, OH

HOLES 6-8 AND 13

In one of the most famous renovations in golf, Inverness brought in George and Tom Fazio in 1977 to remove the short 13th and consolidate the sixth, seventh, and eighth holes into a single 554-yard par 5. Following the mid-sized sixth, the drive-and-pitch seventh gained fame during the 1920 U.S. Open when Englishman Ted Ray drove directly for the green all four days, scoring three birdies and a par en route to winning the championship. The par-3 eighth, on the other hand, was by far the strongest of Inverness's one-shotters. The four new Fazio holes bear little stylistic resemblance to Ross's original 14 but their addition has surely created more of what golf's governing bodies value most in a Major championship site: corporate tent space.

Lost yardages: #6-350, #7-316, #8-210, #13-146

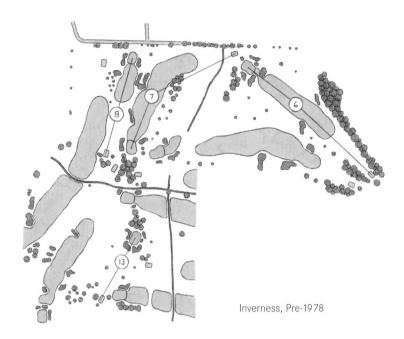

Inverness, Pre-1978

Inverness, Modern

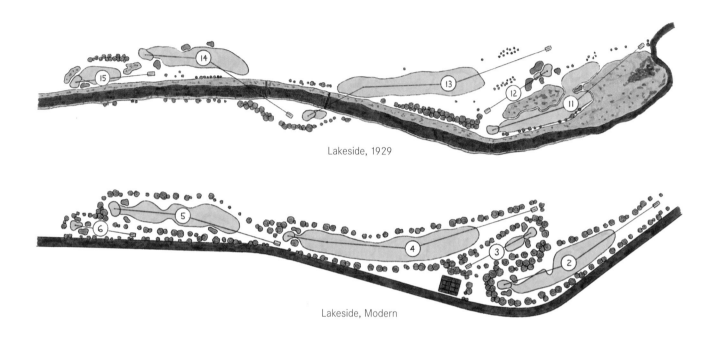

Lakeside, 1929

Lakeside, Modern

LAKESIDE GOLF CLUB

Toluca Lake, CA

HOLES 11-15

Widely considered a classic of its era, Max Behr's 1924 Lakeside design was called "one of the best in the world" by Dr. Alister MacKenzie and was twice photographed for George Thomas's volume *Golf Architecture in America*. Central to its greatness was the incorporation of both some sandy native terrain and the Los Angeles River, particularly on holes 11-15. The par-5 11th, a wonderful split-fairway creation, was probably Lakeside's best, but the backbreaking 13th was surely more famous—a true "untouchable" with its green perched just above the river. The famous Los Angeles flood of 1938 forced the rerouting of the river in the form of a concrete-buttressed channel, and most of the sand has long since become grass. Today, with nines reversed, these former landmark holes have been altered into straightforward, tree-lined affairs with the concrete river more an eyesore than a benefit. The old 13th green lays buried beneath neighboring Universal Studios.

Lost yardages: #11-465, #12-180, #13-595, #14-415, #15-210

LANCASTER
COUNTRY CLUB

Lancaster, PA

HOLES 1,2,6,13, 16, AND 17

William Flynn's 1920 Lancaster design was among his earliest and was shoehorned into a tight piece of land on the north side of the Conestoga River. Expansion in the late 1950s led to a reconfigured site missing six of Flynn's original holes. Of these, the shortest appeared to be most inviting in the form of three drive-and-pitches (the second, 16th and 17th) and the tiny sixth, a tricky one-shotter running down toward the river. Also, holes five and 12, which remain largely in play today, have new green complexes turning each into a dogleg.

Lost yardages: #1-378, #2-269, #6-114, #13-165, #16-333, #17-266

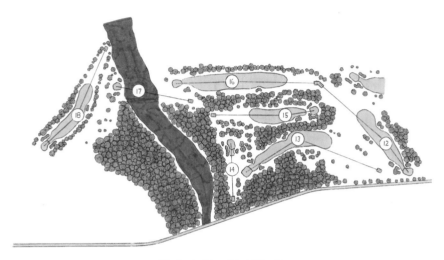

Medinah, Circa World War II

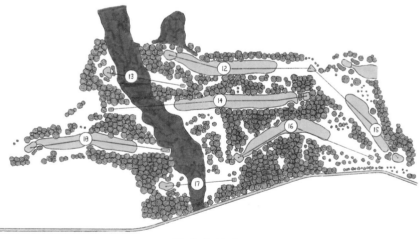

Medinah, Modern

MEDINAH
COUNTRY CLUB (NO.3)

Medinah, IL

HOLES 14, 15, AND 18

Numerous clubs have bowed to the course-altering wishes of the USGA over the years but few so comprehensively as Medinah, which literally rebuilt/reconfigured most of its back nine in preparation for the 1990 U.S. Open. The rather innovative (if not altogether artistic) plan swallowed up the short 14th and 15th holes and plowed under the old 18th while resequencing things considerably. As the old map (circa 1940) illustrates, however, the pre-World War II layout was not terribly elegant and has probably been improved overall. Note: the modern 17th was preceded by a shorter version which was quickly built over by 1996.

Lost yardages: #14-167, #15-318, #18-406

MERION
GOLF CLUB (EAST)

Ardmore, PA

HOLES 1, 10-13

To think that Merion began life with a slightly different configuration from that which we know today is to recall American golf's earliest years, when length wasn't paramount and a small country road like Ardmore Avenue could be played across with little risk to golfer or passerby. The changes made in 1925 were, of course, inevitable and created far better holes than they buried—though the Alps-like 10th, which hints a bit at C.B. Macdonald's consulting role, was an interesting entry.

Lost yardages: #1-335, #10-385, #11-335, #12-460, #13-125

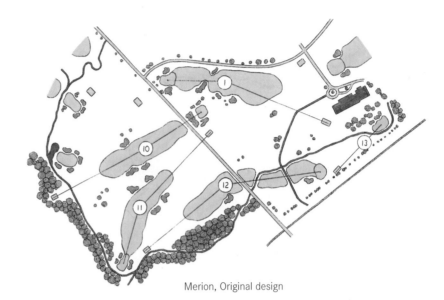

Merion, Original design

Merion, Modern

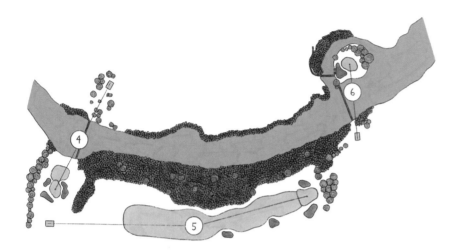

MID-PACIFIC
COUNTRY CLUB

Kailua, HI

HOLES 4-6

Only nine of Seth Raynor's planned 18 holes were initially built at Mid-Pacific (the inward half being constructed in 1949) and by the 1950s, logistical and economic reasons necessitated the loss of three holes crossing or flanking Kaelepulu Stream. Of these, the short, island-greened sixth was surely the most memorable.

Lost yardages: #4-160, #5-440, #6-130

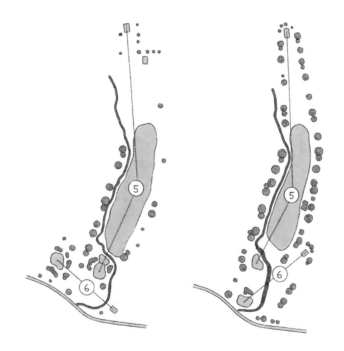

OAK HILL
COUNTRY CLUB (EAST)

Rochester, NY

HOLES 5 AND 6

Prior to the 1980 PGA Championship, the Fazios followed up their work at Inverness with a visit to Oak Hill, replacing holes five and six with distinctly more modern creations. The old fifth (called "one of the best holes I ever played" by Lee Trevino) is mourned to this day.

Lost yardages: #5-180 (originally 371), #6-440 (originally 138)

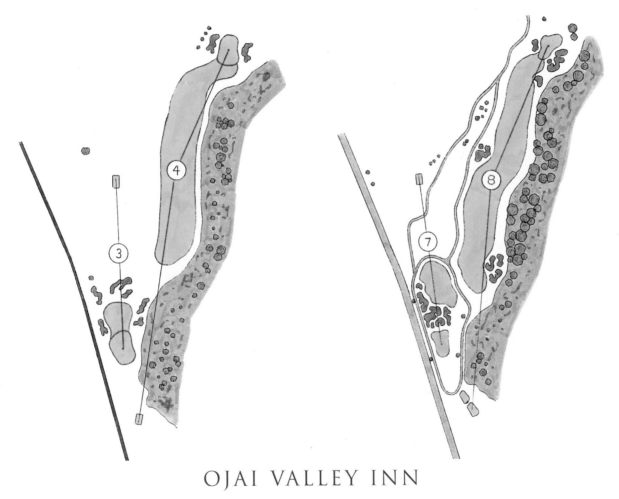

OJAI VALLEY INN

Ojai, CA

HOLES 3 AND 4 ("RESTORED" AS HOLES 7 AND 8)

Much has been made over the years of George Thomas's lost holes at Ojai, particularly the much-photographed par-3 third. Thus a good deal of publicity has surrounded their recent "restoration"—an inappropriate use of the word if ever there was one. One look at the glaring differences between past and present (not a single matching bunker at the third, seven new hazards at the fourth) and we can only conclude that the architect either never saw an old photo or simply didn't care.

Lost yardages: #3-190, #4-400

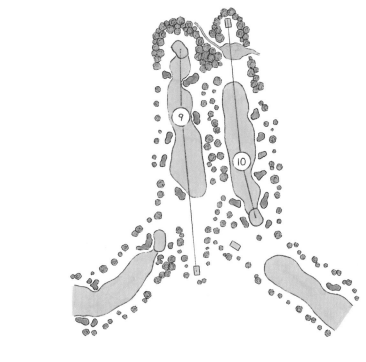

PINEHURST
GOLF CLUB (NO.2)

Pinehurst, NC

HOLES 9 AND 10

In 1935, Donald Ross's perennial tinkering with Pinehurst's featured No. 2 course resulted in the creation of two new holes, the present fourth and fifth. Dropped from the rotation were the then-ninth and 10th, a pair of very poorly documented par 4s whose pregrass (read flat) putting surfaces make it difficult to project their value in the modern era.

Lost yardages: #9-385, #10-338

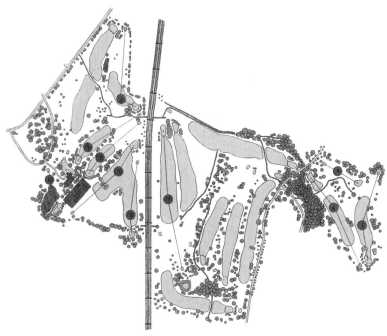

PELHAM COUNTRY CLUB

Pelham, NY

HOLES 2,4-6,9-12,17, AND 18

Pelham Country Club, a 1921 Devereux Emmet design and site of the 1923 PGA Championship, was dramatically altered in 1954 when the New England Thruway was constructed on the west side of today's Conrail tracks. Among the 10 holes lost were a pair of genuine beauties, the 310-yard second (where Gene Sarazen closed out Walter Hagen in a play-off to win the PGA) and the 155-yard 10th, an over-the-water par 3 played to a shallow, sand-ringed putting surface.

Lost yardages: #2-310, #4-154, #5-333, #6-385, #9-294, #10-155, #11-356, #12-255, #17-516, #18-274

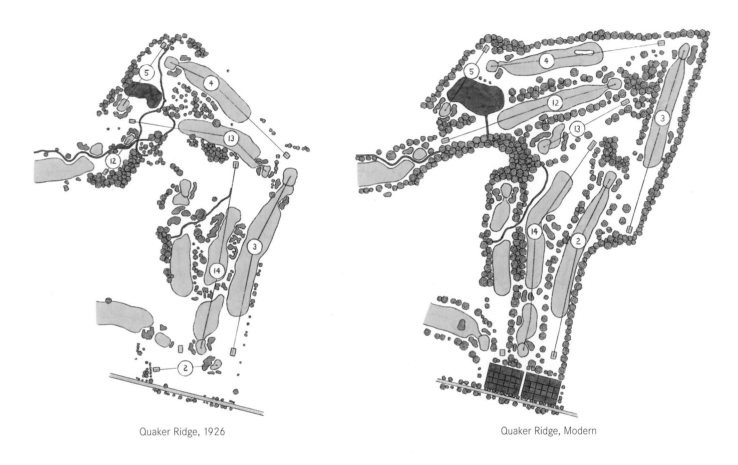

Quaker Ridge, 1926

Quaker Ridge, Modern

QUAKER RIDGE COUNTRY CLUB

Scarsdale, NY

HOLES 2, 4, 12, 13 AND 14

Though frequently considered a "pure" example of A.W. Tillinghast's work, Quaker Ridge was in fact vastly altered even before World War II. Gone were the short, Redan-like second (eventually turned into tennis courts), the tiny 12th and the uphill 13th. Substantially changed were the fine third (today's second) and fourth, plus the extremely difficult two-shot 14th (presently a mid-length par 5). The current third, 12th, and 13th bear no connection to Tillinghast whatsoever, nor, as the drawings illustrate, does the style of Rees Jones's reconfigured bunkering.

Lost yardages: #2-155, #4-355, #12-117, #13-360, #14-445

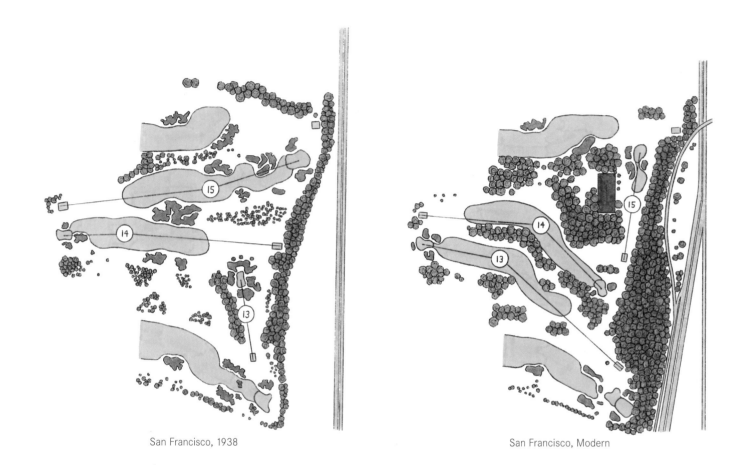

San Francisco, 1938

San Francisco, Modern

SAN FRANCISCO GOLF CLUB

San Francisco, CA

HOLES 13-15

Arguably A.W. Tillinghast's first truly great design (1915), San Francisco Golf Club was substantially altered by Tillie himself in 1924, resulting largely in the layout that we know today. Missing, however, are holes 13 through 15, a relatively short stretch which was replaced – supposedly to accommodate freeway expansion – shortly after World War II. The tiny 13th, known as "Little Tilly" is perhaps the greatest loss, though the mid-length 15th certainly offered bunkering on a memorable scale.

Lost yardages: #13-118, #14-330, #15-385

SKOKIE COUNTRY CLUB

Glencoe, IL

HOLES 3-7 AND 13-16

Donald Ross's 1915 redesign of the Skokie Country Club received a good deal of notoriety after a young Gene Sarazen won the U.S. Open there in 1922. By 1938, however, with the acquisition of previously unavailable land to the southwest, William Langford was brought aboard for a large-scale renovation. Lost in this work were several notable holes including the long third and fifth, the dogleg sixth, and a pair of fine par 3s, the seventh and 13th. Most of the holes that remain have had their bunkering altered somewhat, minimizing whatever Ross features might have been left.

Lost Yardages: #3-440, #4-350, #5-590, #6-390, #7-215, #13-185, #14-315, #15-340, #16-350.

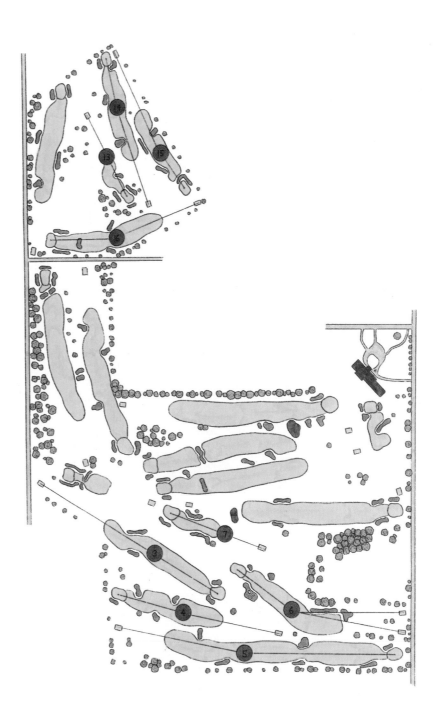

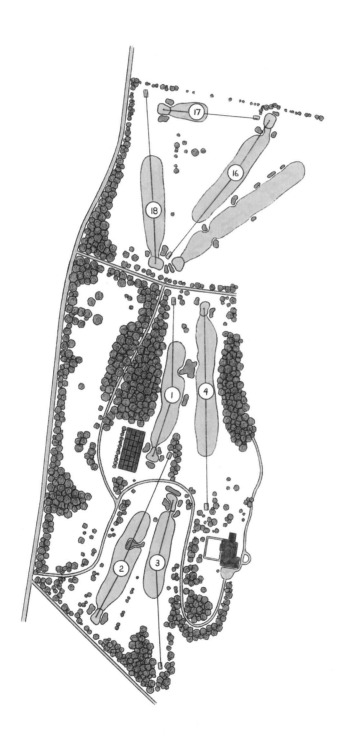

SLEEPY HOLLOW COUNTRY CLUB

Scarborough, NY

HOLES 1-4 AND 16-18

One of America's most historic courses, Sleepy Hollow still boasts a number of original 1911 C.B. Macdonald/Seth Raynor holes, plus five A.W. Tillinghast additions from 1933. Gone, however, are seven holes on the western side of the property, four of which were added in the early 1920s to replace original holes 14-17 when their land was sold off. The Tillinghast additions (which created the present routing) led to the removal of pictured holes two, three, 16, 17, and 18 from the rotation, with numbers one and four being reconfigured into today's first and 18th. Several of these lost holes, it must be noted, still at least partially exist as part of the club's executive-length third nine.

Lost yardages: #1-332, #2-366, #3-345, #4-433, #16-338, #17-198, #18-350

WYKAGYL COUNTRY CLUB

New Rochelle, NY

HOLES 1,2,6,10,11, AND 18

A perennial LPGA Tour stop, Wykagyl's A.W. Tillinghast layout is often overshadowed by such illustrious neighbors as Winged Foot and Quaker Ridge. Interestingly, little of the present routing is Tillie's, with 13 holes dating back to a 1920 Donald Ross redesign of the club's earliest facility. Tillie did obliterate six Ross holes, however: the first, second, 6th, 10th, 11th, and 18th. The opening pair were largely swallowed up by today's practice area, while the others were completely redesigned. Also missing from Ross's layout are some especially grand bunkers at holes four, 12, and 13 (colored in red).

Lost yardages: #1-350, #2-320, # 6-318, #10-241, #11-447 (par 5), #18-542

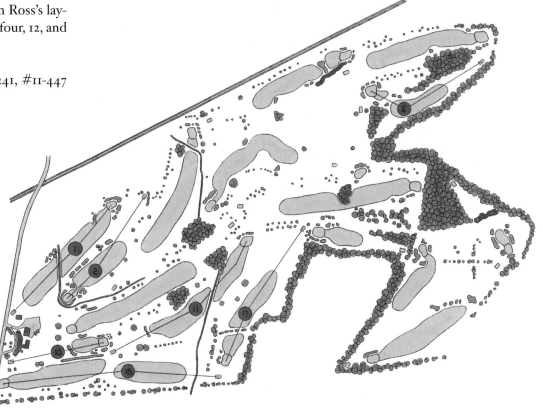

MAPS OF PROMINENT
GOLFING CITIES

*T*he following 8 maps represent lost courses in some of America's most prominent Golden Age golfing cities. Each has been created from a variety of period sources and is drawn to scale. Yardages and par figures are listed where available, as are architectural credits. Generally, only regulation-sized facilities are included (i.e., no "executive" or par-3 layouts), though benefit of the doubt has occasionally been extended where specifics were unavailable. Courses are limited to those built or rebuilt during the Golden Age. Rudimentary layouts known to predate World War I have been deliberately omitted, even if still present between the wars. Due to source inconsistencies, the occasional inadvertent omission may unfortunately come to light.

Defunct courses are marked in green, completely altered layouts of significance in blue. Major airports appear in gray.

Maps for New York, Chicago, and Los Angeles appear in *The Missing Links*.

BOSTON

1. Wellesley Country Club - 3,010 yds Par 35
A 1911 Donald Ross nine which was built over by Stiles & Van Kleek well before the club's 1961 expansion to 18 holes.

2. Woodland Golf Club - 6,222 yds Par 71
Woodland's original course was an early Wayne Stiles design which was replaced, in 1928, by a Donald Ross 18.

3. Albemarle Country Club - 5,200 yds Par 70
A short but highly rated Wayne Stiles layout which was reduced to nine holes during the Depression. Converted to today's Albemarle Park in 1979.

4. Waltham Country Club - 3,132 yds Par 35
A 1921 Donald Ross nine-holer built on a site currently occupied by the Gore Place Society. Gone prior to World War II.

5. Newton Commonwealth Golf Course
Originally a 1921 Donald Ross design, this public layout just north of Boston College was rebuilt by Stiles and Van Kleek, probably in the late 1920s.

6. Weld Golf Club - 3,000 yds Par 35
An early Stiles and Van Kleek nine-holer located off Church St. in West Roxbury. Gone before the war.

7. Wollaston Golf Club - 6,150 yds Par 71
Originally built in 1895 by George Wright, Wollaston remained a high-profile layout well past the turn of the century. Wayne Stiles overhauled it completely in 1920, but subsequent modernizations have removed any trace of the prewar design.

8. Stony Brae Golf Club - 5,160 yds Par 67
A Wayne Stiles solo design on the site of today's Furnace Brook CC. Built over by William Mitchell in 1947.

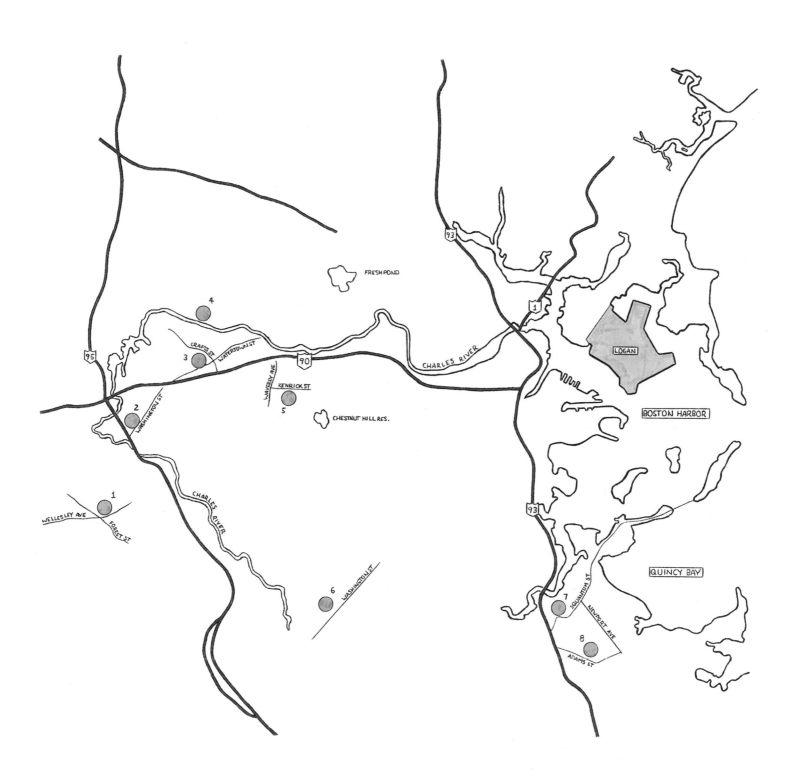

DETROIT

1. Aviation Country Club (Page 94)

2. Lancaster Hills Golf Course
   A nine-hole facility located on the northeast corner of
   Twelve Mile and Telegraph Rds.

3. River Bank Golf Course
   Located off the old Northwestern Highway, north of
   Eleven Mile Rd. and east of Telegraph Rd. Buried
   beneath the 696 freeway.

4. Northville Golf Club
   An 18-holer located at the southwest corner of
   Newburgh and Seven Mile Roads, near the present
   Whispering Willow GC.

5. Hawthorne Valley Golf Club
   The 1931 *American Annual Golf Guide* listed
   Hawthorne Valley as a 90-hole public facility with five
   courses (all par 72) measuring 6,340, 6,300, 6,250, 6,500,
   and 6,240 yards. Located on land that includes today's
   nine-hole Hawthorne Valley CC, it remains a rather
   grand footnote to Detroit-area golf history.

6. Fairway Golf Club
   This public 18-holer lay just a short distance from Lake
   St. Clair, on the south side of Ten Mile Rd.

7. Beverly Hills Public Golf Course
   Yet another deceased public 18, Beverly Hills was
   located at the southwest corner of Thirteen Mile Rd.
   and Earle Memorial Highway.

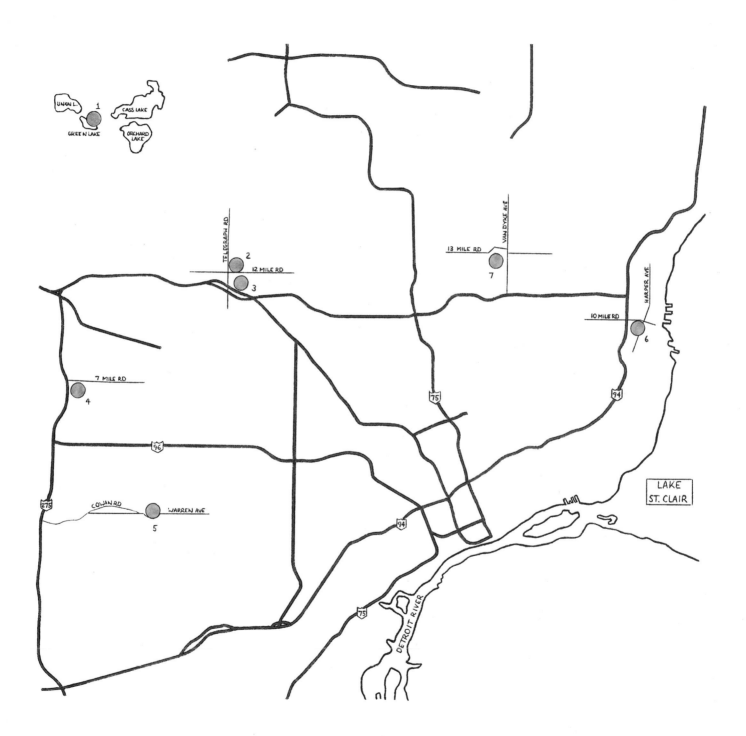

MIAMI

1. Shriners Golf Course
A nondescript pre-1926 hurricane nine located just across Route 1 (the Dixie Highway) from the University of Miami.

2. West Flagler Golf Course
A poorly documented post-hurricane layout located just south of today's Melrose Golf Course, between West Flagler St. and NW 7th St. Adjacent to the West Flagler Kennel Club.

3. Miami Country Club (Page 146)

4. Miami Municipal Golf Course - 6,310 yds Par 70
A good deal of William Langford's 1923 routing remains intact here, but nearly all of its original bunkering and character are gone. Very well thought of, once upon a time.

5. Miami Beach Golf Course - 6,130 yds Par 72
A very early (ca.1915) layout frequently pictured in period brochures. Located just southeast of Bay Shore Golf Course on land comprising today's City Park.

6. Flamingo Golf Course
A short-lived nine-hole facility belonging to the nearby Flamingo Hotel, Miami Beach's first luxury hostelry. Gone well before WWII, the site is largely occupied by today's Flamingo Park.

7. Miami Shores Country Club (Page 148)

8. South Florida Golf & Country Club - 6,300 yds Par 72
H.C. Tippett's original 1925 layout, a high-profile venture initially represented by Gene Sarazen, was largely washed away by the 1926 hurricane. Its WWII-era reincarnation has evolved into today's Westview CC.

9. Miami Golf Course
William Flynn drew impressive plans for this site, but it is not yet known whether the short-lived course was actually his or someone else's. The land today comprises the eastern half of Opa-Locka Airport. Gone before WWII.

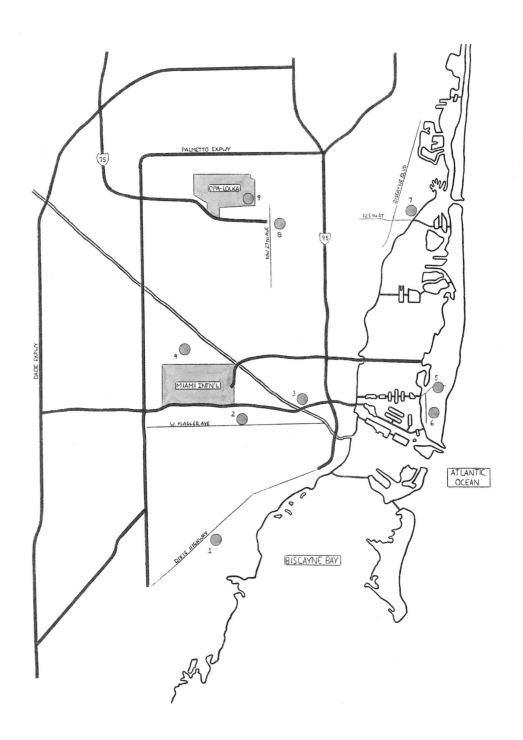

PALMETTO EXPWY

75

OPA-LOCKA
9

8
NW 27th AVE

95

BISCAYNE BLVD
7
125 th ST

DADE EXPWY

4

MIAMI INTN'L

3

2
W. FLAGLER AVE

5

6

ATLANTIC
OCEAN

DIXIE HIGHWAY
1

BISCAYNE BAY

MINNEAPOLIS/ST. PAUL

1. Columbia Park Golf Course
Golf at Columbia Park dates back to 1919. The present course, however, dates only to E.L. Packard's thorough makeover in 1965.

2. Hilltop Public Golf Links
Located on the north side of County Road E, this 18-holer filled land now occupied by Driftwood Park and the United Theological Seminary of the Twin Cities.

3. Matoska Golf Club - 2,650 yds Par 34
Golf is still played on this site just southwest of White Bear Lake, but on a nine-holer dating only to 1955.

4. Northwood Country Club - 3,362 yds Par 37
Located across Holloway Ave. from today's Maplewood Middle School, this public nine-holer has been replaced by residences and an eponymous park.

5. Keller Golf Club - 6,650 yds Par 72
Little remains of one of the nation's better public courses, a once-regular PGA Tour stop and two-time host of the PGA Championship. Neglected, remodeled, and underappreciated.

6. Phalen Public Golf Club
Like several other Twin Cities municipal tracks, Phalen has been completely rebuilt, burying holes dating back to 1929.

7. Como Park Golf Course - 3,115 yds Par 36
See entry number six—this one courtesy of Don Herfort in 1986.

8. Westwood Hills Golf Course
This 27-hole daily-fee facility was an immediate northern neighbor to the present Minneapolis Golf Club. Its land, including Westwood Lake, is now Westdale Park.

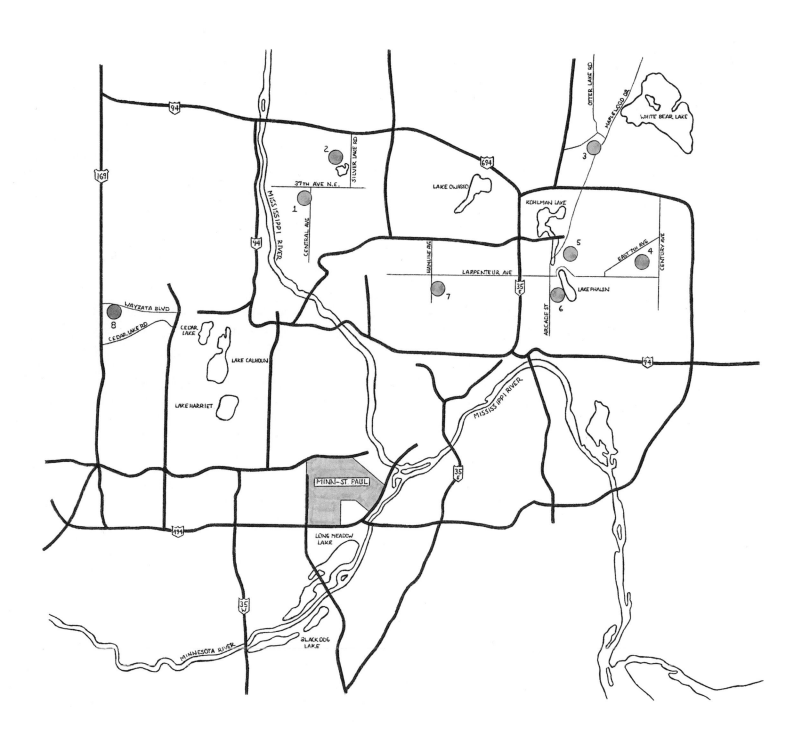

PHILADELPHIA

1. Cooper River Parkway Country Club - 6,150 yds Par 71
Located in Camden, NJ, this Devereux Emmet layout opened in 1929 on land which is today part of Camden County Park.

2. Pennsylvania Golf Club - 6,432 yds Par 73
Located on a triangular plot across Township Line Rd. from the Philadelphia Electric CC. In disrepair by the war years.

3. Overbrook Country Club
This 6,215-yard layout was a much-altered Donald Ross design for a club with roots dating back to 1900. Lankenau Hospital occupies the site today as the club moved to suburban Radnor in 1952.

4. Radnor Golf Club
This little-documented facility was located slightly south of today's Valley Forge Military Academy, on either side of East Lancaster Avenue.

5. Mary Lyon's School Golf Course
Long-gone facility located just north of the present Springhaven GC and west of the 476 freeway. Tract size suggested only nine holes.

6. Swarthmore Golf Club
As with Mary Lyon's, likely a nine-hole layout situated southeast of Springhaven GC, across Chester Rd.

7. Aberfoyle Country Club
The third in this cluster of lost courses, Aberfoyle lay east of Brookhaven Rd., on land which presently encompasses a residential neighborhood and city park.

8. Tully Memorial Country Club
Later known as Tully-Secane CC, this club was best known for pro Henry Williams Jr., who won the 1952 Tucson Open and reached the match-play finals of the 1950 PGA.

9. Sunnybrook Country Club - 6,430 yds Par 73
This challenging Donald Ross design lives on – barely – in the form of the present Flourtown CC, where several original holes remain in play.

10. Cedarbrook Country Club (Page 116)

11. Old York Road Country Club
Only nine rather altered holes remain at this A.W. Tillinghast-modified facility. The lost nine would not fall among Tillie's elite.

12. Baederwood Country Club (Page 96)

13. Rydal Golf Club
Par-68 layout which was rated easiest among Philadelphia-area courses in 1949.

14. Wissahickon Golf & Country Club
This club lies buried beneath the intersection of the Pennsylvania Turnpike and Route 309, just north of the Penn Central railroad tracks.

15. Beverly Hills Golf Club
Likely a nine-holer, this facility was situated just east of Delaware County Memorial Hospital, on land encompassing today's Beverly Hills Recreation Area.

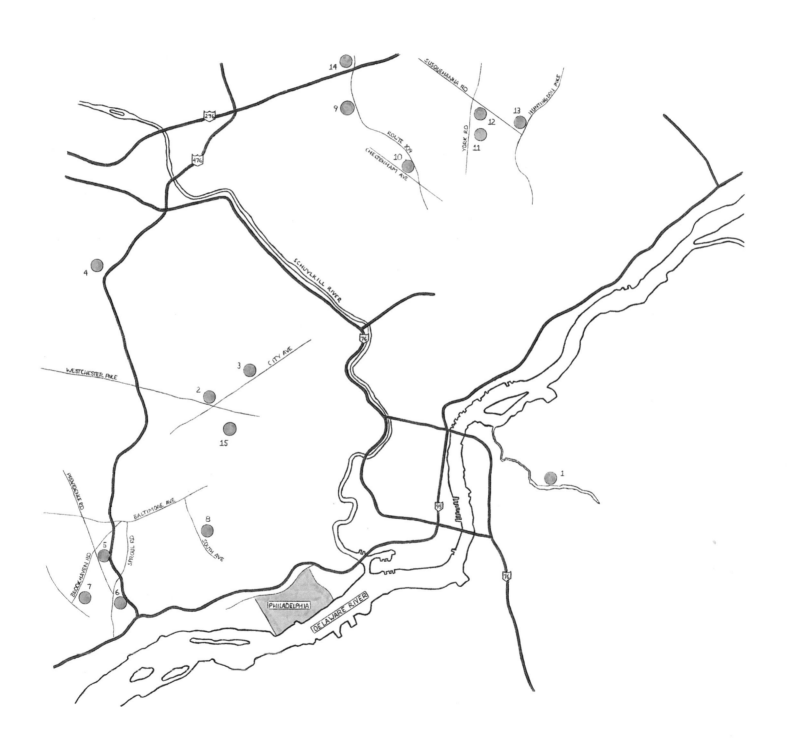

SAN DIEGO

1. Point Loma Golf Club - 6,027 yds Par 72
Originally built by Tom Bendelow in 1912, this early
facility was reduced to nine holes in 1921 after Congress
funded construction of the San Diego Naval Hospital.
It disappeared entirely in 1928.

2. Coronado Country Club - 6,605 yds Par 72
San Diego's second oldest course (1901), this waterfront
facility was upgraded several times, including an A.W.
Tillinghast touch-up in 1937. Two-time U.S. Open
champ Alex Smith was the first pro here.

3. Balboa Park Municipal Golf Course - 5,772 yds Par 69
Golf continues to be played on this site, but little
remains of either the original (1915) sand-and-dirt
course or Billy Bell's Golden Age redesign (1921).

4. Emerald Hills Country Club
This very popular public course was located south of
Highway 94 near the Kelton off-ramp. A victim of
suburban expansion, it closed in 1956.

5. La Mesa Country Club - 6,145 yds Par 70
Built in 1924, this private club turned public during the
Depression before ultimately being sold off for residential
development in 1950.

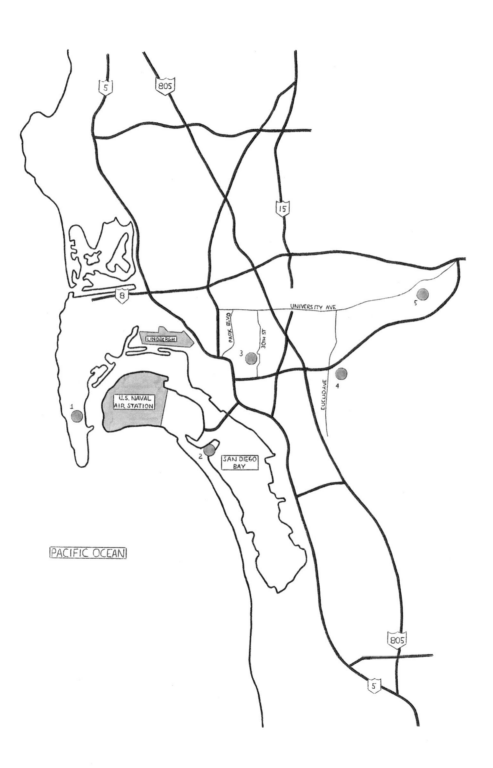

SAN FRANCISCO BAY AREA

1. Olympic Club (Ocean Course) - 6,606 yds Par 74
Willie Watson and Sam Whiting (see *The Missing Links*).

1A. Lakeside Golf & Country Club - 6,410 yds Par 75
This 1917 Wilfrid Reid design was the short-lived predecessor of today's Olympic Club. A hilly layout that sat mostly upon the present Lake course, it was plowed under completely when Willie Watson created 36 new holes in 1924.

2. Lake Merced Golf & Country Club (Page 140)

3. California Golf Club - 6,172 yds Par 71

4. Sharp Park Golf Course - 6,154 yds Par 71
Dr. Alister MacKenzie (see *The Missing Links*).

5. Capuchino Golf & Country Club - 6,371 yds Par 72
A short-lived 18 (circa 1927) located immediately north of today's Green Hills CC. Subdivided decades ago.

6. Crystal Springs Golf Club
Originally built by Herbert Fowler in 1920, this once-important design has, over several remodels, been altered largely out of existence.

7. Burlingame Country Club
One of several clubs with claims as the oldest course west of the Mississippi River, Burlingame's Golden Age Herbert Fowler layout (1922) has been systematically modified into oblivion.

8. Emerald Lake Golf Club - 2,622 yds Par 35
Defunct nine-holer, circa 1925.

9. Oakland Golf Club
Short-lived pioneer of East Bay golf, founded in 1897 on the north shore of Lake Merritt. Gone by 1903.

10. Oak Knoll Country Club - 6,625 yds Par 71
Circa-1927 18 was located slightly northwest of today's Sequoyah CC, on land now occupied by the Oak Knoll Naval Medical Center.

11. Belvedere Golf & Country Club - 1,957 yds Par 30
Noted centerpiece of the upscale Belvedere real estate development, located at the peninsula's northern tip.

12. Marin Golf & Country Club - 2,833 yds Par 35
A very early nine-holer located just north of San Rafael Creek. Long since subdivided.

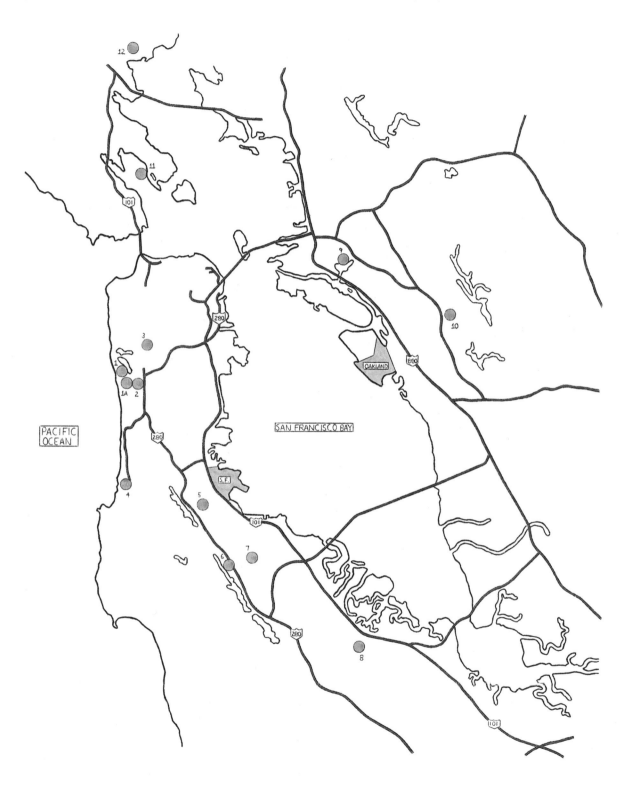

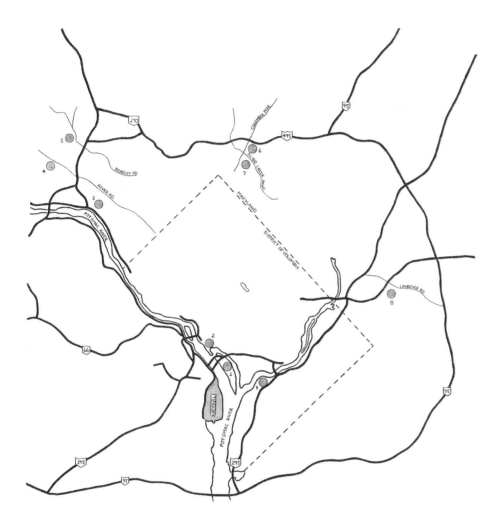

WASHINGTON, DC (AND SURROUNDS)

1. East Potomac Park Golf Courses
This William Flynn redesign of a Robert White original retains its Golden Age routing but has lost nearly all of Flynn's considerable bunkering. A shadow of its former self.

2. West Potomac Park Golf Course
A sand-greened nine-holer. A bit less grand than its East Potomac partner.

3. Bannockburn Golf Club (Page 100)

4. Congressional Country Club (Page 192)

5. Women's National Country Club
A mysteriously undocumented Bradley Road layout listed on a 1934 AAA area map.

6. Indian Springs Golf Club
This 6,642-yard Donald Ross layout, located slightly east of Sligo Park, was likely renovated by William Flynn (or others) prior to World War II. The club still exists today, at a William & David Gordon-designed facility several miles to the north.

7. Montgomery County Country Club
Another poorly documented facility, this 18-holer located at Pershing Dr. and Springvale Rd. was subdivided by 1941.

8. Prince George's Country Club (Page 166)

9. Anacostia Park Golf Course - 3,140 yds Par 36
Former nine-holer situated along the southern bank of the Anacostia river.

ACKNOWLEDGMENTS

On behalf of all golfers, I must first thank the Amateur Athletic Foundation of Los Angeles for providing a splendid new home for the Ralph W. Miller Golf Library, with Wayne Wilson and Shannon Boyd especially acknowledged for their contributions to this volume. Similarly, I am forever indebted to Saundra Sheffer and Marge Dewey, the library's former guardians in the City of Industry, who so strongly supported my endeavors from the very beginning.

Khris Januzik, formerly of the Given Memorial Library, will surely recognize her input throughout this book, as will Stephanie Breaux of the Fairchild Aerial Photography Collection at Whittier College. And a very special thank you goes to both the aerial photography researchers of the National Archives and Records Administration in College Park, Maryland, and the staff of King Visual Technology, without whose great efforts and forbearance neither this book nor *The Missing Links* could possibly have been written.

I have also been extremely fortunate to enjoy the aid and support of several outstanding researchers, authors, and historians from across the country including Craig Disher (who truly came to the aid of the party), Tommy Naccarato, Tom MacWood, Wayne Morrison, George Bahto, and Bob Labbance, among others.

Also: Nancy Stulack and Patty Moran at the USGA library, Tom Paul, Ran Morrissett, Gil Hanse, L.E. Eustis, Tom Doak, Hank Pela, Ray Cross, Doug Lonnstrom, Robert Conte, Rick Wolffe, Philip Young, David Rowland, Hart Huffines, John Morsut, Bo Links, Jeffrey Myers, and Dave Ward.

Among the many, many public libraries: Boston, Cleveland, Dallas, Detroit, Kingsport (TN), Knox County (IN), Martin County (FL), Multnomah County (OR), Petersburg (VA), Philadelphia, Pontiac (MI), Enoch Pratt (MD), San Francisco, Seattle, the Florida State Library, and the Michigan State Archives.

On the private side: Algonac/Clay Township (MI) Historical Society, Ardsley Country Club, Baker Library (Dartmouth College), Boca Raton Resort & Club, Bostonian Society, Cincinnati Historical Society,